Liebestrasse™

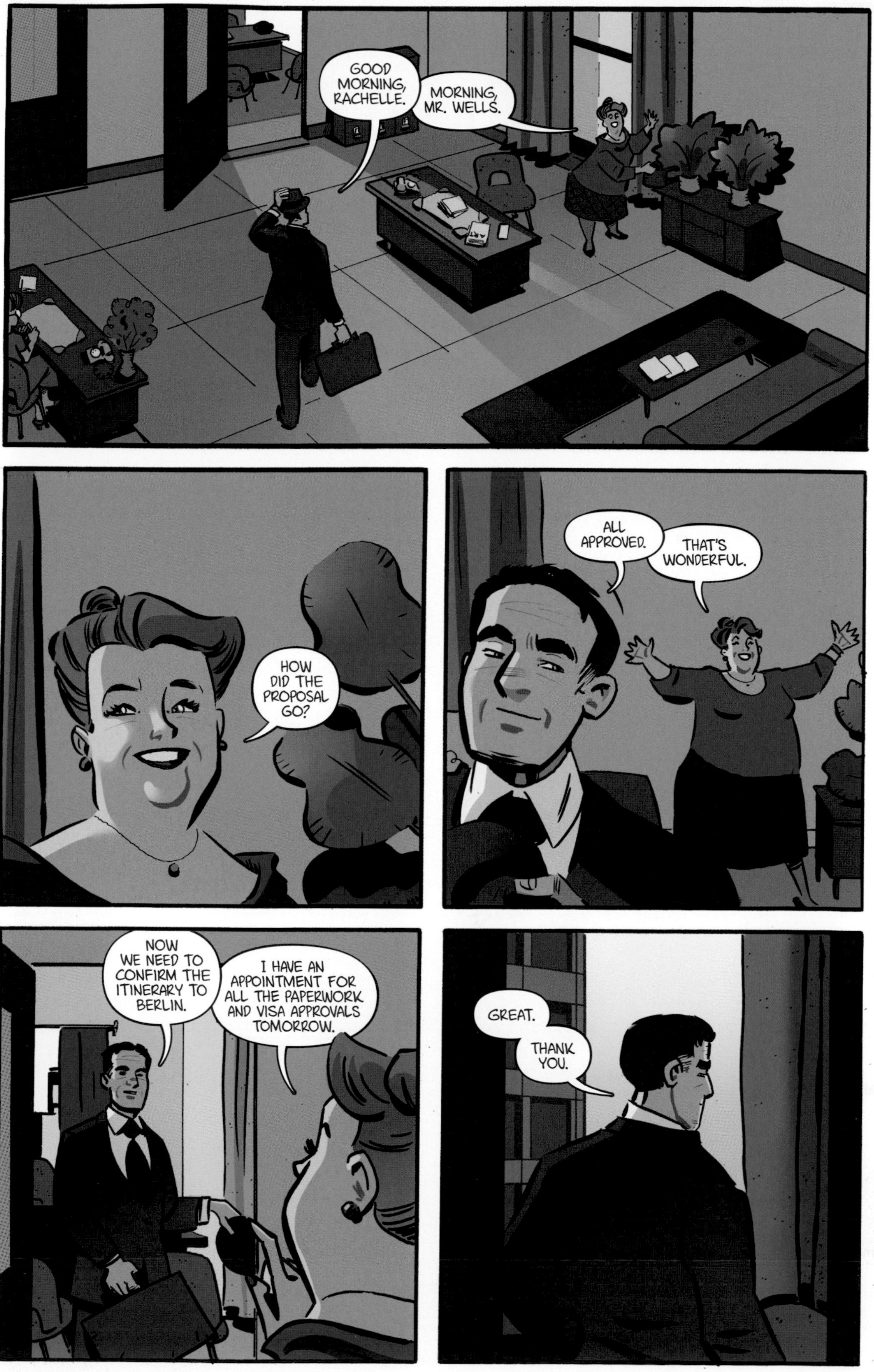
GOOD MORNING, RACHELLE.
MORNING, MR. WELLS.
HOW DID THE PROPOSAL GO?
ALL APPROVED.
THAT'S WONDERFUL.
NOW WE NEED TO CONFIRM THE ITINERARY TO BERLIN.
I HAVE AN APPOINTMENT FOR ALL THE PAPERWORK AND VISA APPROVALS TOMORROW.
GREAT.
THANK YOU.

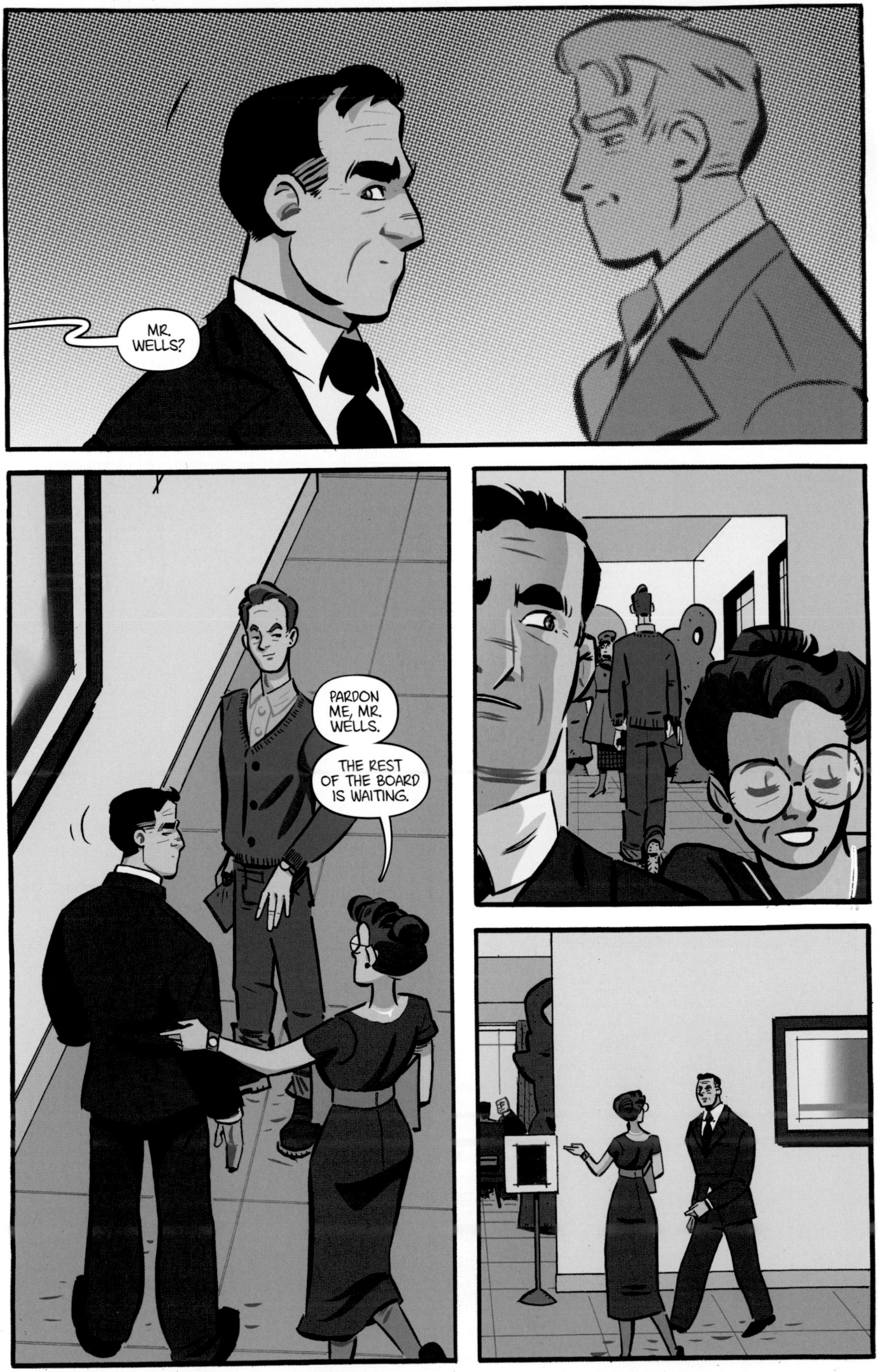
MR. WELLS?
PARDON ME, MR. WELLS.
THE REST OF THE BOARD IS WAITING.

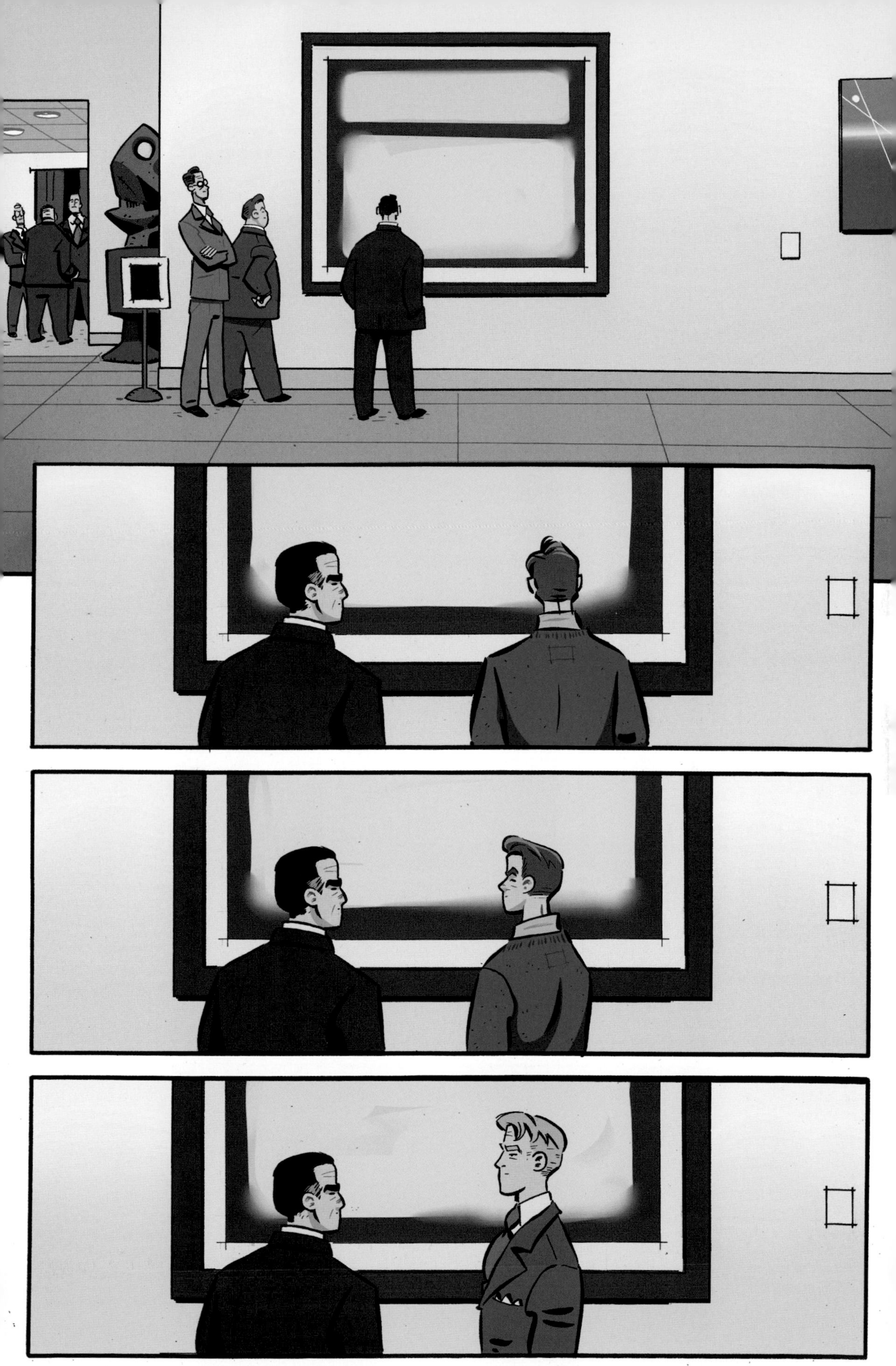

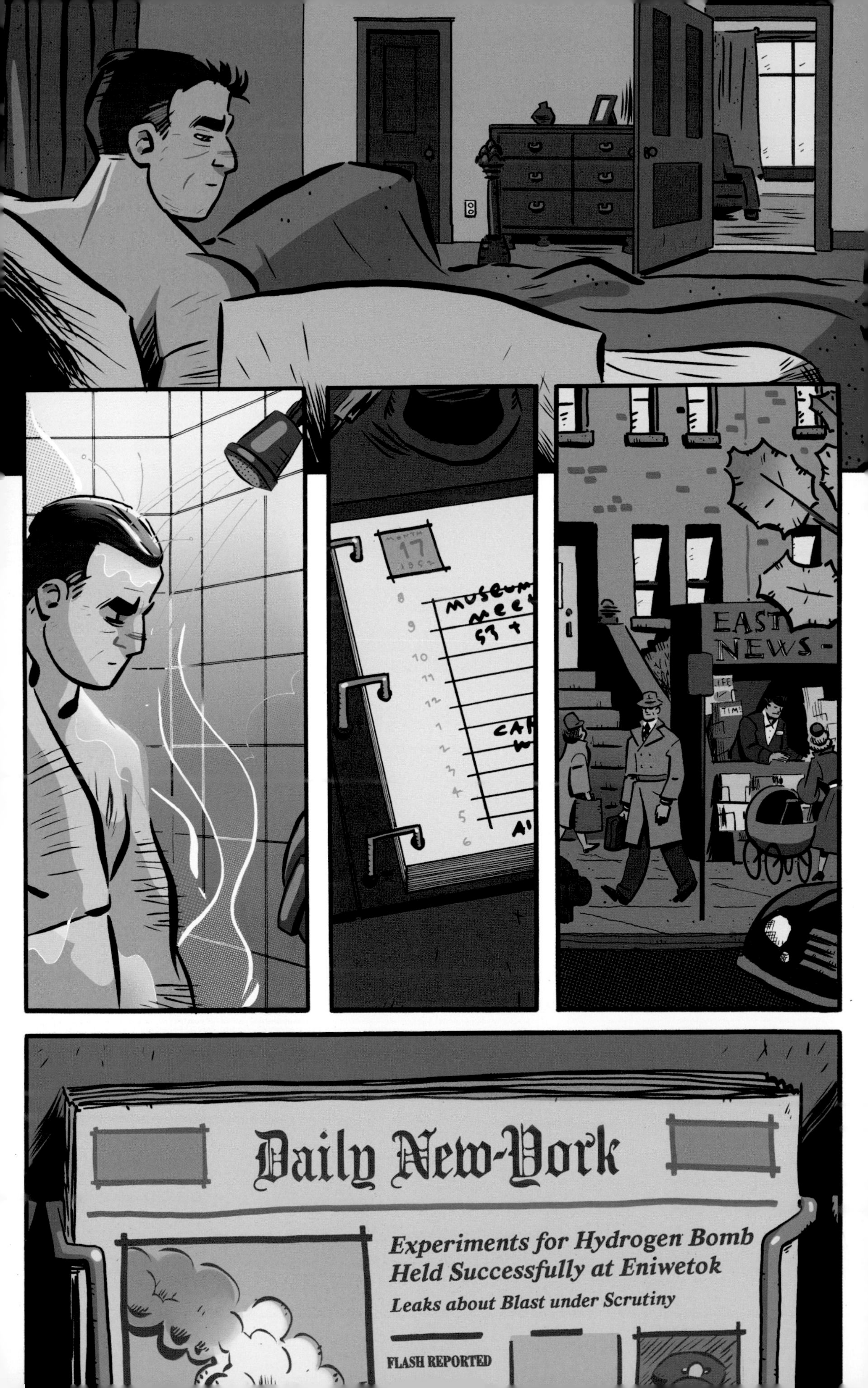
MONTH
17
1952
EAST
NEWS
TIME
Daily New-York
Experiments for Hydrogen Bomb Held Successfully at Eniwetok
Leaks about Blast under Scrutiny
FLASH REPORTED

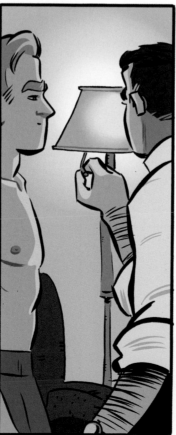

click

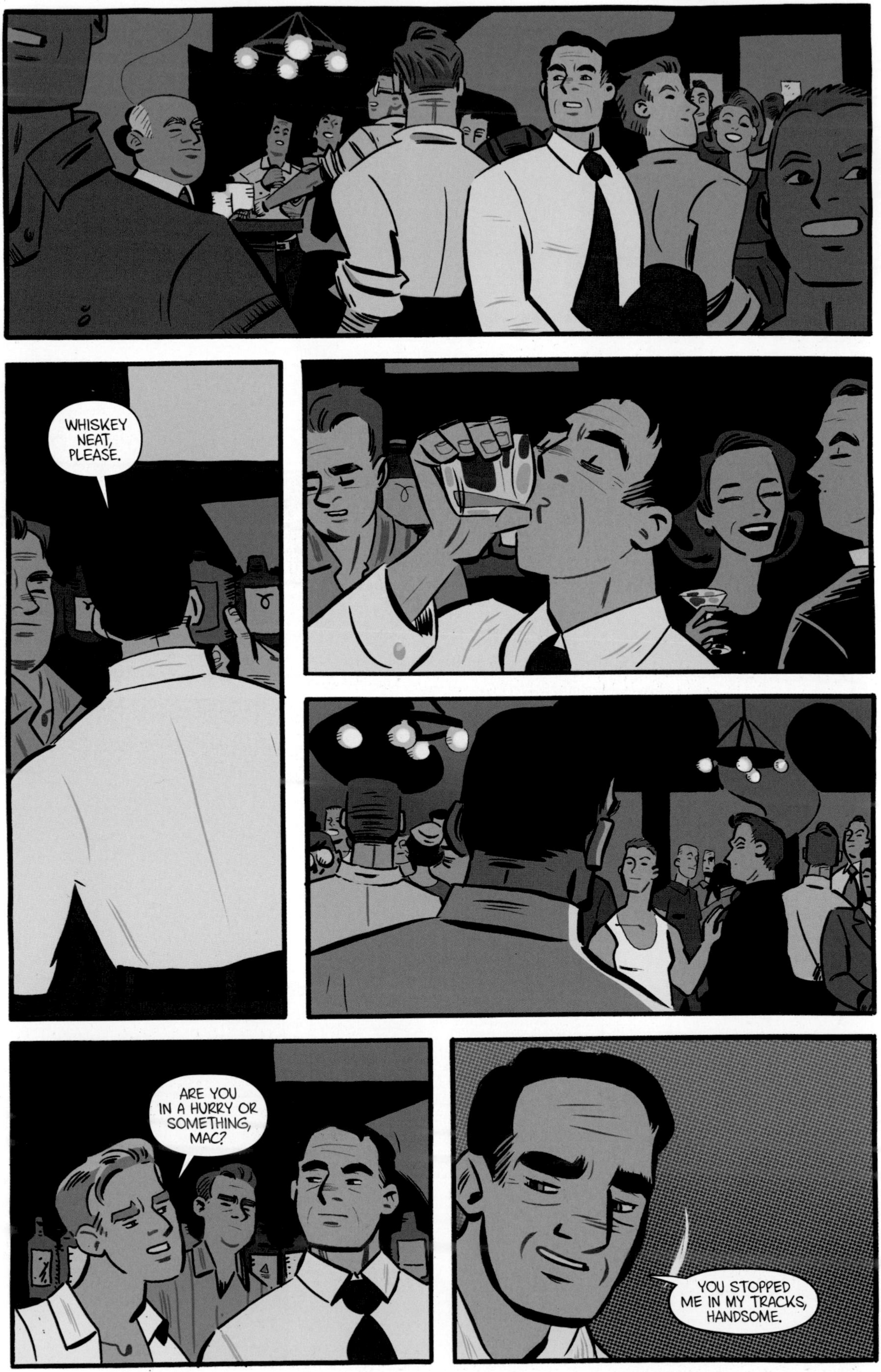
WHISKEY NEAT, PLEASE.
ARE YOU IN A HURRY OR SOMETHING, MAC?
YOU STOPPED ME IN MY TRACKS, HANDSOME.

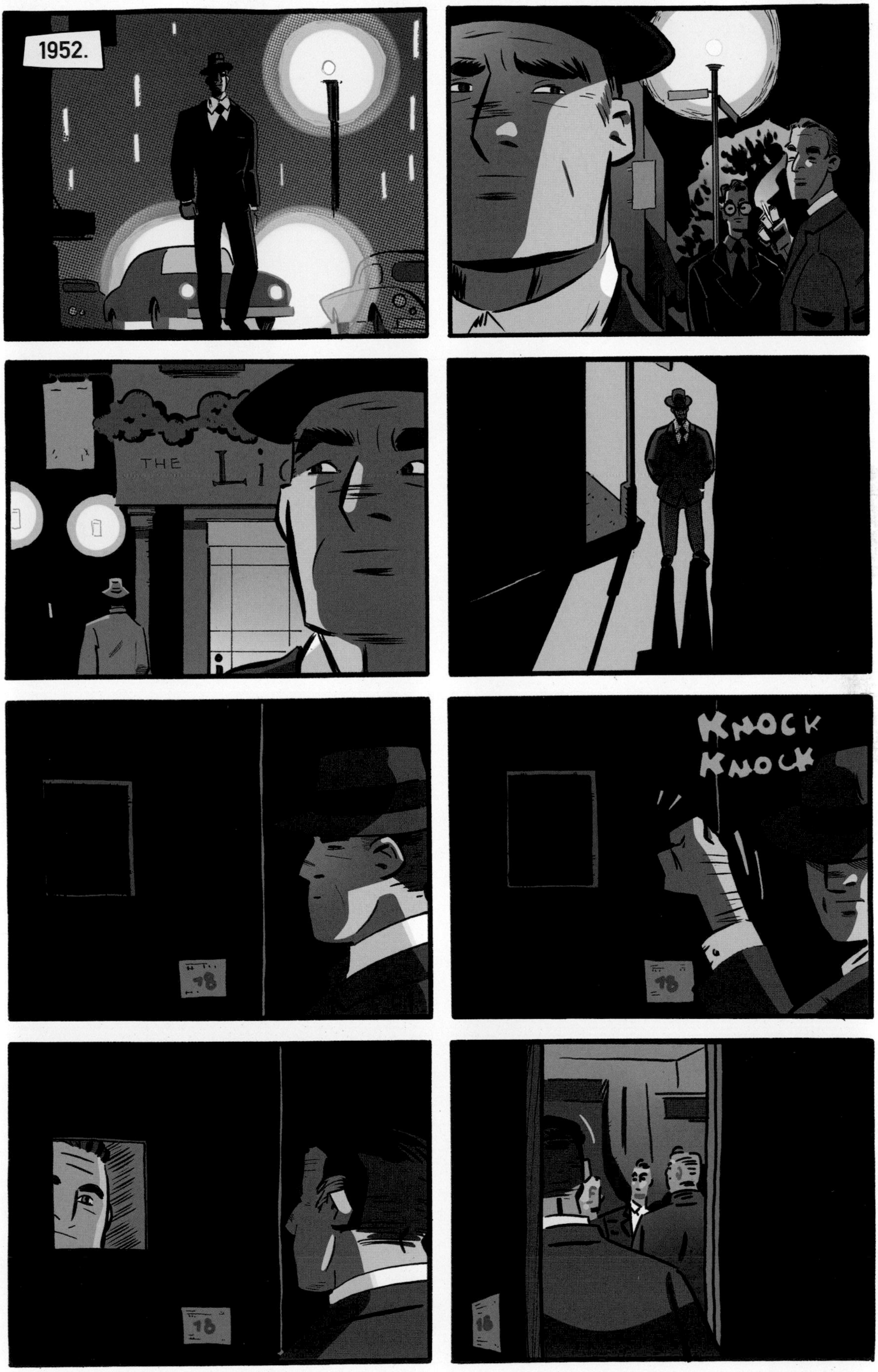
1952.
THE Li
18
KNOCK
KNOCK
18
18
18

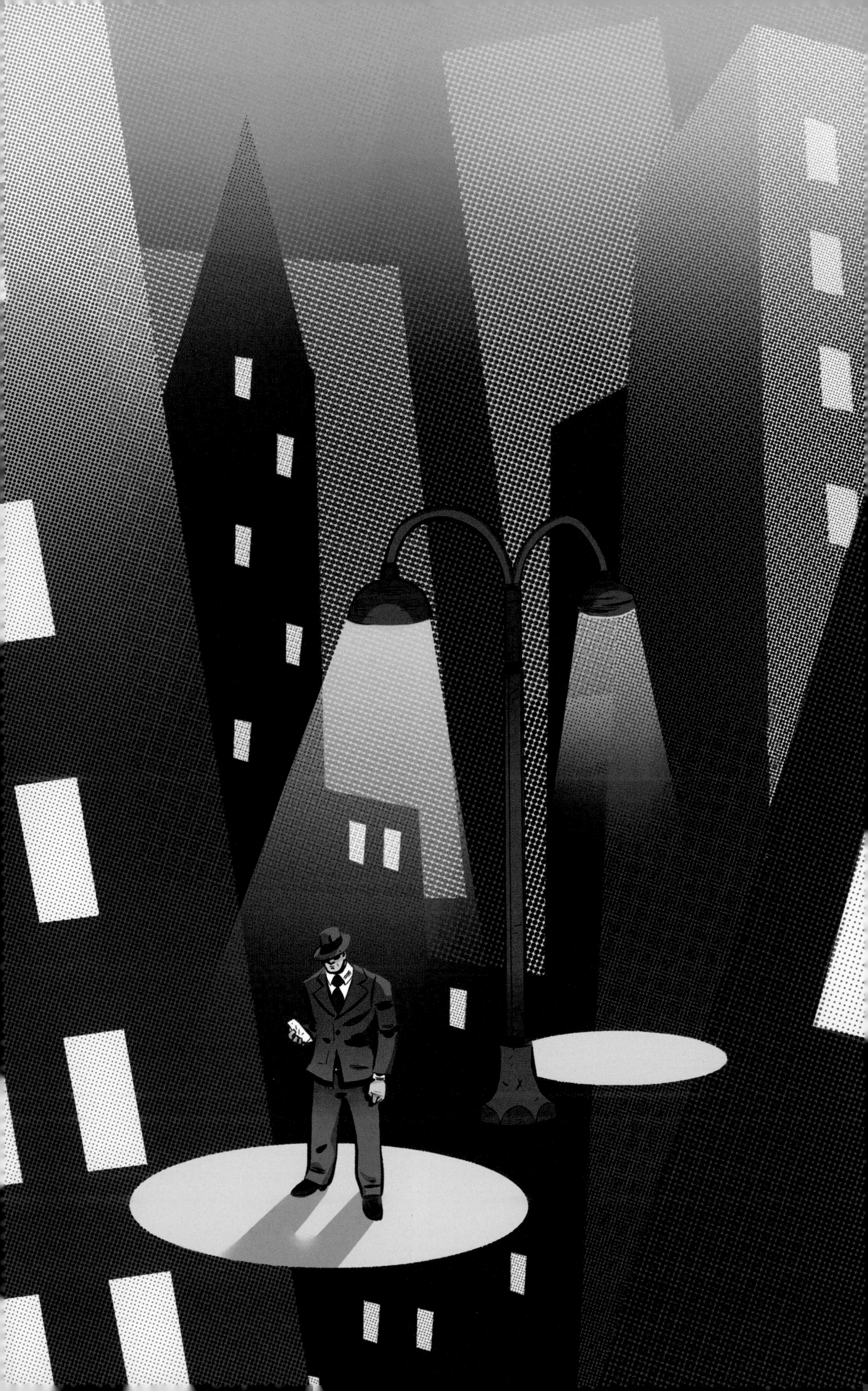

.

This book is dedicated to all the silenced voices of LGBTQ+ individuals around the world. We will never take our freedoms for granted and we will never stop fighting against the repetition of these histories.

.

SPECIAL THANKS

David Steinberger

Chip Mosher

Bryce Gold

Jack Mahan

Lynn and Greg Lockard Sr.

David Hyde and Pamela Mullin-Horvath
from Superfan Promotions

.

DARK HORSE TEAM

Mike Richardson
PRESIDENT AND PUBLISHER

Daniel Chabon
EDITOR

Chuck Howitt AND Konner Knudsen
ASSISTANT EDITORS

Kathleen Barnett
DESIGNER

Jason Rickerd
DIGITAL ART TECHNICIAN

EXECUTIVE VICE PRESIDENT **NEIL HANKERSON** | CHIEF FINANCIAL OFFICER **TOM WEDDLE** | CHIEF INFORMATION OFFICER **DALE LAFOUNTAIN** | VICE PRESIDENT OF LICENSING **TIM WIESCH** | VICE PRESIDENT OF MARKETING **MATT PARKINSON** | VICE PRESIDENT OF PRODUCTION AND SCHEDULING **VANESSA TODD-HOLMES** | VICE PRESIDENT OF BOOK TRADE AND DIGITAL SALES **MARK BERNARDI** | VICE PRESIDENT OF PRODUCT DEVELOPMENT **RANDY LAHRMAN** | GENERAL COUNSEL **KEN LIZZI** | EDITOR IN CHIEF **DAVE MARSHALL** | EDITORIAL DIRECTOR **DAVEY ESTRADA** | SENIOR BOOKS EDITOR **CHRIS WARNER** | DIRECTOR OF SPECIALTY PROJECTS **CARY GRAZZINI** | ART DIRECTOR **LIA RIBACCHI** | DIRECTOR OF DIGITAL ART AND PREPRESS **MATT DRYER** | SENIOR DIRECTOR OF LICENSED PUBLICATIONS **MICHAEL GOMBOS** | DIRECTOR OF CUSTOM PROGRAMS **KARI YADRO** | DIRECTOR OF INTERNATIONAL LICENSING **KARI TORSON**

Published by Dark Horse Books
A division of Dark Horse Comics LLC
10956 SE Main Street
Milwaukie, OR 97222

First edition: June 2022
Trade paperback ISBN: 978-1-50672-455-3

1 3 5 7 9 10 8 6 4 2

Printed in Singapore

Comic Shop Locator Service: comicshoplocator.com

Liebestrasse™

.

Greg Lockard
WRITER

Tim Fish
ARTIST

Héctor Barros
COLORIST

Lucas Gattoni
LETTERER & DESIGNER

Will Dennis
EDITOR

.

Dark Horse Books

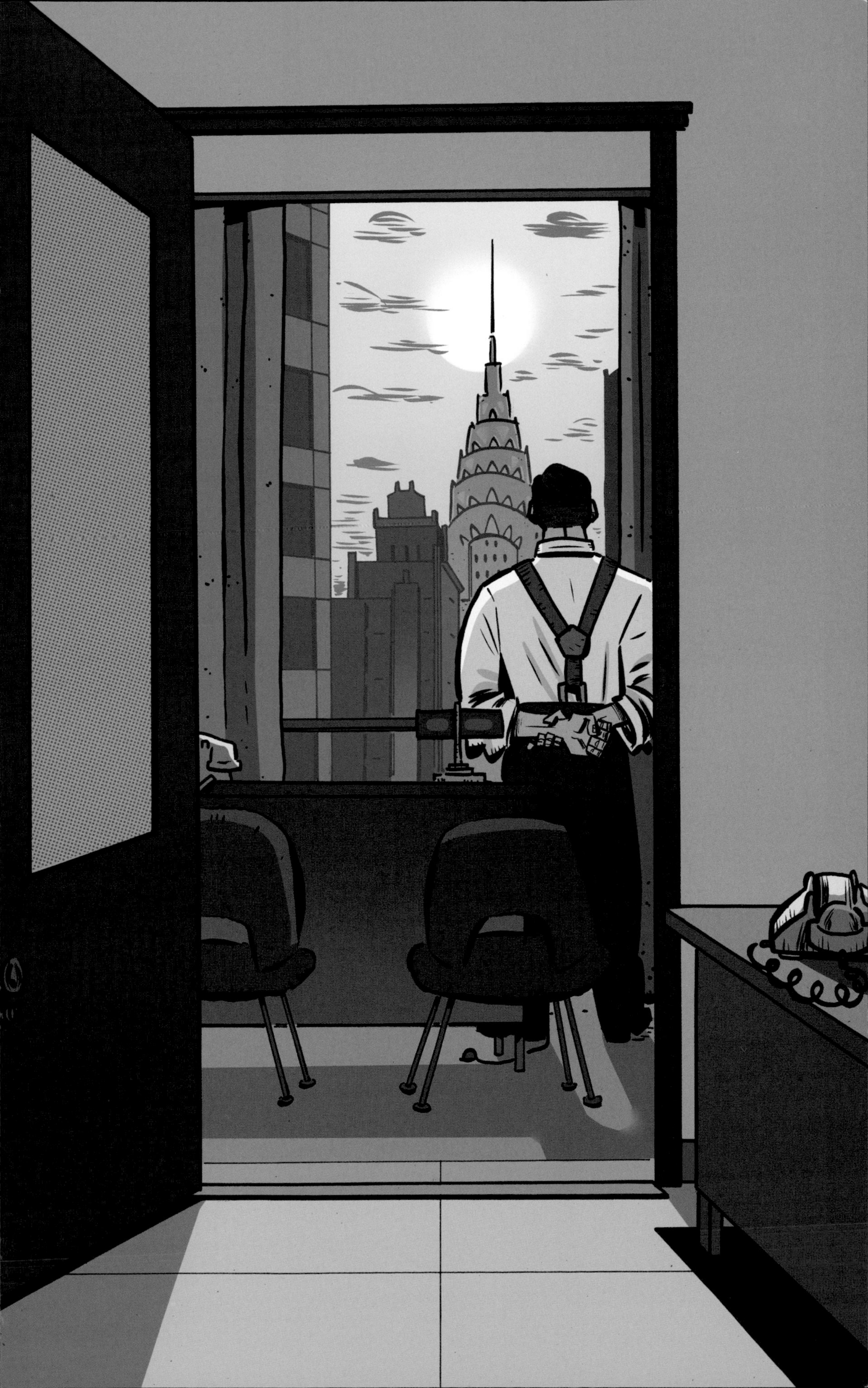

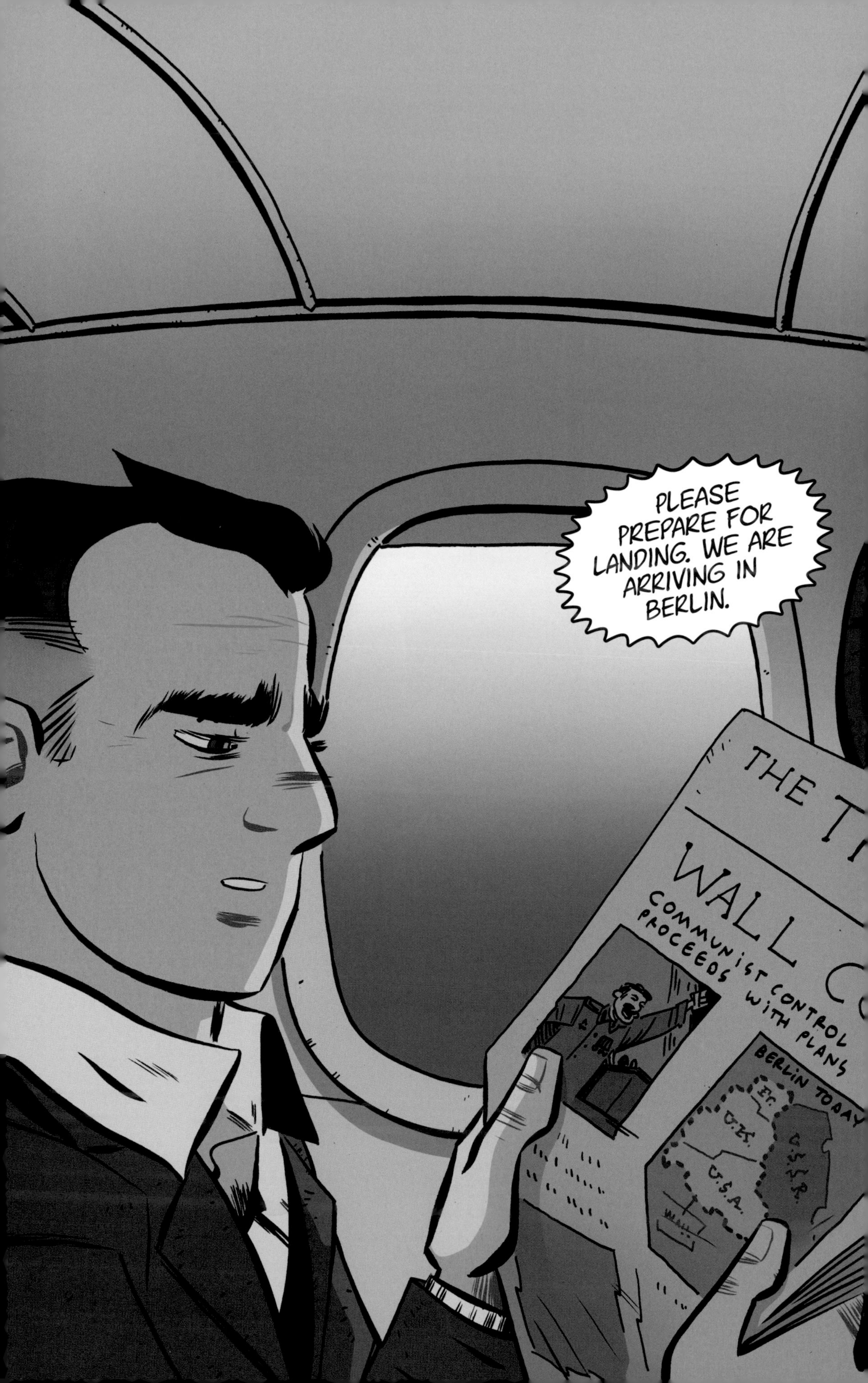
PLEASE PREPARE FOR LANDING. WE ARE ARRIVING IN BERLIN.
THE T
WALL C
COMMUNIST CONTROL PROCEEDS WITH PLANS
BERLIN TODAY
FR.
U.K.
U.S.A.
U.S.S.R.

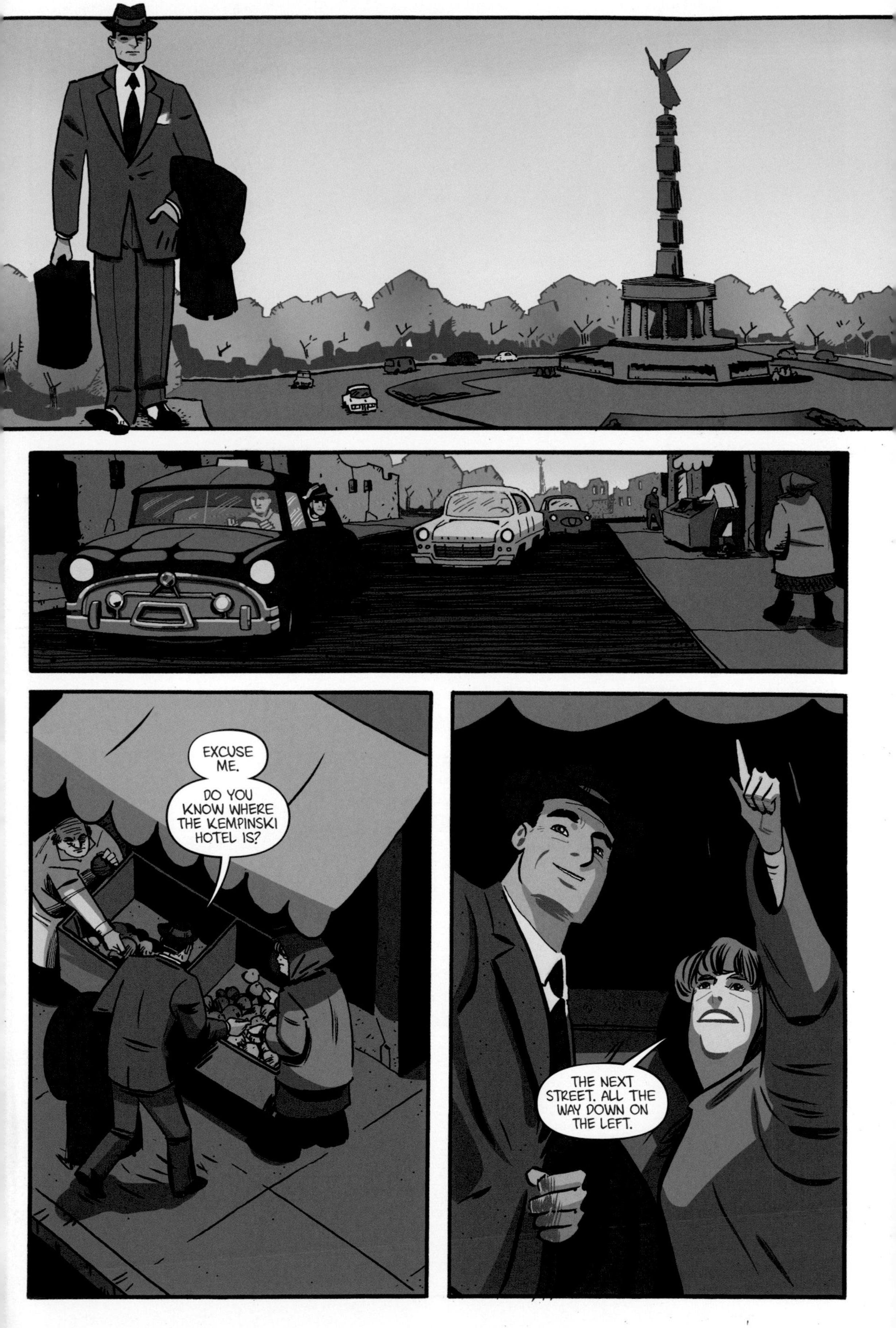
EXCUSE ME.
DO YOU KNOW WHERE THE KEMPINSKI HOTEL IS?
THE NEXT STREET. ALL THE WAY DOWN ON THE LEFT.

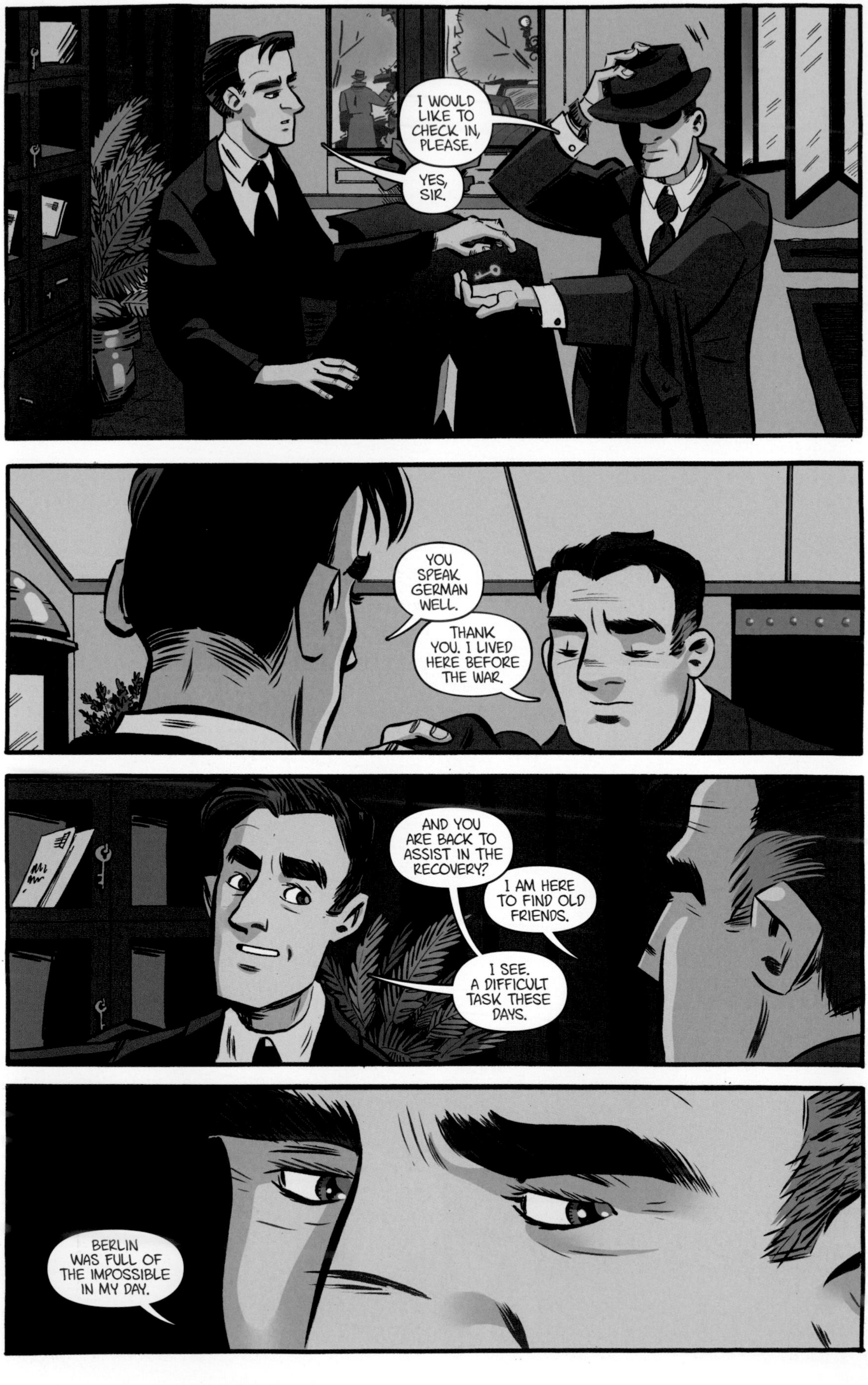
I WOULD LIKE TO CHECK IN, PLEASE.
YES, SIR.
YOU SPEAK GERMAN WELL.
THANK YOU. I LIVED HERE BEFORE THE WAR.
AND YOU ARE BACK TO ASSIST IN THE RECOVERY?
I AM HERE TO FIND OLD FRIENDS.
I SEE. A DIFFICULT TASK THESE DAYS.
BERLIN WAS FULL OF THE IMPOSSIBLE IN MY DAY.

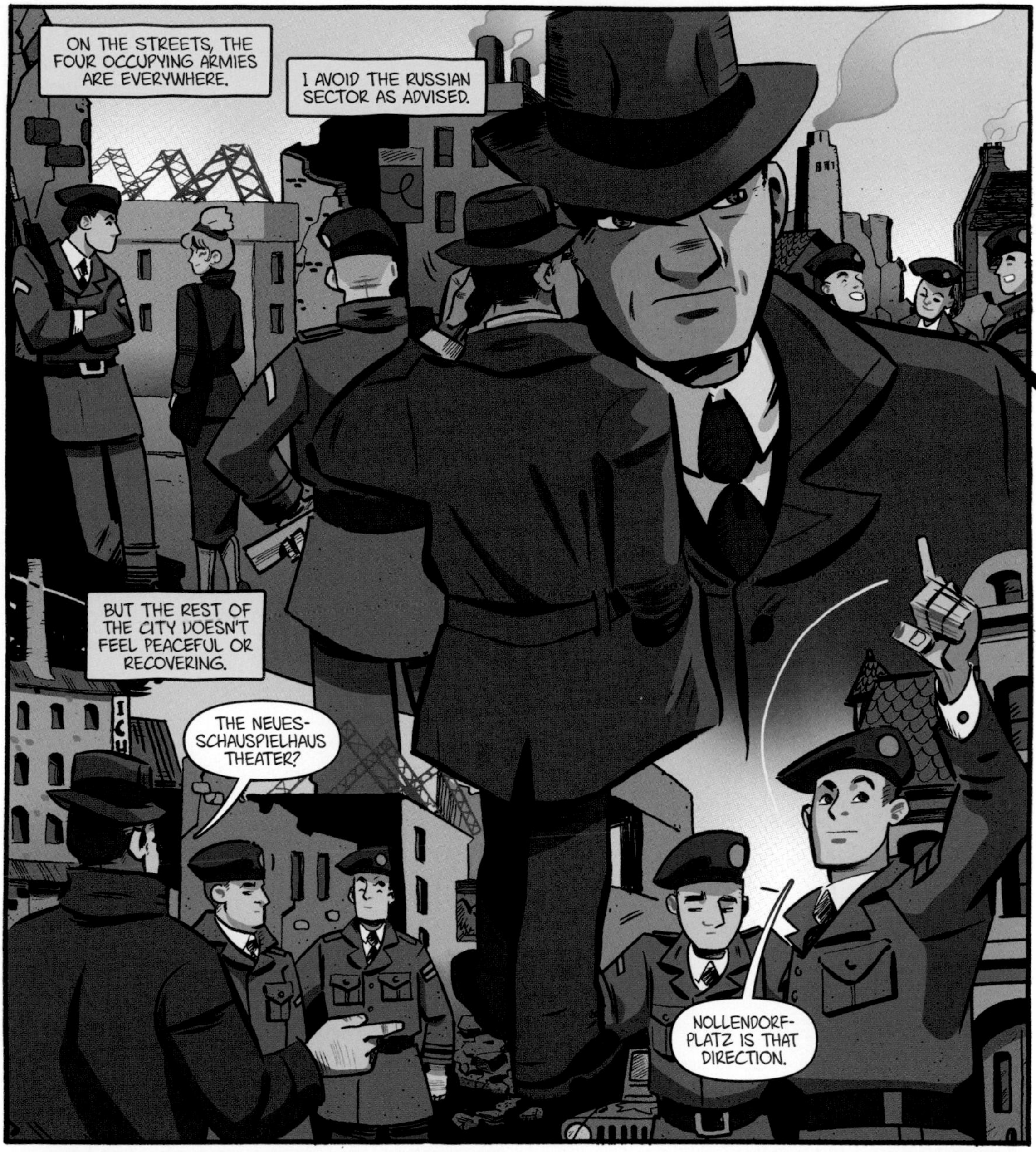
ON THE STREETS, THE FOUR OCCUPYING ARMIES ARE EVERYWHERE.
I AVOID THE RUSSIAN SECTOR AS ADVISED.
BUT THE REST OF THE CITY DOESN'T FEEL PEACEFUL OR RECOVERING.
THE NEUES-SCHAUSPIELHAUS THEATER?
NOLLENDORF-PLATZ IS THAT DIRECTION.

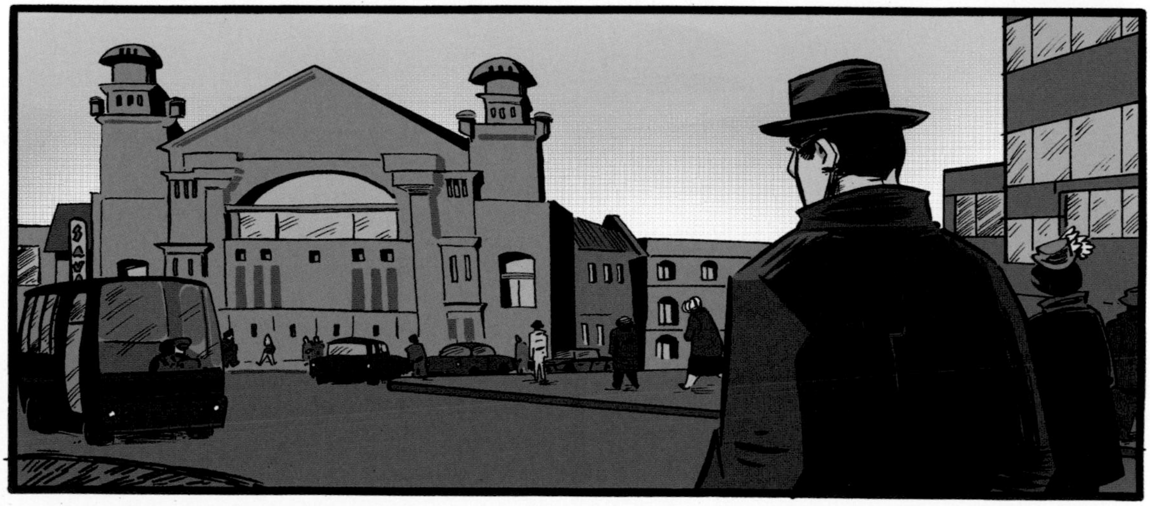

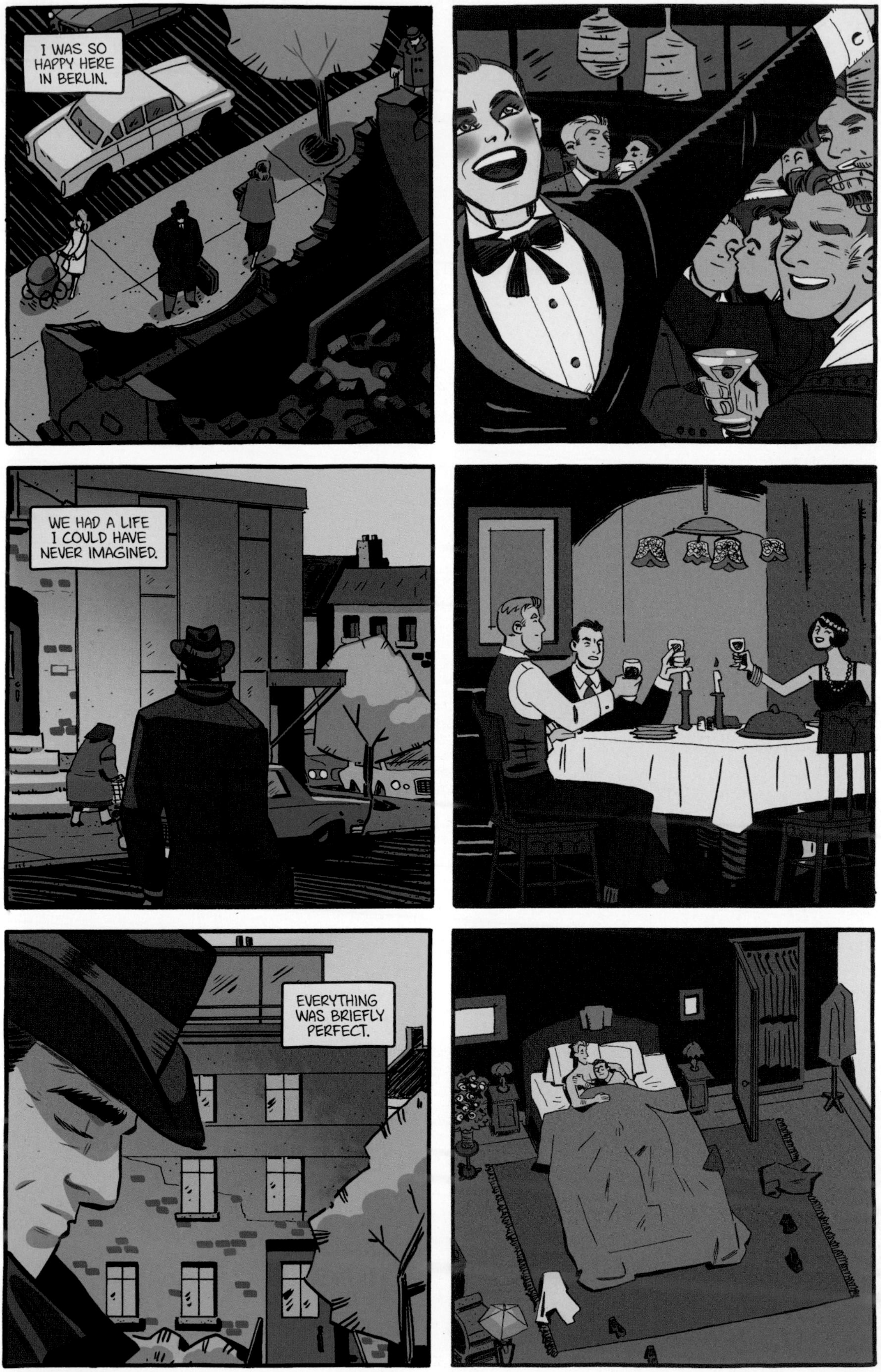
I WAS SO HAPPY HERE IN BERLIN.
WE HAD A LIFE I COULD HAVE NEVER IMAGINED.
EVERYTHING WAS BRIEFLY PERFECT.

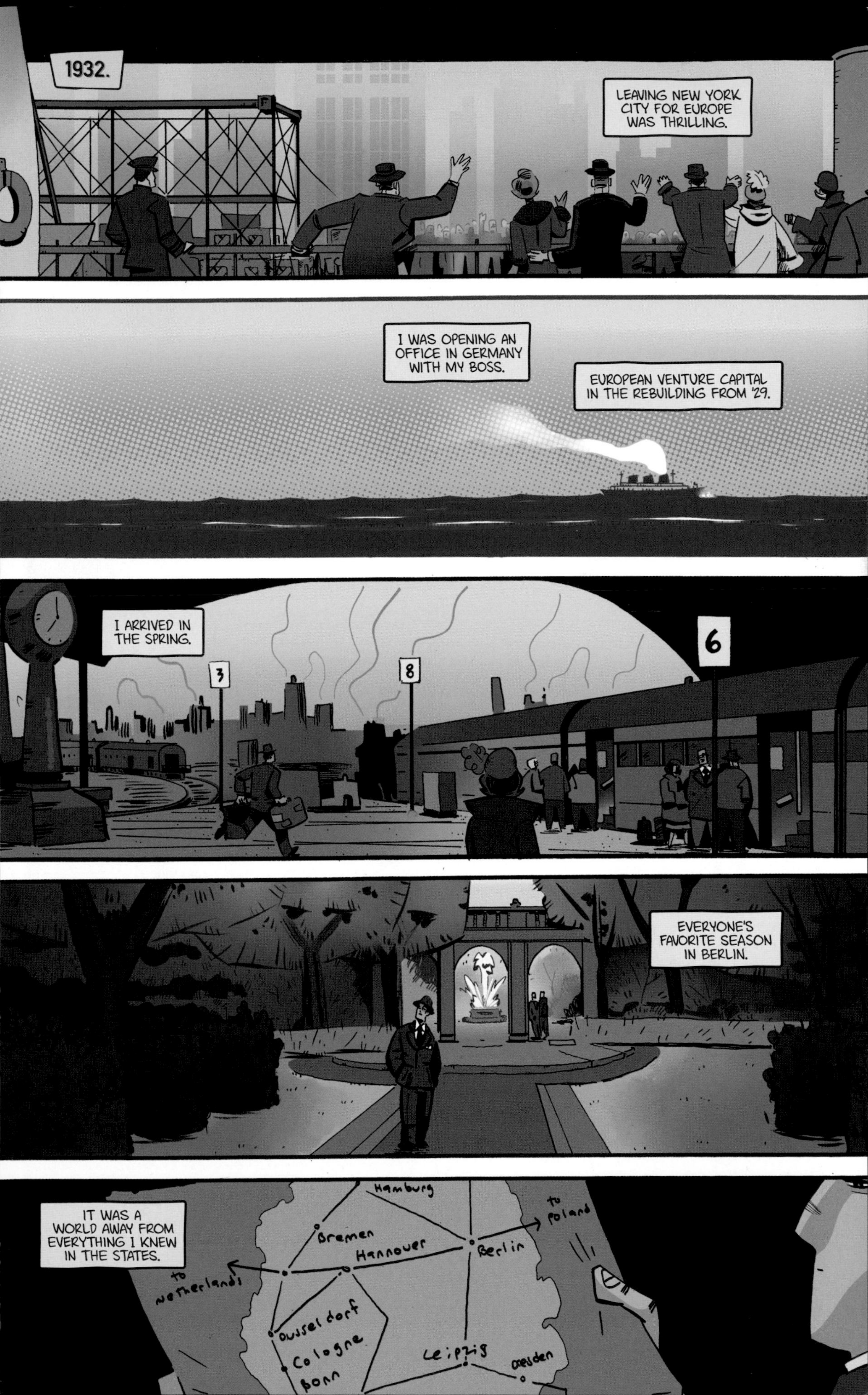
1932.
LEAVING NEW YORK CITY FOR EUROPE WAS THRILLING.
I WAS OPENING AN OFFICE IN GERMANY WITH MY BOSS.
EUROPEAN VENTURE CAPITAL IN THE REBUILDING FROM '29.
I ARRIVED IN THE SPRING.
3
8
6
EVERYONE'S FAVORITE SEASON IN BERLIN.
IT WAS A WORLD AWAY FROM EVERYTHING I KNEW IN THE STATES.
Hamburg
to Poland
Bremen
Hannover
Berlin
to Netherlands
Dusseldorf
Cologne
Bonn
Leipzig
Dresden

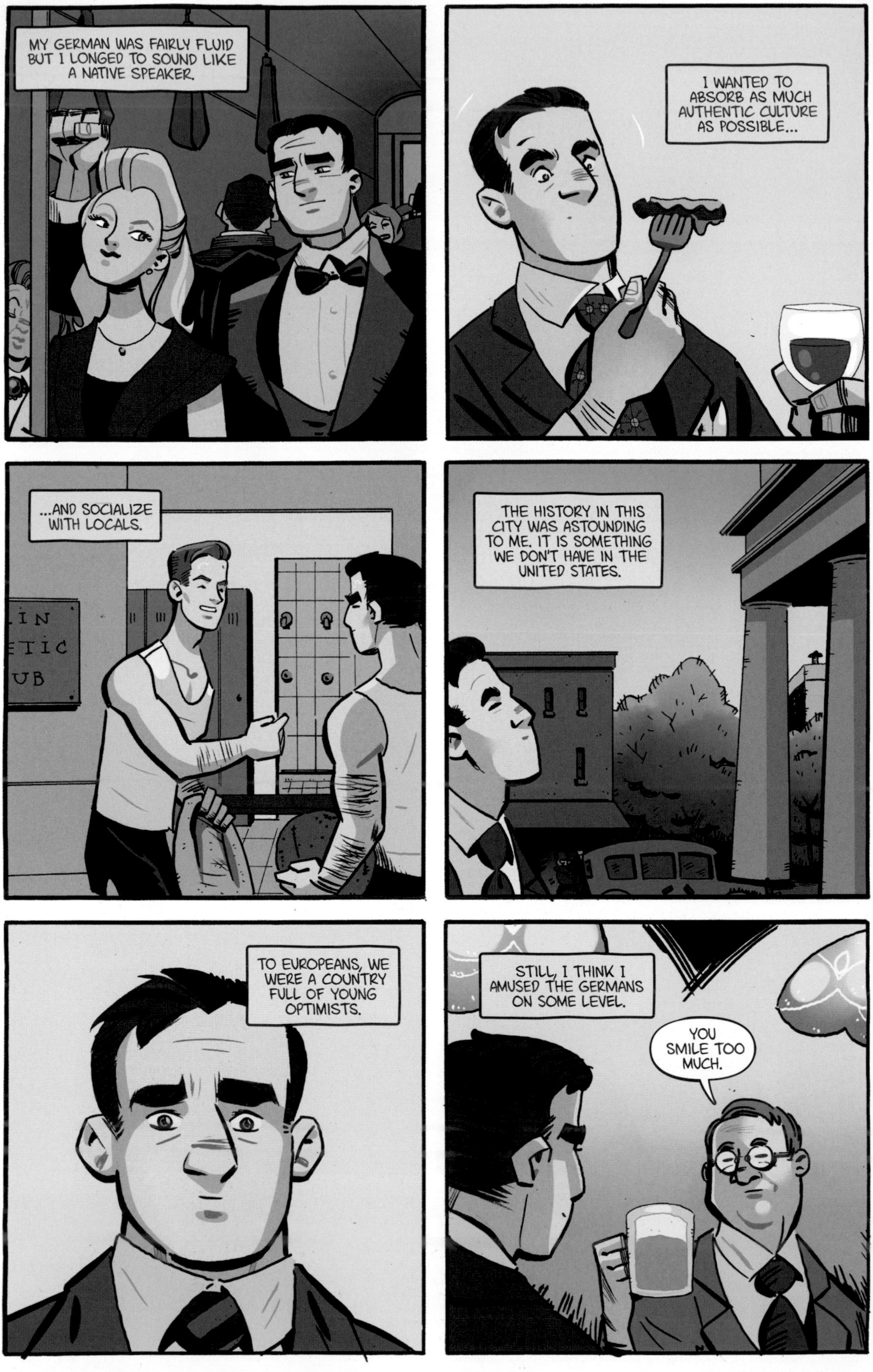
MY GERMAN WAS FAIRLY FLUID BUT I LONGED TO SOUND LIKE A NATIVE SPEAKER.
I WANTED TO ABSORB AS MUCH AUTHENTIC CULTURE AS POSSIBLE...
...AND SOCIALIZE WITH LOCALS.
THE HISTORY IN THIS CITY WAS ASTOUNDING TO ME. IT IS SOMETHING WE DON'T HAVE IN THE UNITED STATES.
TO EUROPEANS, WE WERE A COUNTRY FULL OF YOUNG OPTIMISTS.
STILL, I THINK I AMUSED THE GERMANS ON SOME LEVEL.
YOU SMILE TOO MUCH.

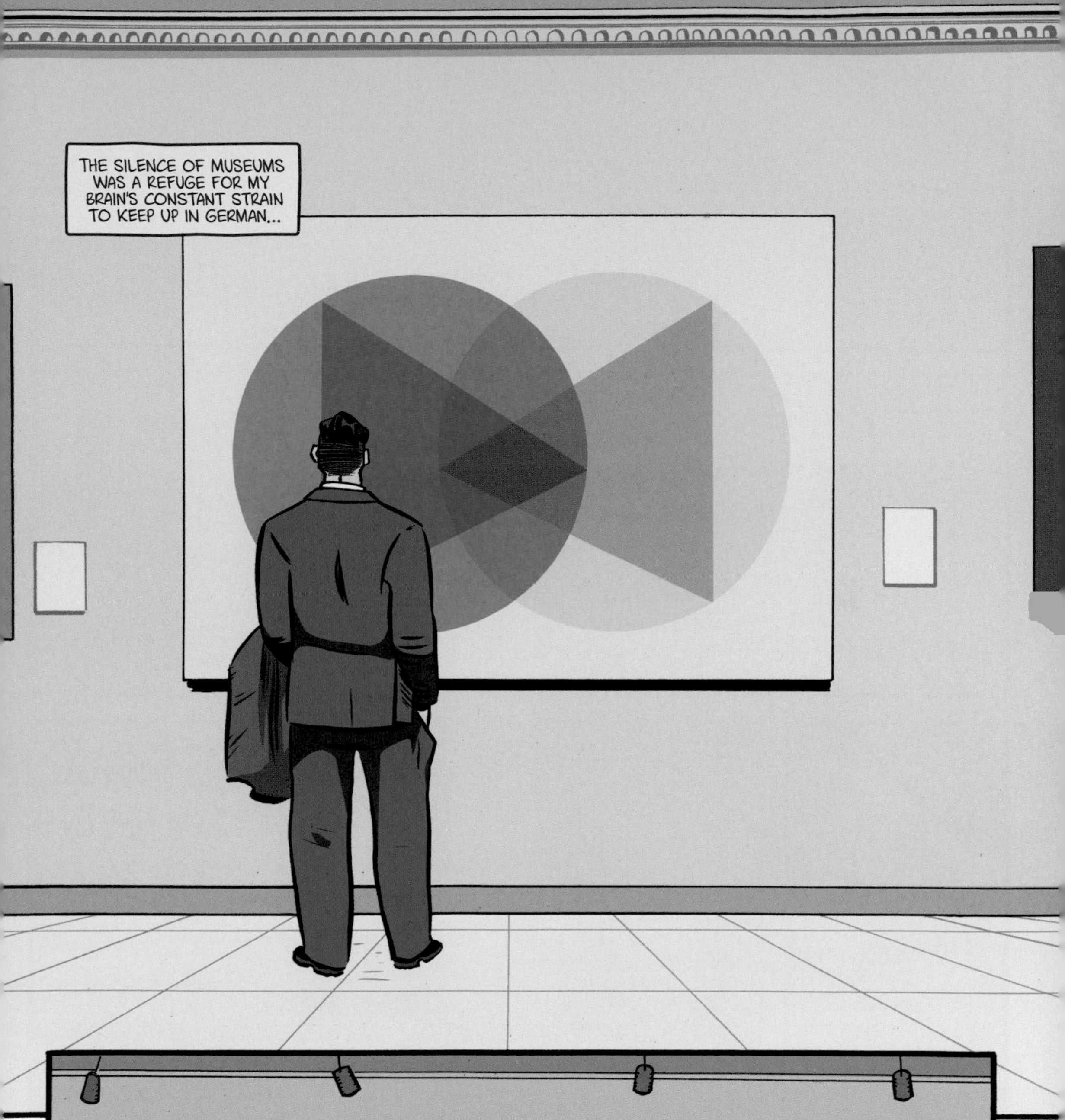
THE SILENCE OF MUSEUMS WAS A REFUGE FOR MY BRAIN'S CONSTANT STRAIN TO KEEP UP IN GERMAN...

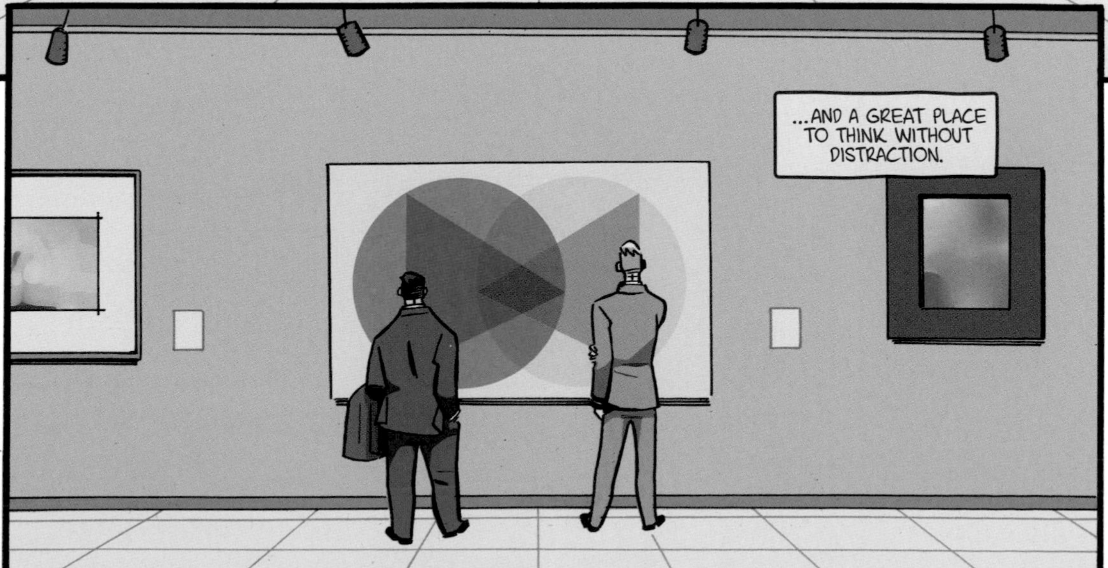
...AND A GREAT PLACE TO THINK WITHOUT DISTRACTION.

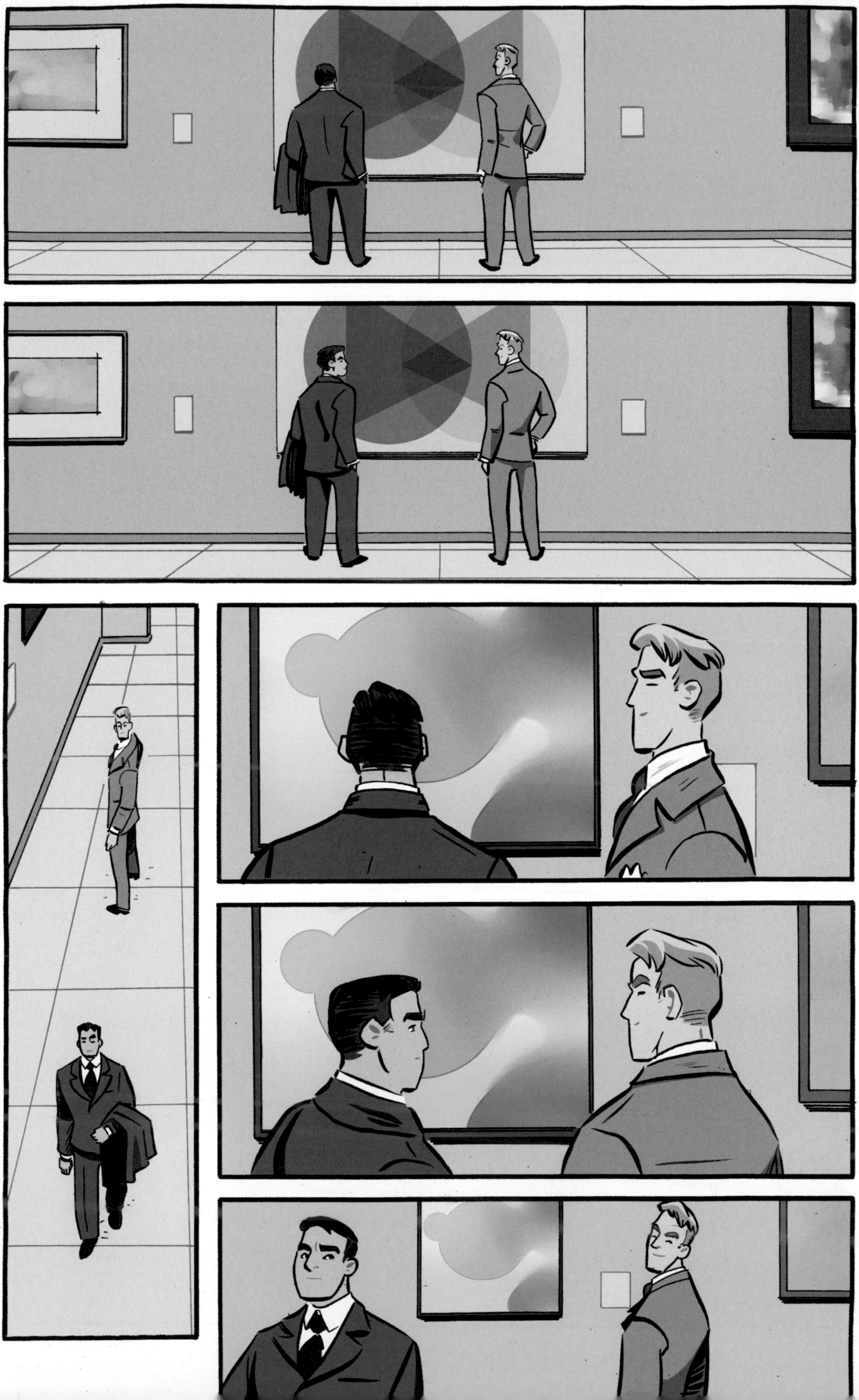

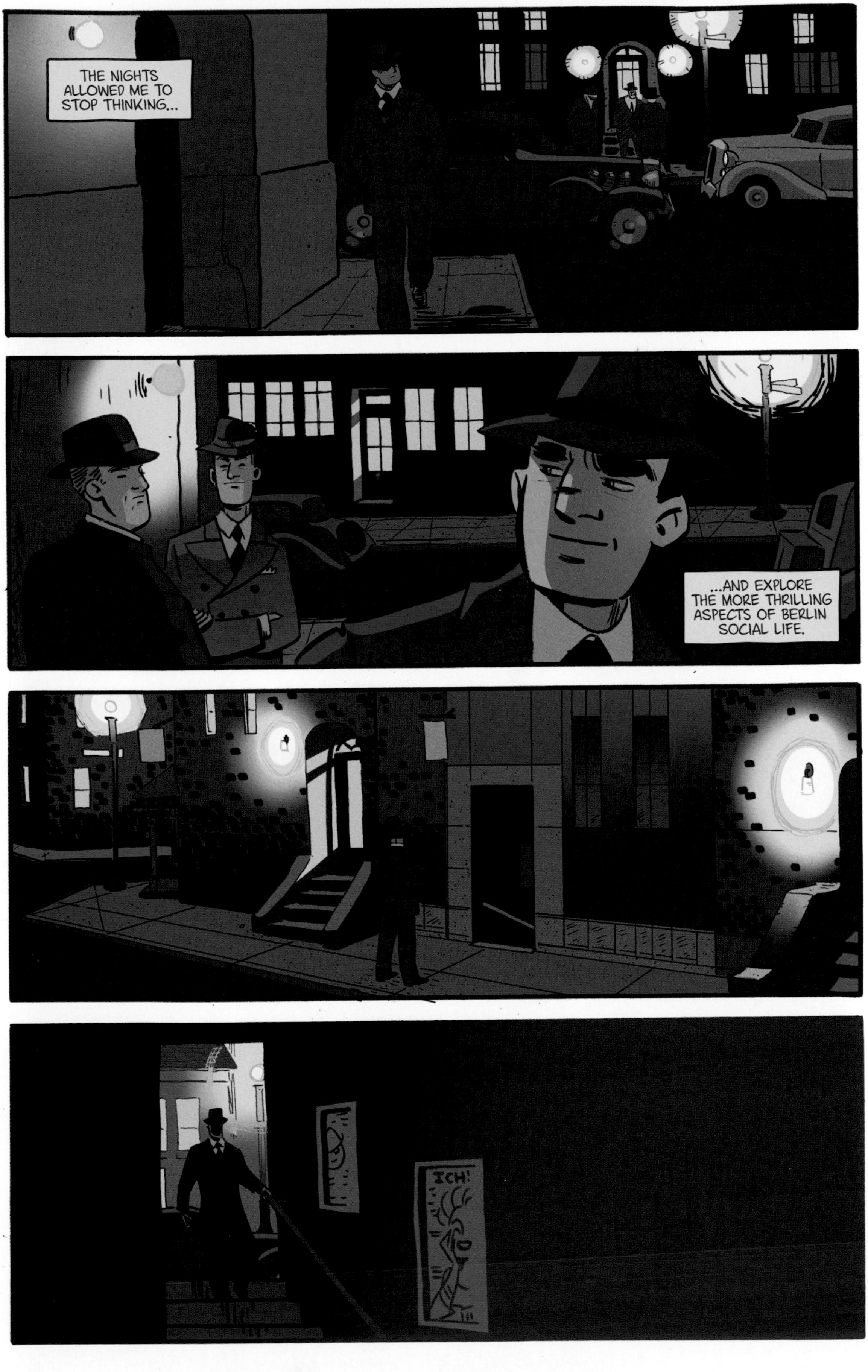
THE NIGHTS ALLOWED ME TO STOP THINKING...
...AND EXPLORE THE MORE THRILLING ASPECTS OF BERLIN SOCIAL LIFE.
ICH!

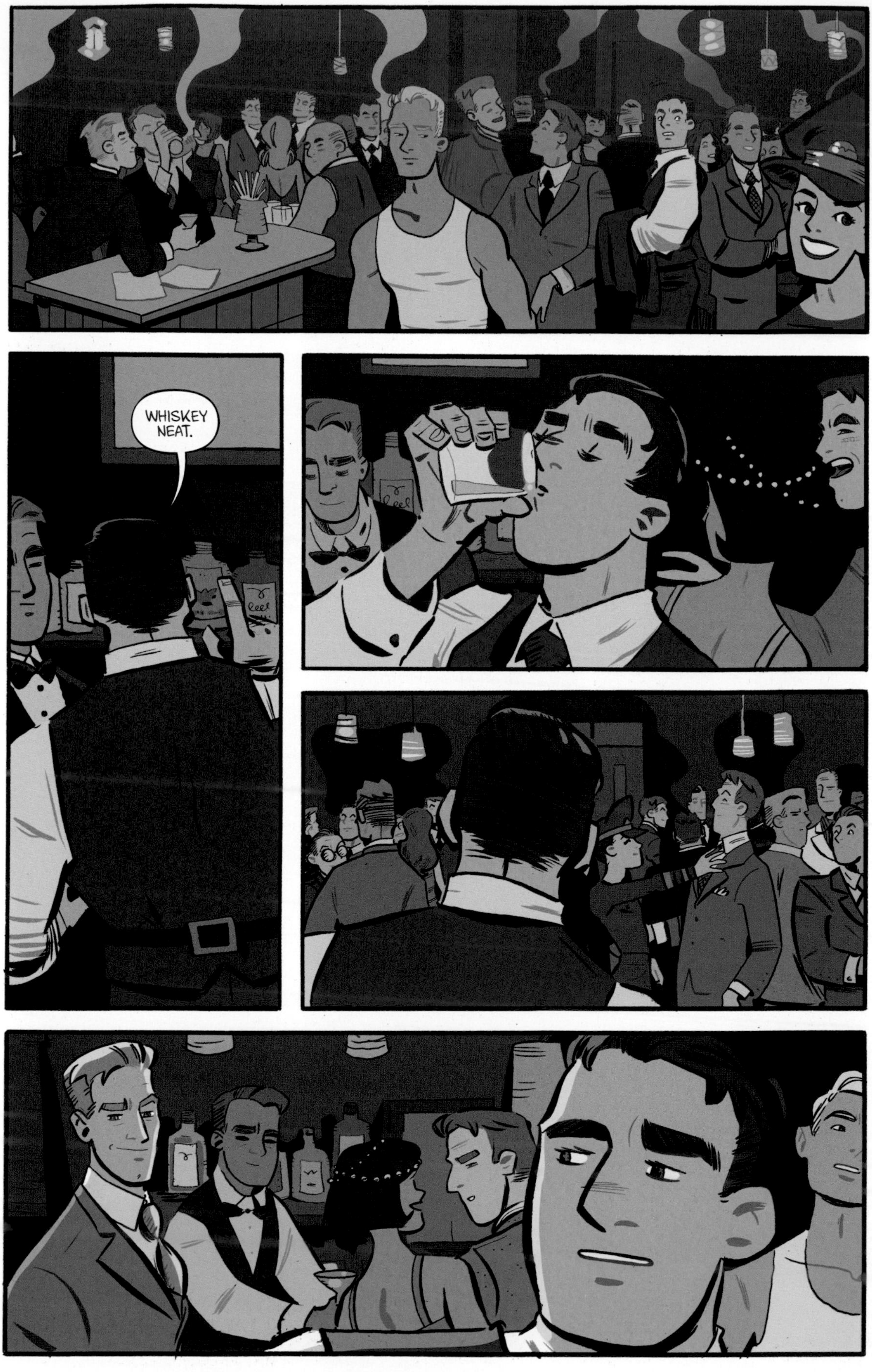
WHISKEY NEAT.

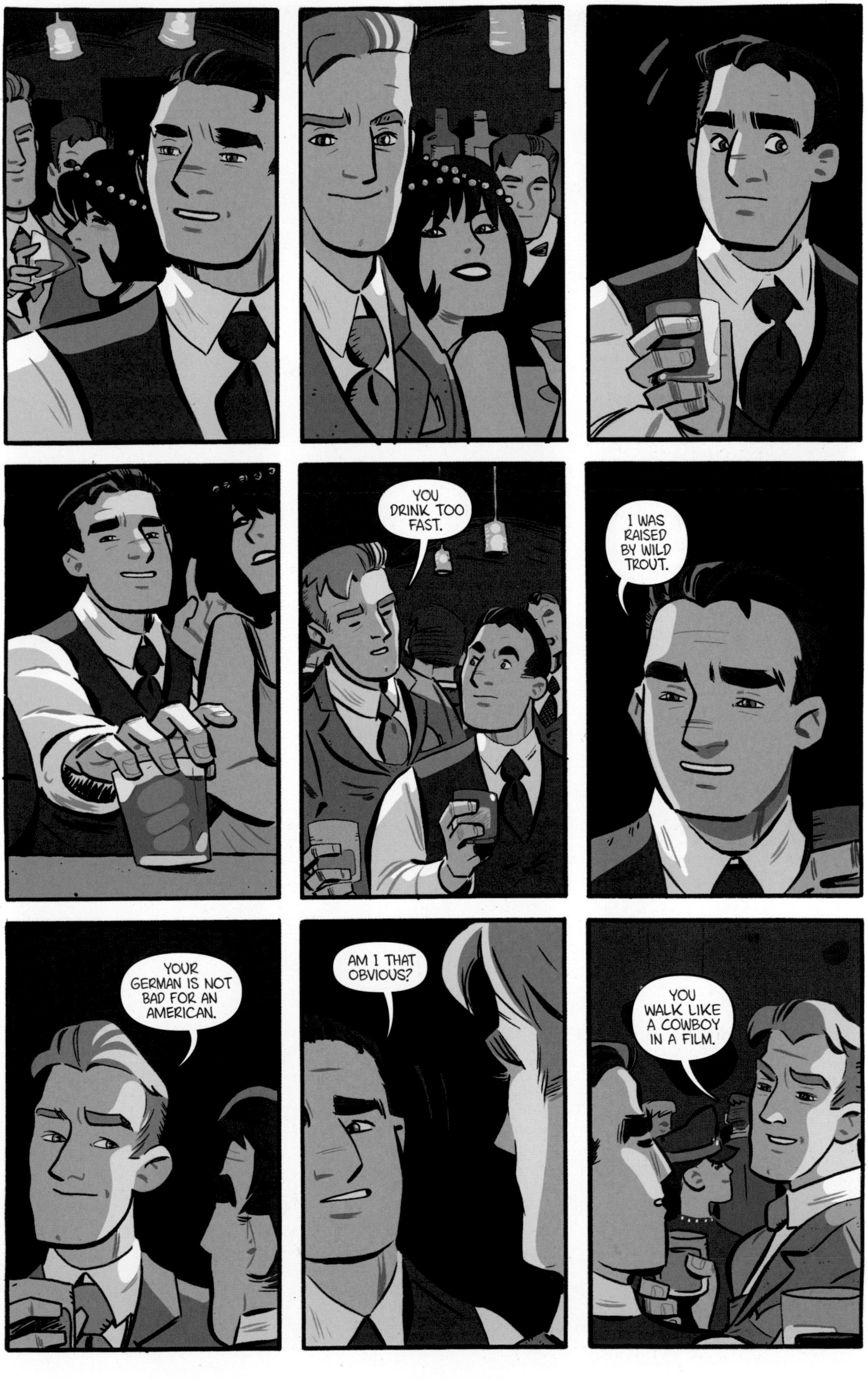
YOU DRINK TOO FAST.
I WAS RAISED BY WILD TROUT.
YOUR GERMAN IS NOT BAD FOR AN AMERICAN.
AM I THAT OBVIOUS?
YOU WALK LIKE A COWBOY IN A FILM.

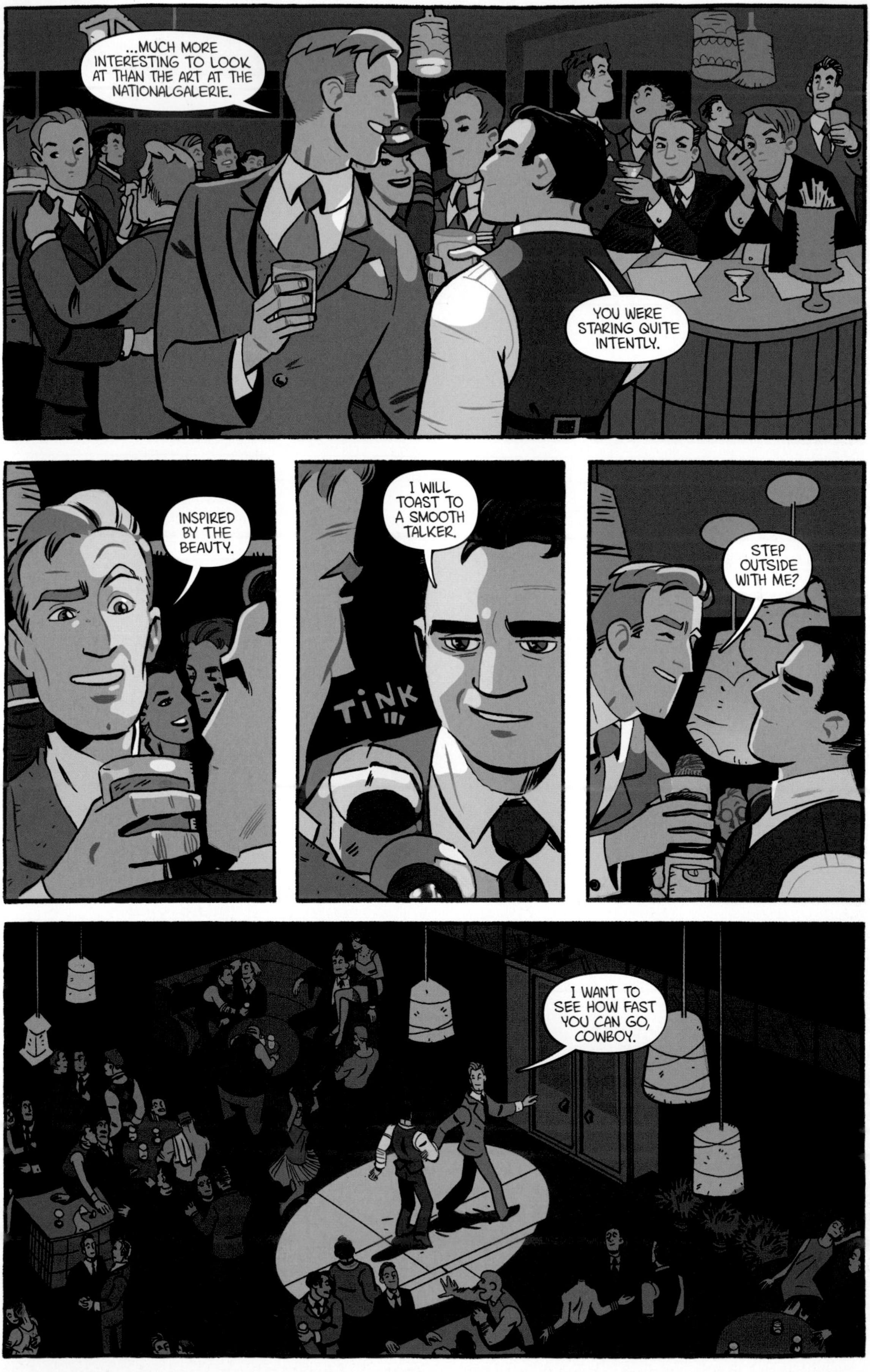
...MUCH MORE INTERESTING TO LOOK AT THAN THE ART AT THE NATIONALGALERIE.
YOU WERE STARING QUITE INTENTLY.
INSPIRED BY THE BEAUTY.
I WILL TOAST TO A SMOOTH TALKER.
TINK
STEP OUTSIDE WITH ME?
I WANT TO SEE HOW FAST YOU CAN GO, COWBOY.

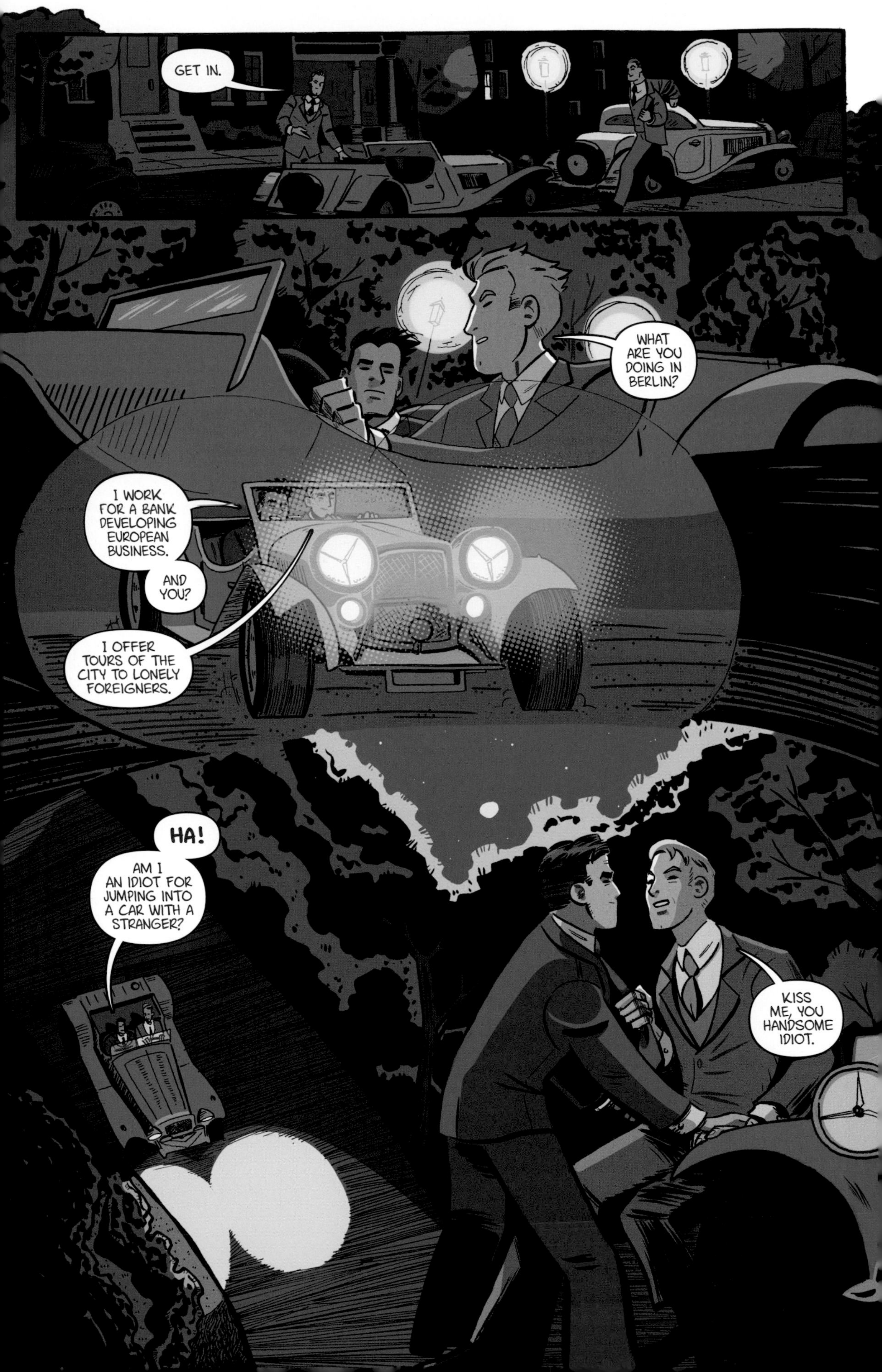
GET IN.
WHAT ARE YOU DOING IN BERLIN?
I WORK FOR A BANK DEVELOPING EUROPEAN BUSINESS.
AND YOU?
I OFFER TOURS OF THE CITY TO LONELY FOREIGNERS.
HA!
AM I AN IDIOT FOR JUMPING INTO A CAR WITH A STRANGER?
KISS ME, YOU HANDSOME IDIOT.

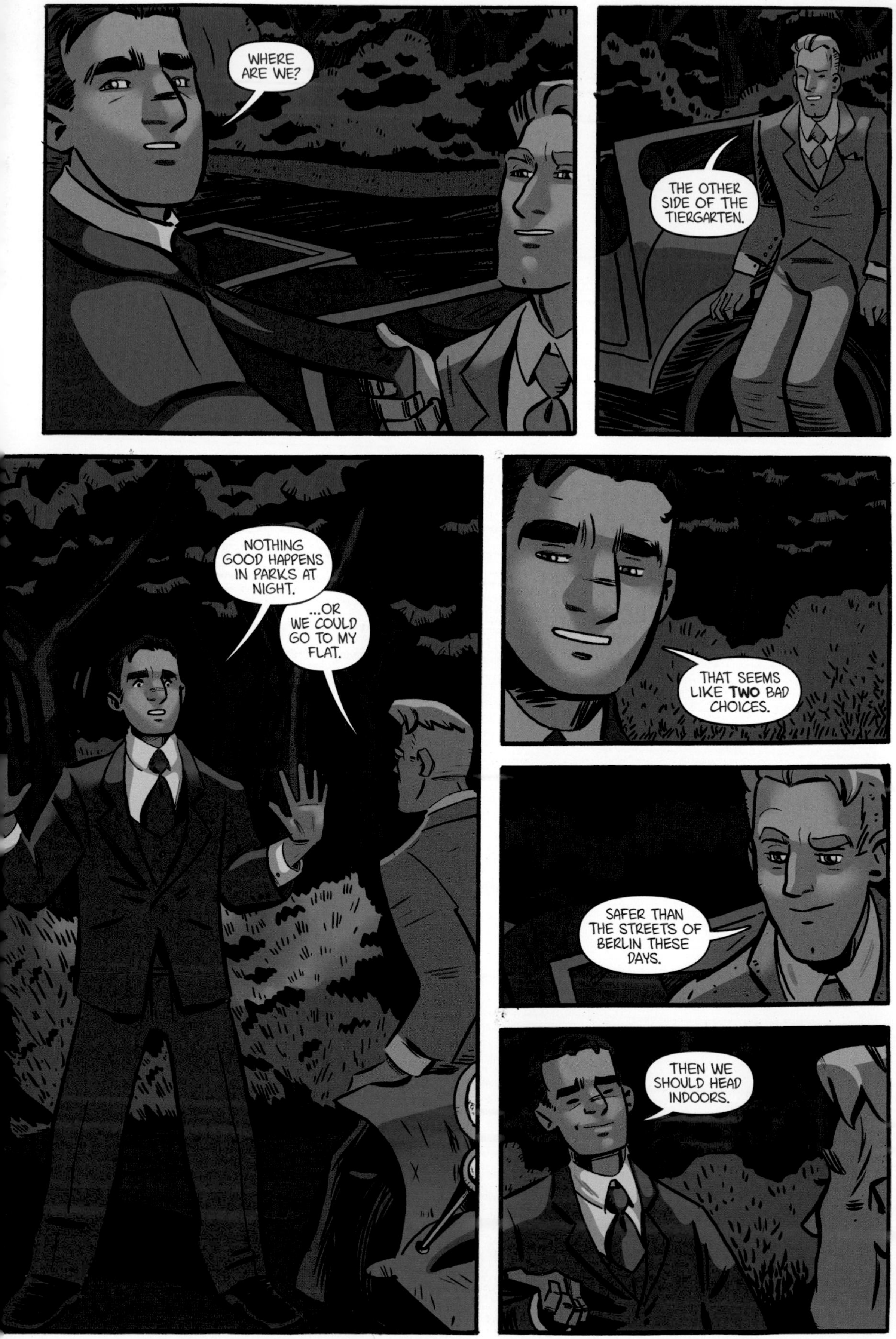
WHERE ARE WE?
THE OTHER SIDE OF THE TIERGARTEN.
NOTHING GOOD HAPPENS IN PARKS AT NIGHT.
...OR WE COULD GO TO MY FLAT.
THAT SEEMS LIKE TWO BAD CHOICES.
SAFER THAN THE STREETS OF BERLIN THESE DAYS.
THEN WE SHOULD HEAD INDOORS.

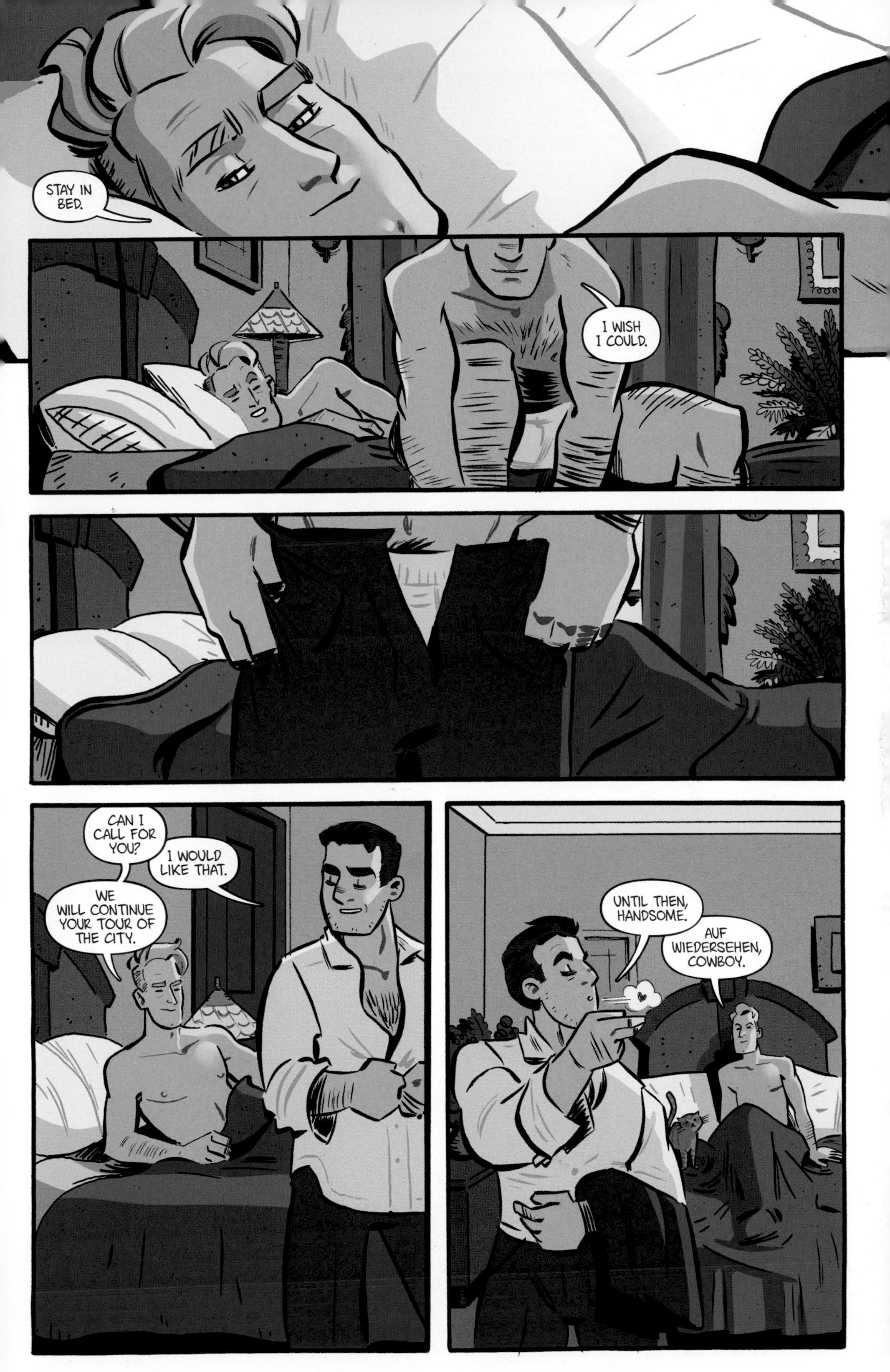
STAY IN BED.
I WISH I COULD.
CAN I CALL FOR YOU?
I WOULD LIKE THAT.
WE WILL CONTINUE YOUR TOUR OF THE CITY.
UNTIL THEN, HANDSOME.
AUF WIEDERSEHEN, COWBOY.

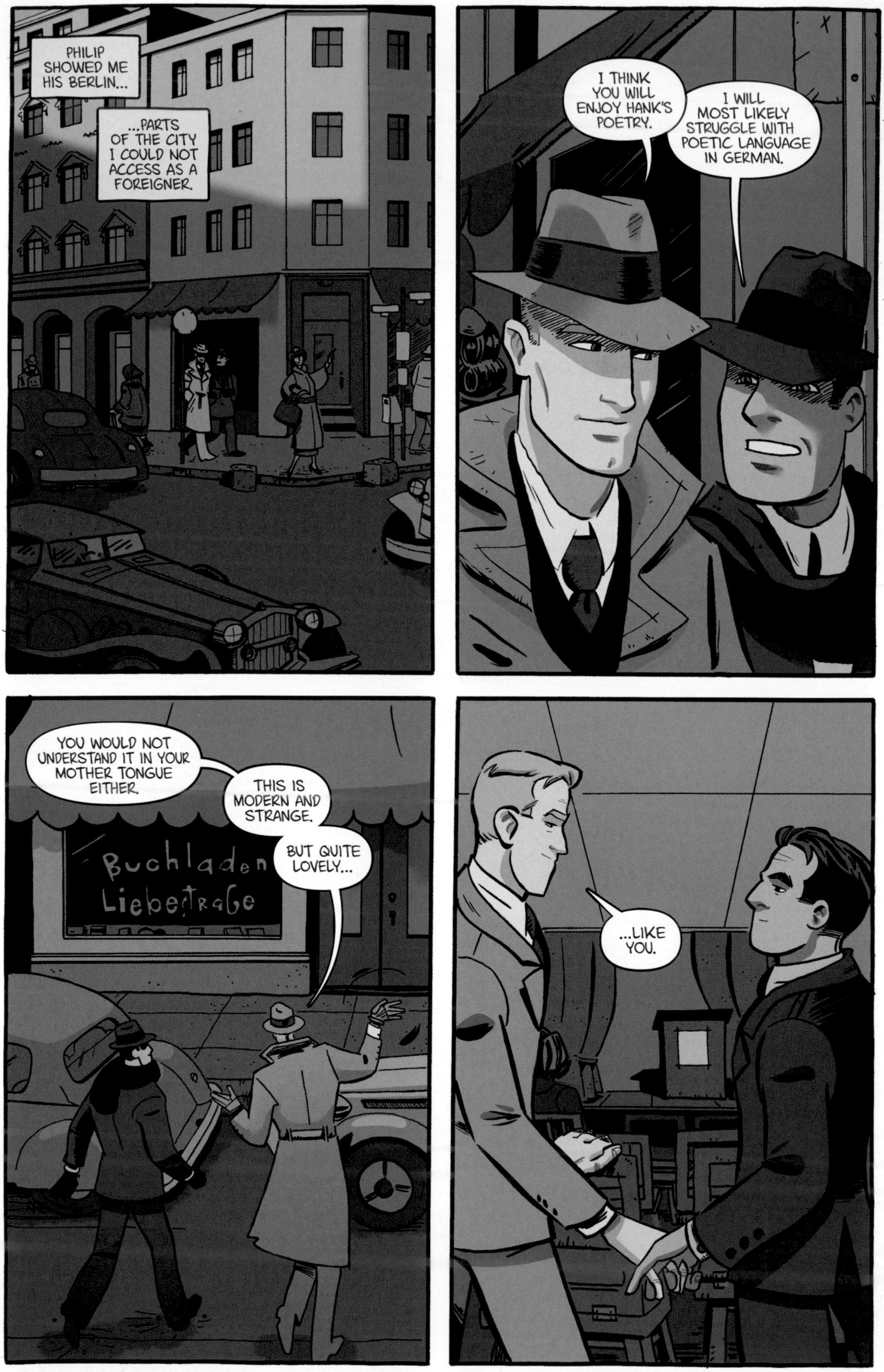
PHILIP SHOWED ME HIS BERLIN...
...PARTS OF THE CITY I COULD NOT ACCESS AS A FOREIGNER.
I THINK YOU WILL ENJOY HANK'S POETRY.
I WILL MOST LIKELY STRUGGLE WITH POETIC LANGUAGE IN GERMAN.
YOU WOULD NOT UNDERSTAND IT IN YOUR MOTHER TONGUE EITHER.
THIS IS MODERN AND STRANGE.
BUT QUITE LOVELY...
Buchladen
...LIKE YOU.

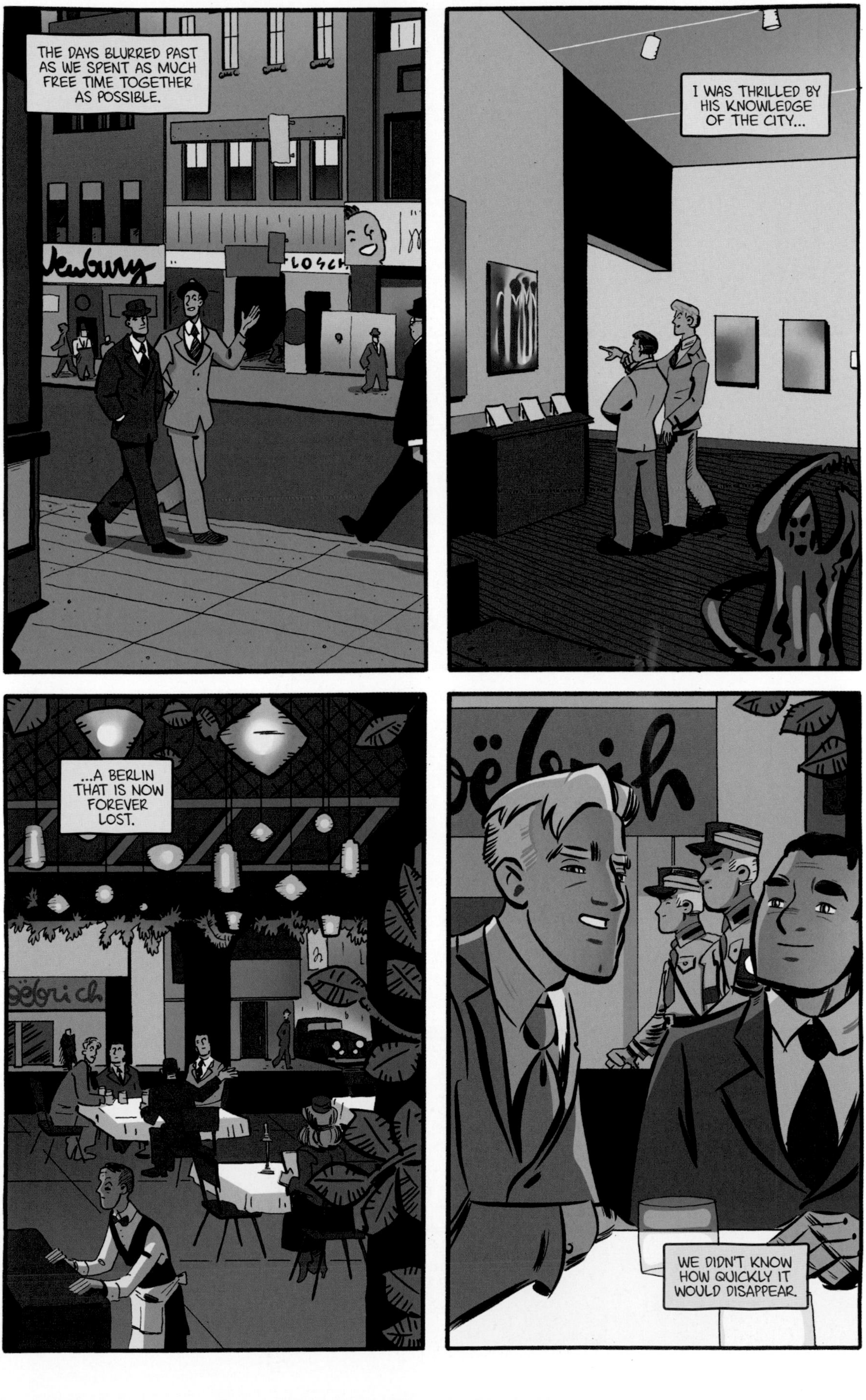
THE DAYS BLURRED PAST AS WE SPENT AS MUCH FREE TIME TOGETHER AS POSSIBLE.
I WAS THRILLED BY HIS KNOWLEDGE OF THE CITY...
...A BERLIN THAT IS NOW FOREVER LOST.
WE DIDN'T KNOW HOW QUICKLY IT WOULD DISAPPEAR.

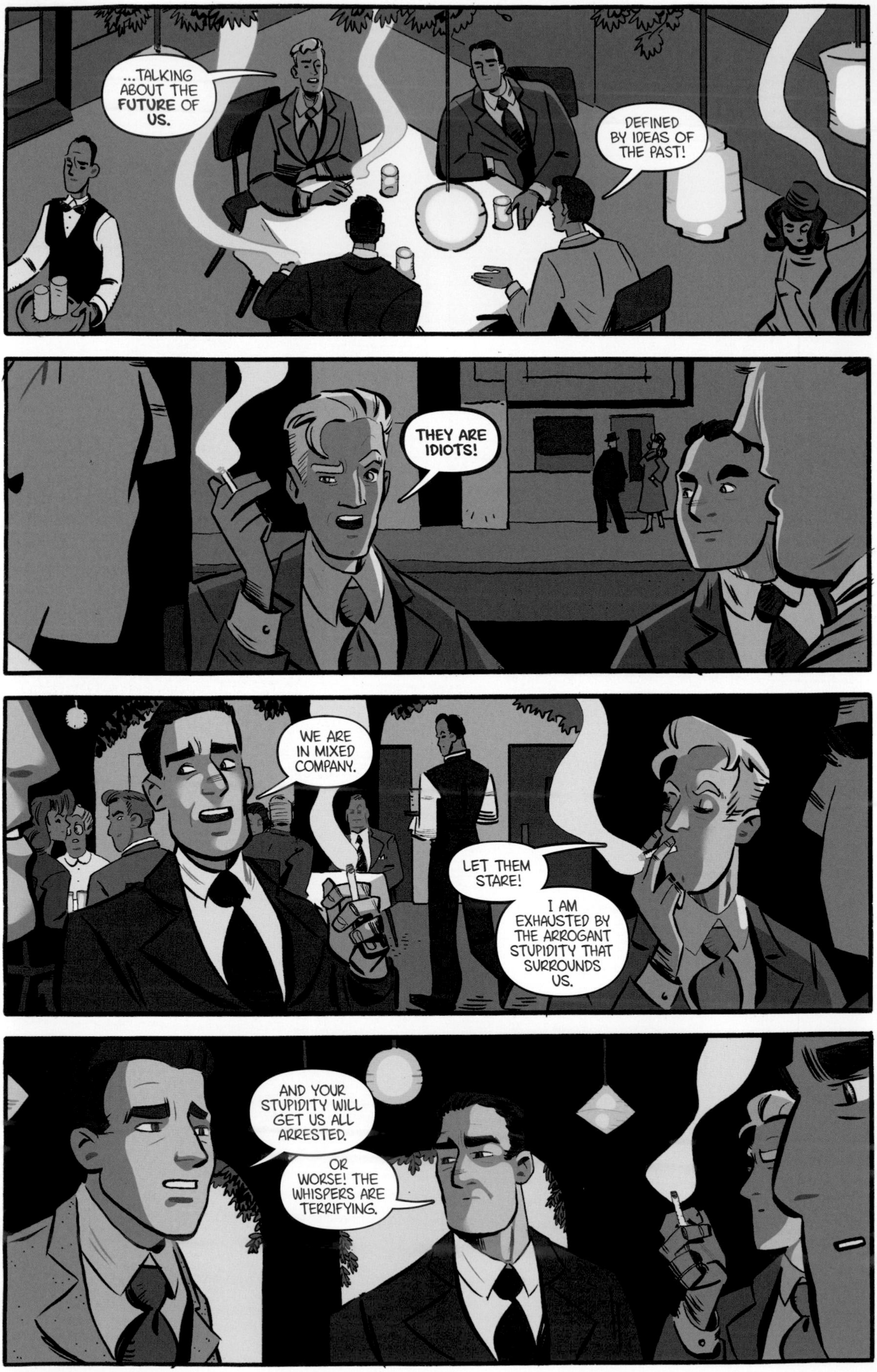
...TALKING ABOUT THE FUTURE OF US.
DEFINED BY IDEAS OF THE PAST!
THEY ARE IDIOTS!
WE ARE IN MIXED COMPANY.
LET THEM STARE!
I AM EXHAUSTED BY THE ARROGANT STUPIDITY THAT SURROUNDS US.
AND YOUR STUPIDITY WILL GET US ALL ARRESTED.
OR WORSE! THE WHISPERS ARE TERRIFYING.

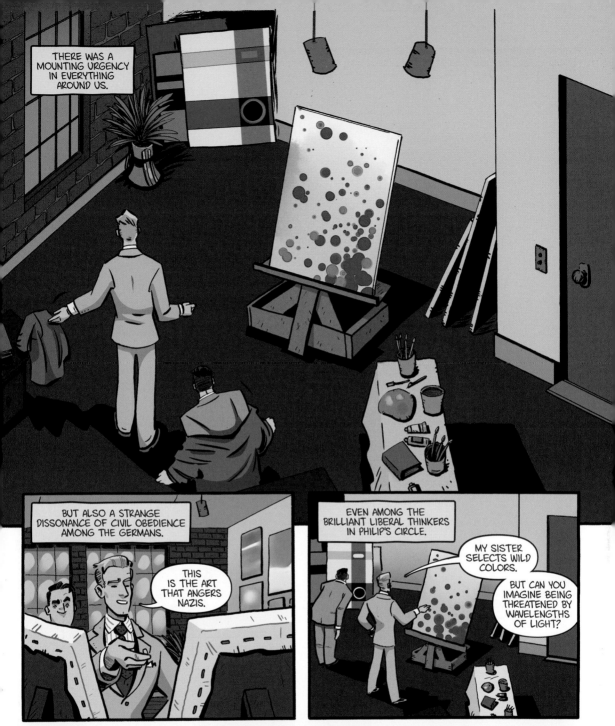

THERE WAS A MOUNTING URGENCY IN EVERYTHING AROUND US.

BUT ALSO A STRANGE DISSONANCE OF CIVIL OBEDIENCE AMONG THE GERMANS.

THIS IS THE ART THAT ANGERS NAZIS.

EVEN AMONG THE BRILLIANT LIBERAL THINKERS IN PHILIP'S CIRCLE.

MY SISTER SELECTS WILD COLORS.

BUT CAN YOU IMAGINE BEING THREATENED BY WAVELENGTHS OF LIGHT?

DEAR BROTHER, STOP HAWKING MY PAINTINGS LIKE PRODUCE.

SAMUEL, THIS IS HILDE.

VERY NICE TO MEET YOU.

LIKEWISE.

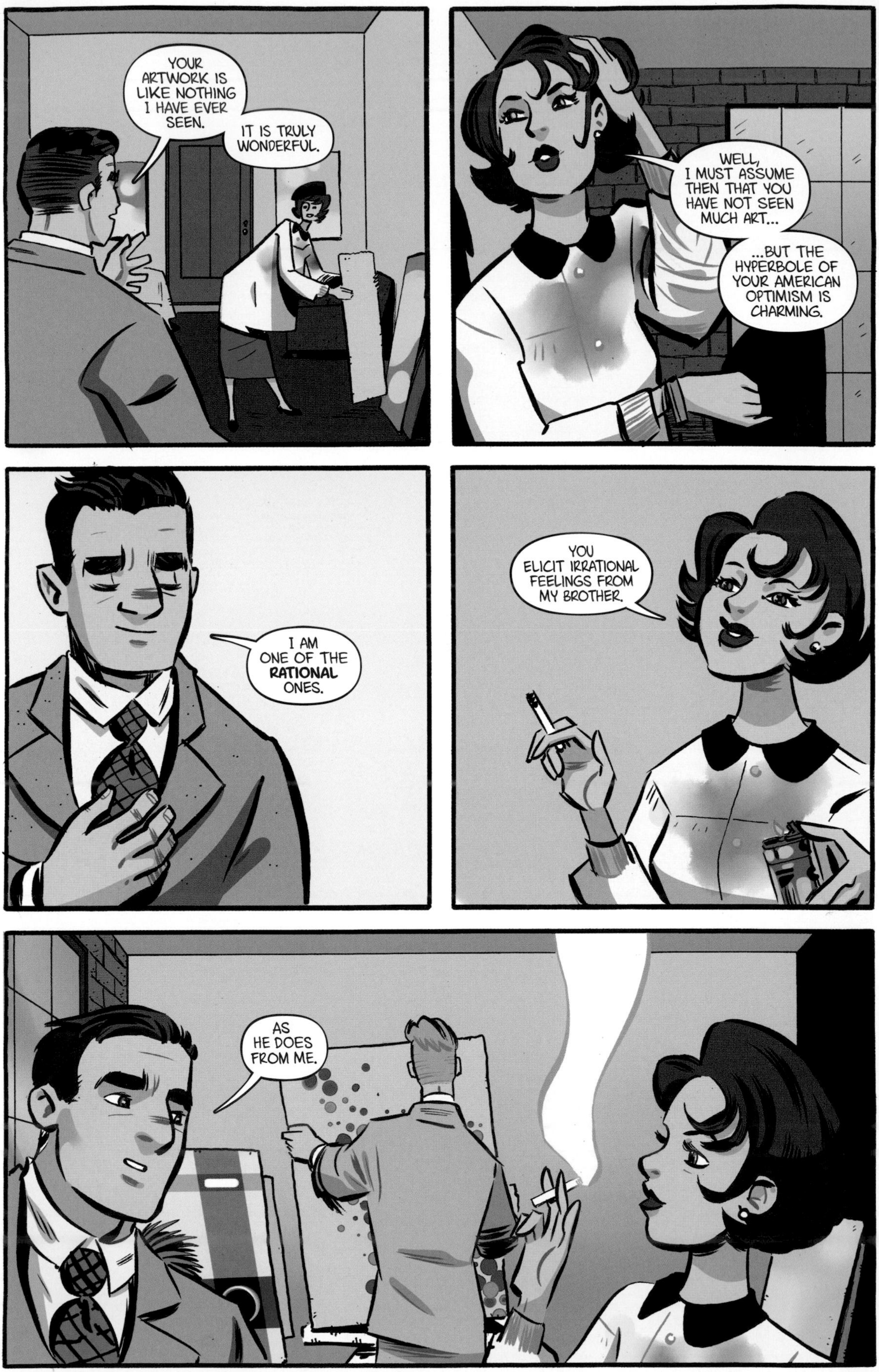
YOUR ARTWORK IS LIKE NOTHING I HAVE EVER SEEN.
IT IS TRULY WONDERFUL.
WELL, I MUST ASSUME THEN THAT YOU HAVE NOT SEEN MUCH ART...
...BUT THE HYPERBOLE OF YOUR AMERICAN OPTIMISM IS CHARMING.
I AM ONE OF THE **RATIONAL** ONES.
YOU ELICIT IRRATIONAL FEELINGS FROM MY BROTHER.
AS HE DOES FROM ME.

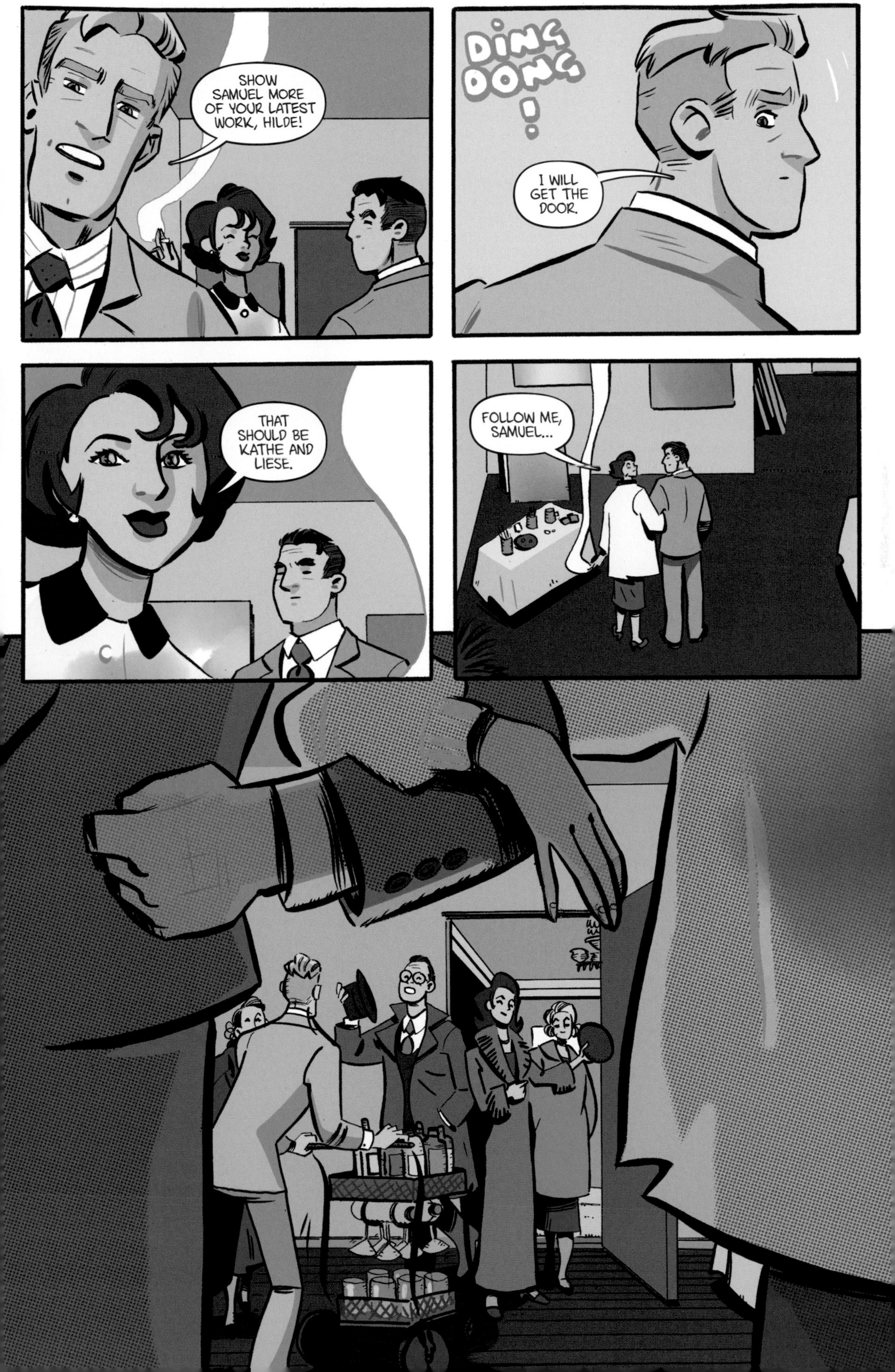
SHOW SAMUEL MORE OF YOUR LATEST WORK, HILDE!
DING DONG!
I WILL GET THE DOOR.
THAT SHOULD BE KATHE AND LIESE.
FOLLOW ME, SAMUEL...

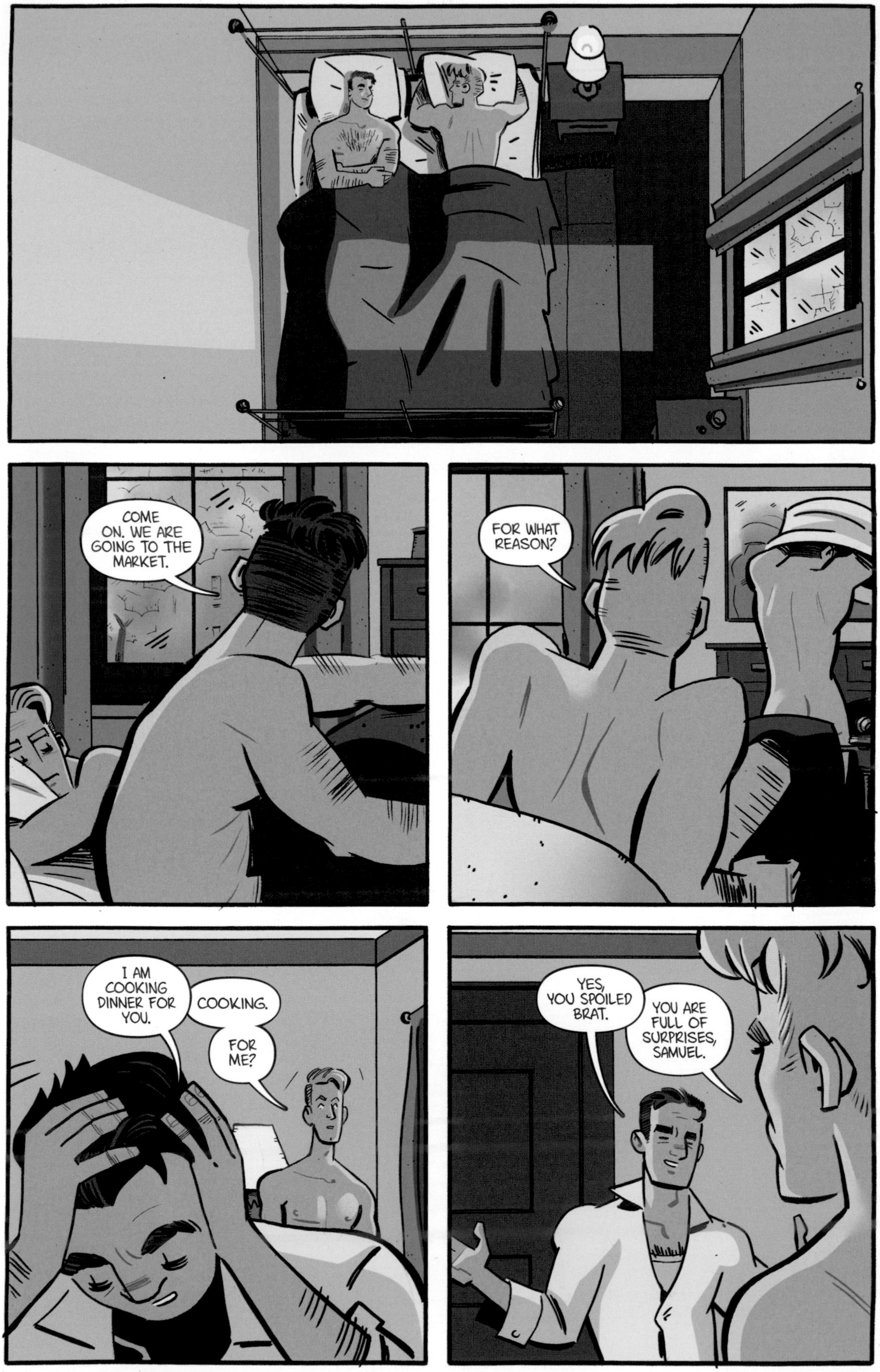
COME ON. WE ARE GOING TO THE MARKET.
FOR WHAT REASON?
I AM COOKING DINNER FOR YOU.
COOKING.
FOR ME?
YES, YOU SPOILED BRAT.
YOU ARE FULL OF SURPRISES, SAMUEL.

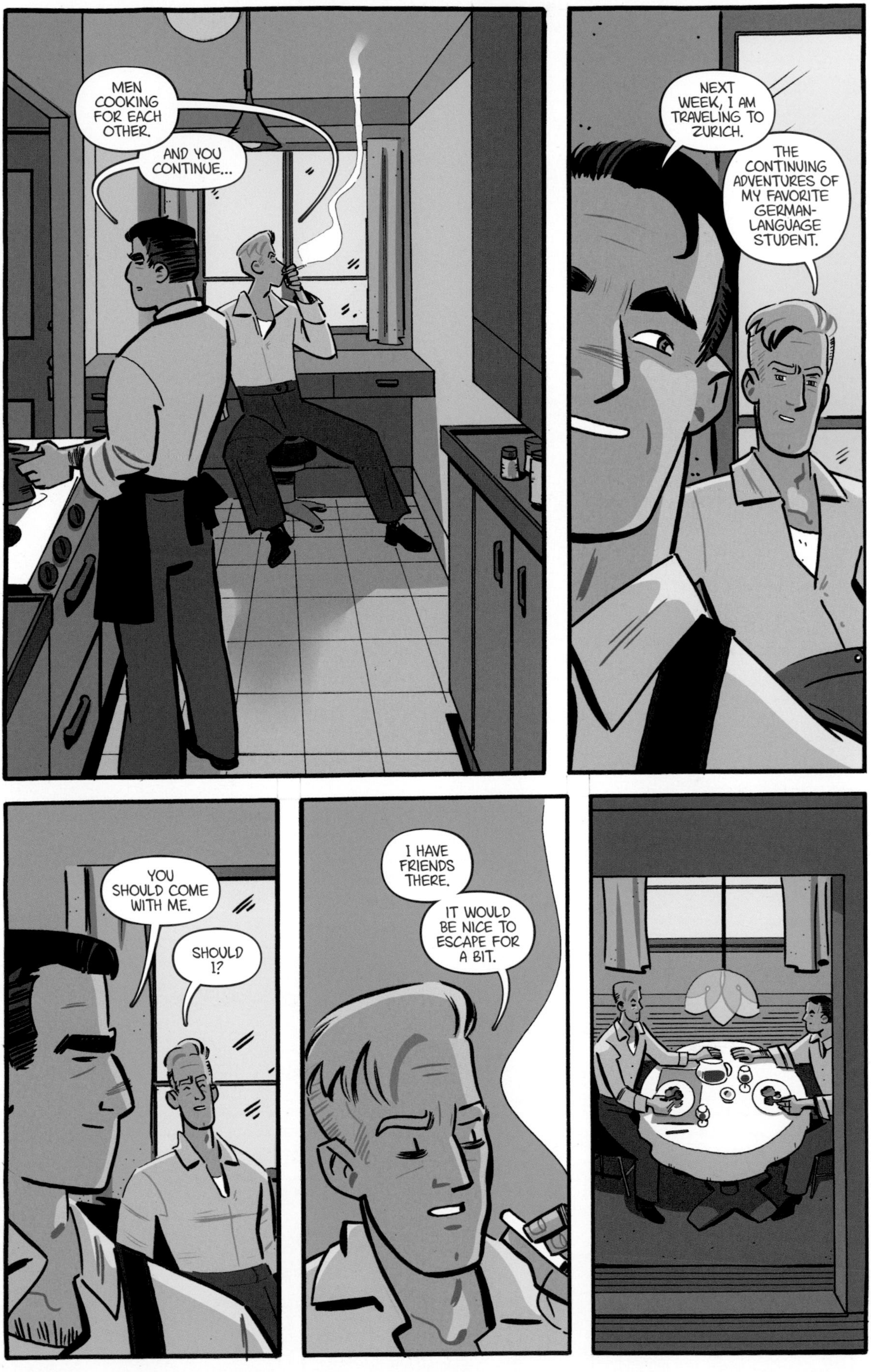
MEN COOKING FOR EACH OTHER.
AND YOU CONTINUE...
NEXT WEEK, I AM TRAVELING TO ZURICH.
THE CONTINUING ADVENTURES OF MY FAVORITE GERMAN-LANGUAGE STUDENT.
YOU SHOULD COME WITH ME.
SHOULD I?
I HAVE FRIENDS THERE.
IT WOULD BE NICE TO ESCAPE FOR A BIT.

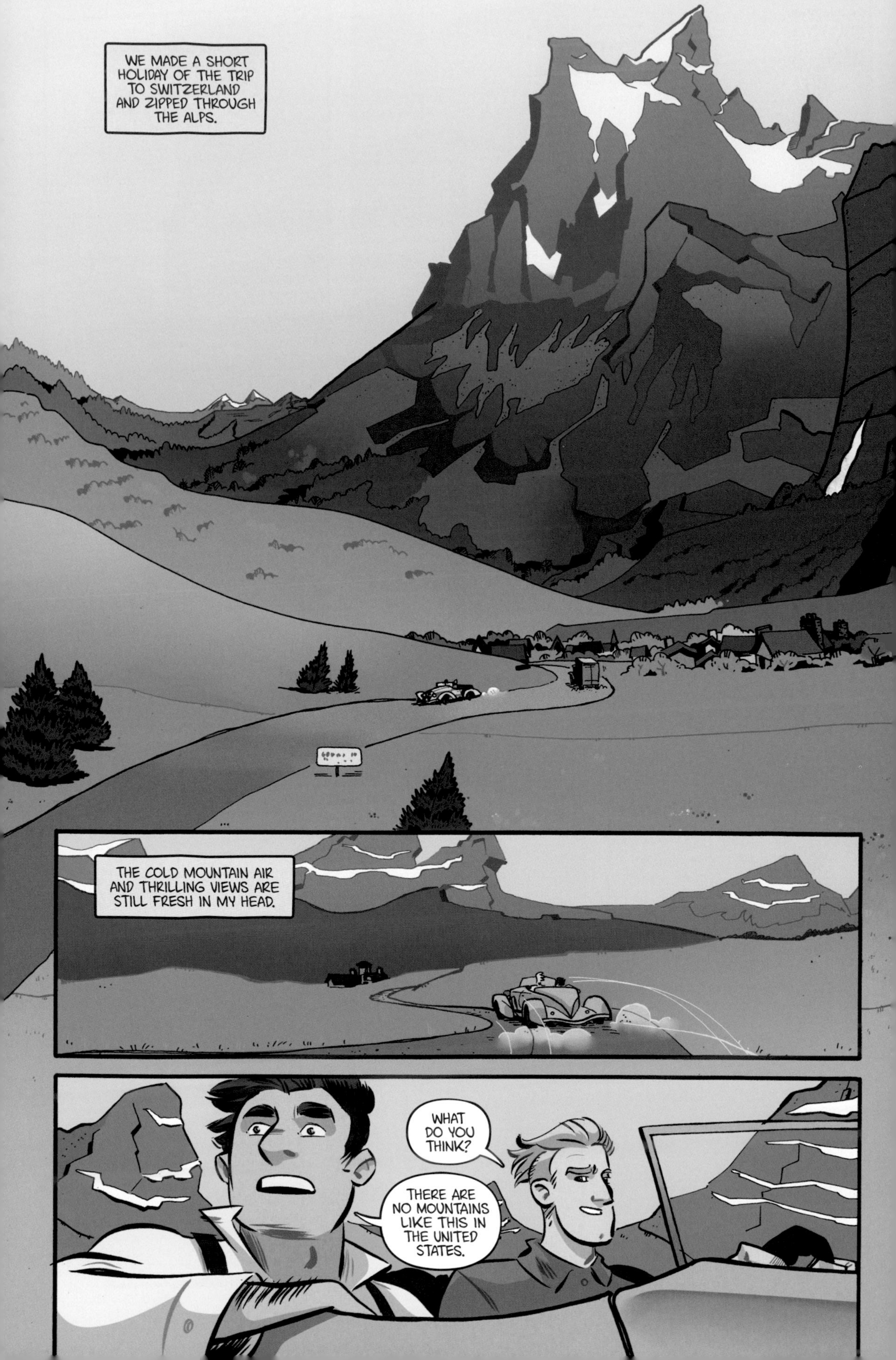
WE MADE A SHORT HOLIDAY OF THE TRIP TO SWITZERLAND AND ZIPPED THROUGH THE ALPS.
THE COLD MOUNTAIN AIR AND THRILLING VIEWS ARE STILL FRESH IN MY HEAD.
WHAT DO YOU THINK?
THERE ARE NO MOUNTAINS LIKE THIS IN THE UNITED STATES.

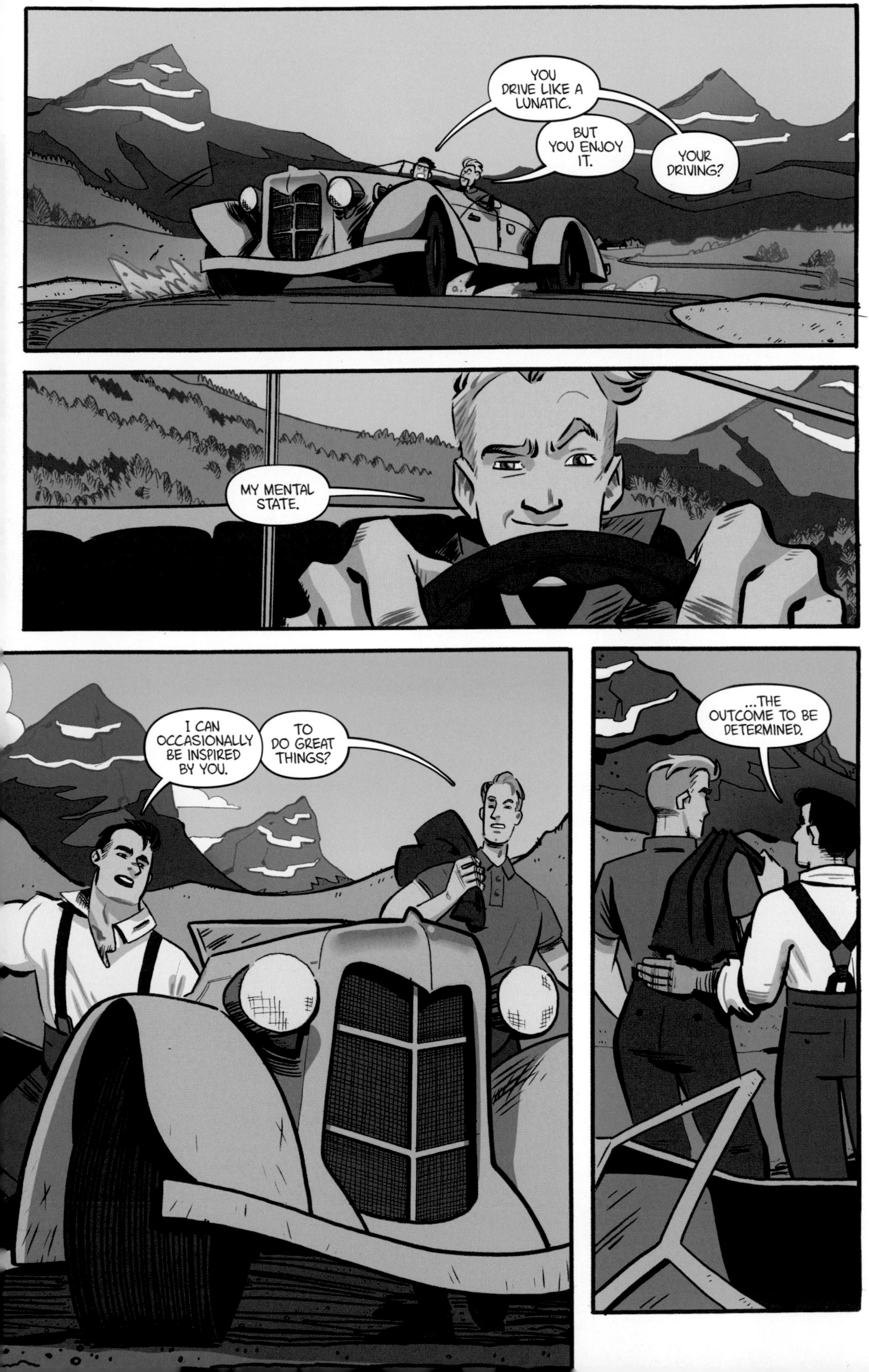
YOU DRIVE LIKE A LUNATIC.
BUT YOU ENJOY IT.
YOUR DRIVING?
MY MENTAL STATE.
I CAN OCCASIONALLY BE INSPIRED BY YOU.
TO DO GREAT THINGS?
...THE OUTCOME TO BE DETERMINED.

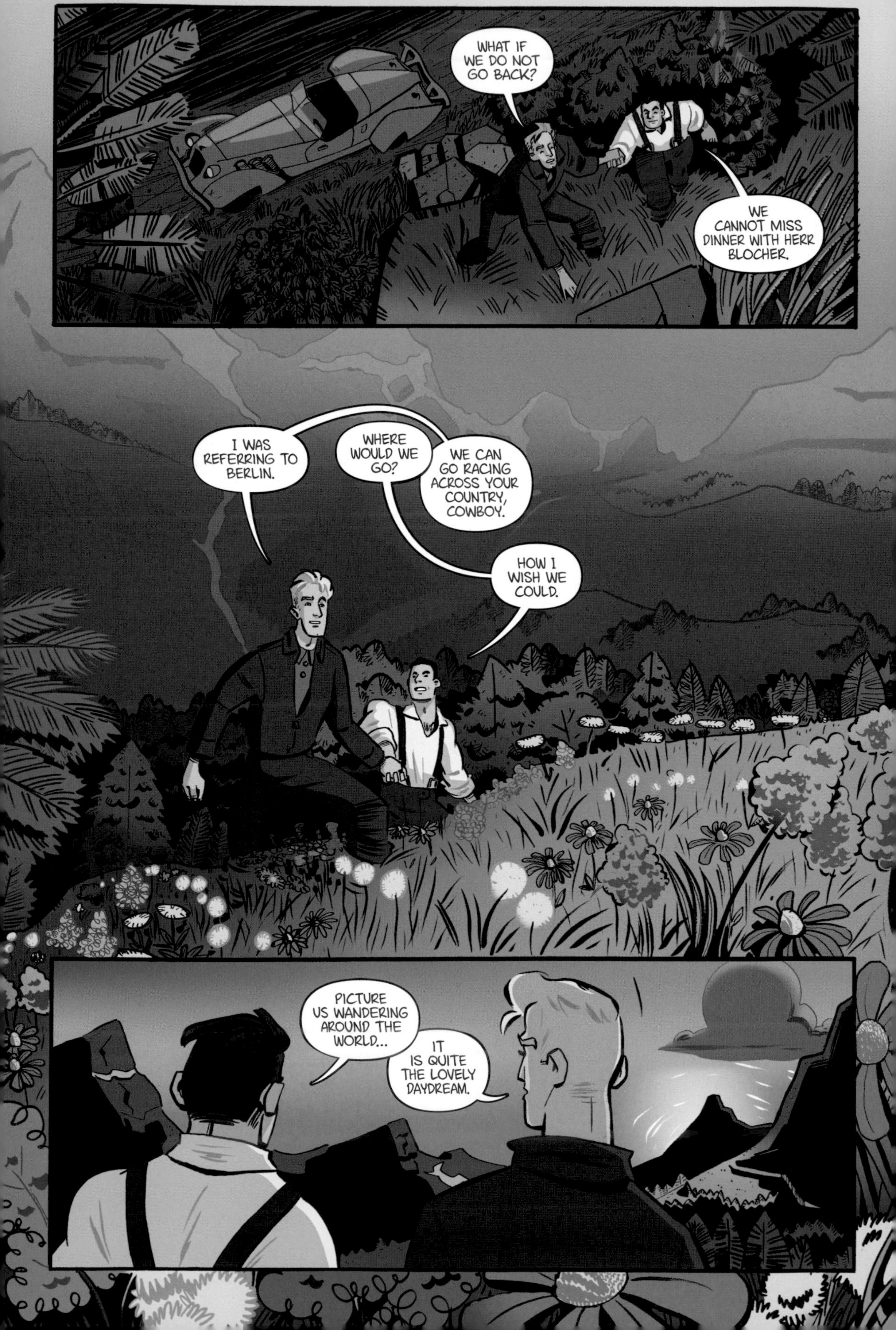
WHAT IF WE DO NOT GO BACK?
WE CANNOT MISS DINNER WITH HERR BLOCHER.
I WAS REFERRING TO BERLIN.
WHERE WOULD WE GO?
WE CAN GO RACING ACROSS YOUR COUNTRY, COWBOY.
HOW I WISH WE COULD.
PICTURE US WANDERING AROUND THE WORLD...
IT IS QUITE THE LOVELY DAYDREAM.

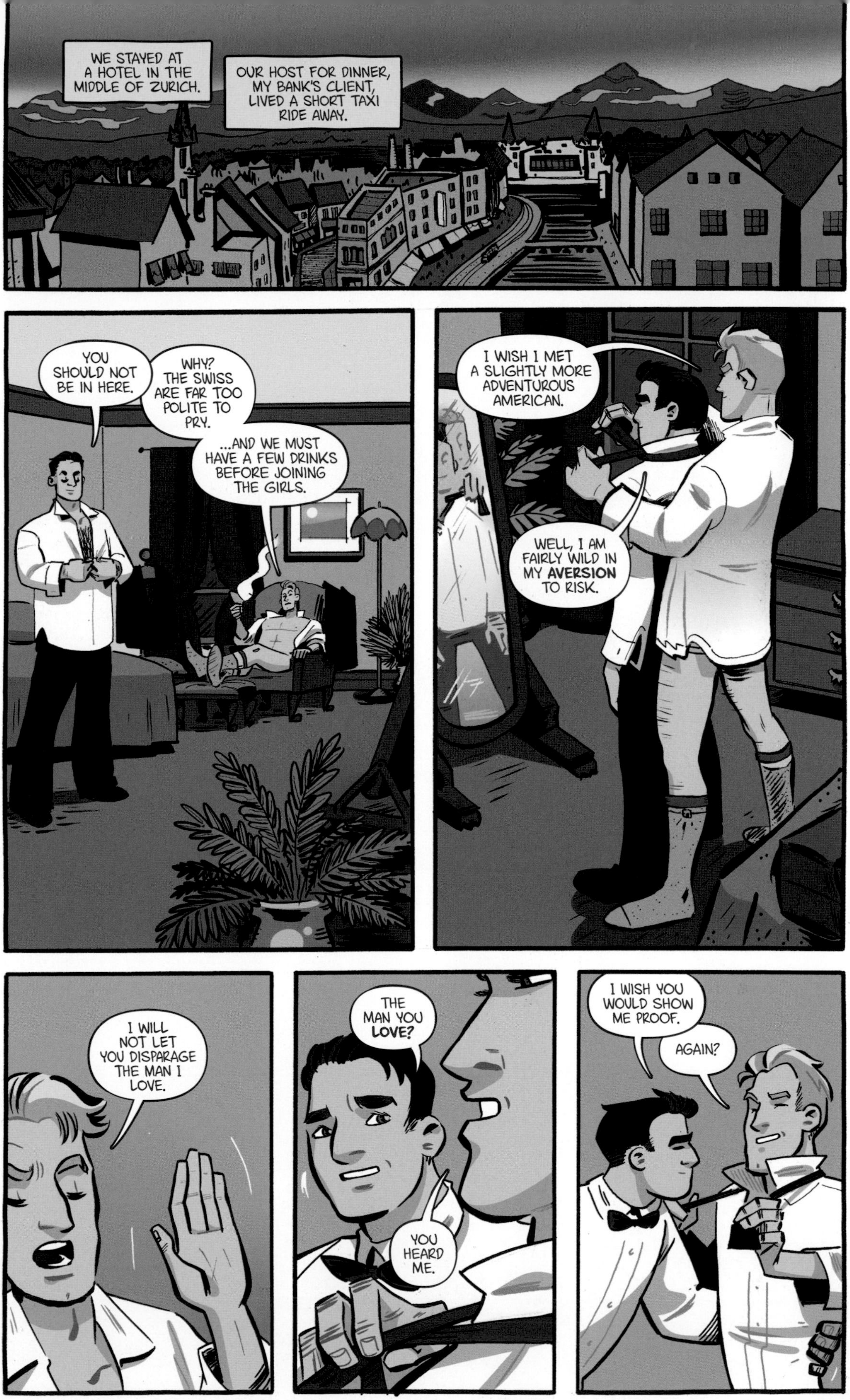

WE STAYED AT A HOTEL IN THE MIDDLE OF ZURICH.
OUR HOST FOR DINNER, MY BANK'S CLIENT, LIVED A SHORT TAXI RIDE AWAY.
YOU SHOULD NOT BE IN HERE.
WHY? THE SWISS ARE FAR TOO POLITE TO PRY.
...AND WE MUST HAVE A FEW DRINKS BEFORE JOINING THE GIRLS.
I WISH I MET A SLIGHTLY MORE ADVENTUROUS AMERICAN.
WELL, I AM FAIRLY WILD IN MY **AVERSION** TO RISK.
I WILL NOT LET YOU DISPARAGE THE MAN I LOVE.
THE MAN YOU **LOVE?**
YOU HEARD ME.
I WISH YOU WOULD SHOW ME PROOF.
AGAIN?

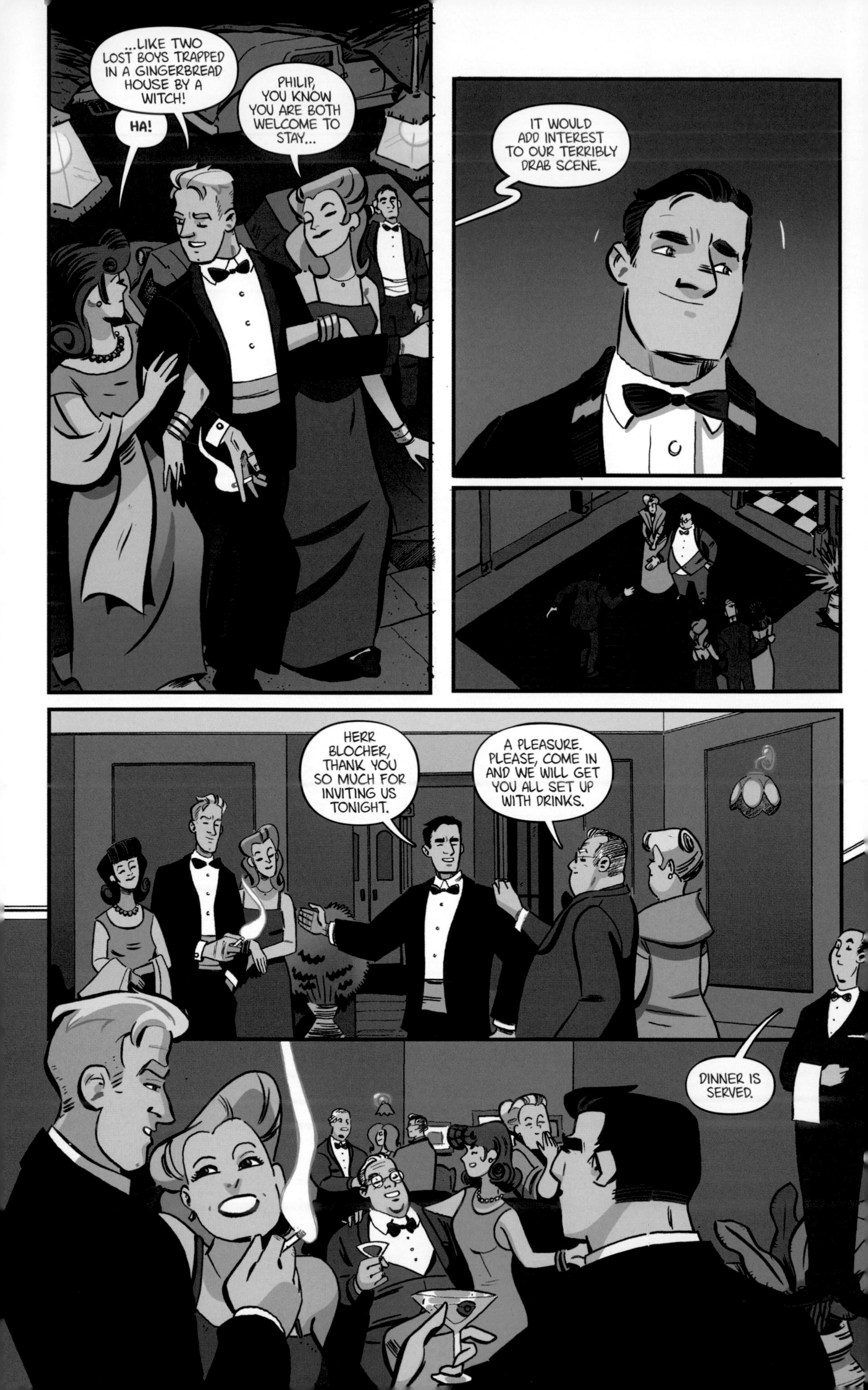
...LIKE TWO LOST BOYS TRAPPED IN A GINGERBREAD HOUSE BY A WITCH!
HA!
PHILIP, YOU KNOW YOU ARE BOTH WELCOME TO STAY...
IT WOULD ADD INTEREST TO OUR TERRIBLY DRAB SCENE.
HERR BLOCHER, THANK YOU SO MUCH FOR INVITING US TONIGHT.
A PLEASURE. PLEASE, COME IN AND WE WILL GET YOU ALL SET UP WITH DRINKS.
DINNER IS SERVED.

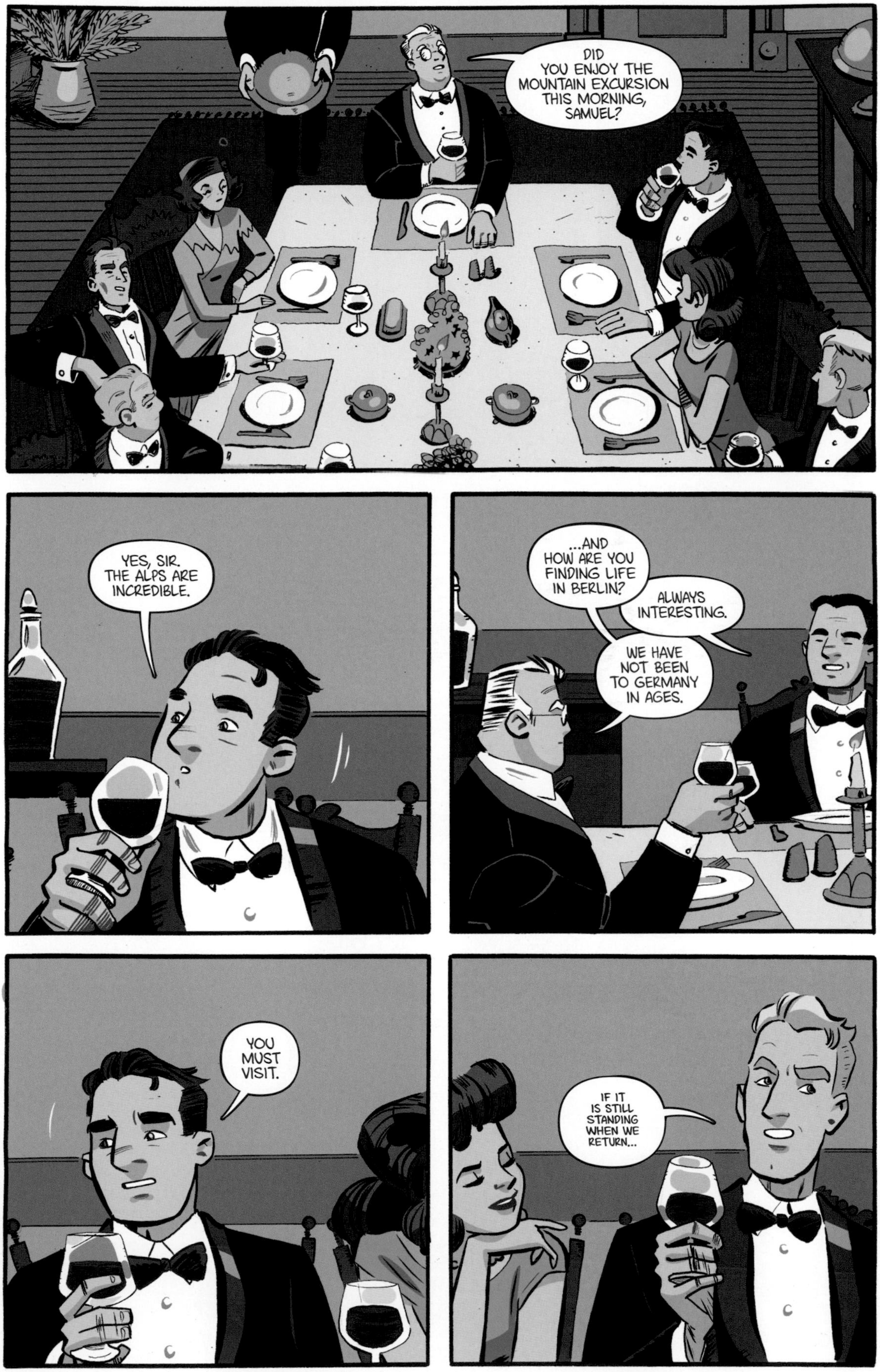
DID YOU ENJOY THE MOUNTAIN EXCURSION THIS MORNING, SAMUEL?
YES, SIR. THE ALPS ARE INCREDIBLE.
...AND HOW ARE YOU FINDING LIFE IN BERLIN?
ALWAYS INTERESTING.
WE HAVE NOT BEEN TO GERMANY IN AGES.
YOU MUST VISIT.
IF IT IS STILL STANDING WHEN WE RETURN...

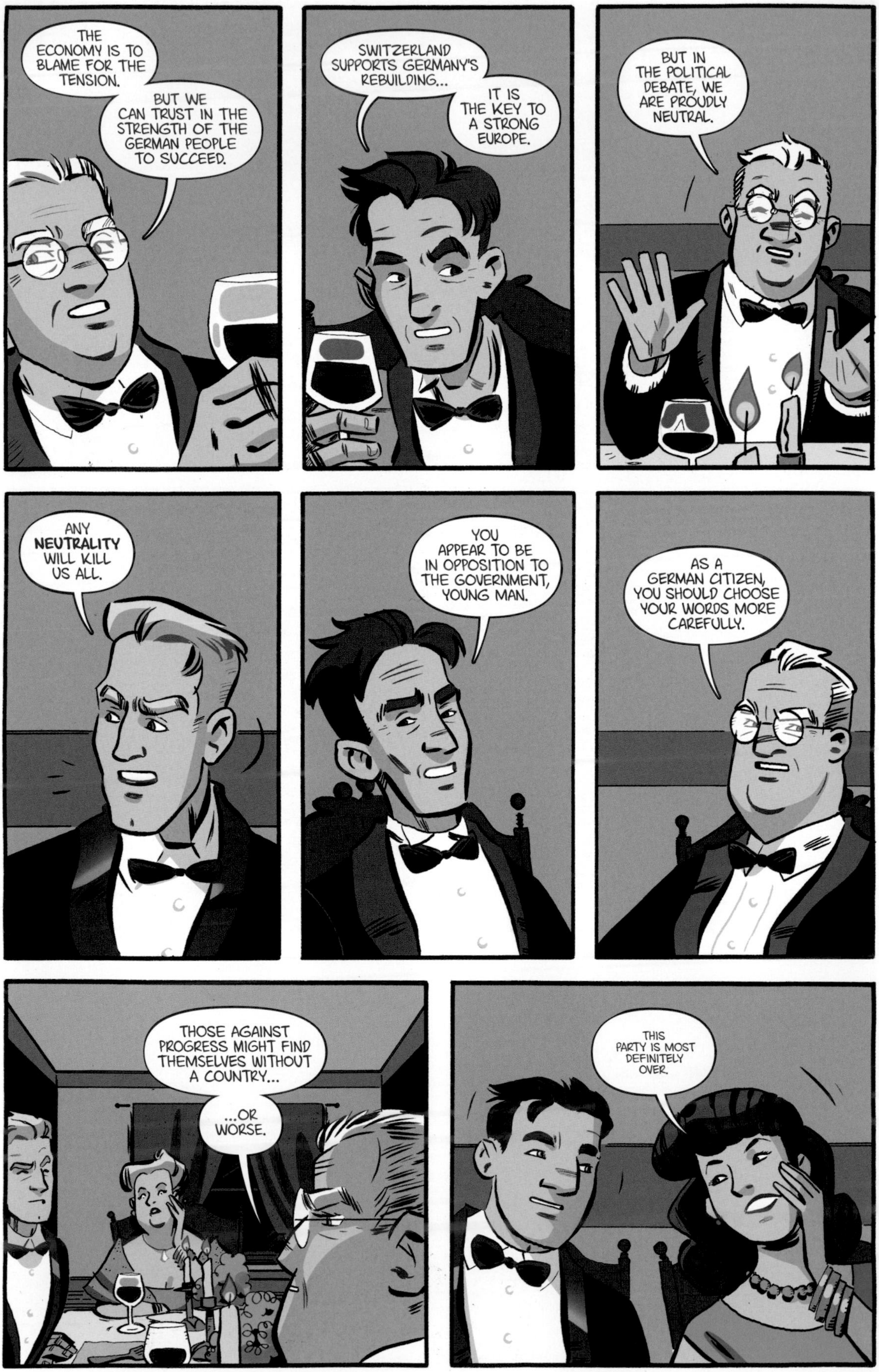
THE ECONOMY IS TO BLAME FOR THE TENSION.
BUT WE CAN TRUST IN THE STRENGTH OF THE GERMAN PEOPLE TO SUCCEED.
SWITZERLAND SUPPORTS GERMANY'S REBUILDING...
IT IS THE KEY TO A STRONG EUROPE.
BUT IN THE POLITICAL DEBATE, WE ARE PROUDLY NEUTRAL.
ANY **NEUTRALITY** WILL KILL US ALL.
YOU APPEAR TO BE IN OPPOSITION TO THE GOVERNMENT, YOUNG MAN.
AS A GERMAN CITIZEN, YOU SHOULD CHOOSE YOUR WORDS MORE CAREFULLY.
THOSE AGAINST PROGRESS MIGHT FIND THEMSELVES WITHOUT A COUNTRY...
...OR WORSE.
THIS PARTY IS MOST DEFINITELY OVER.

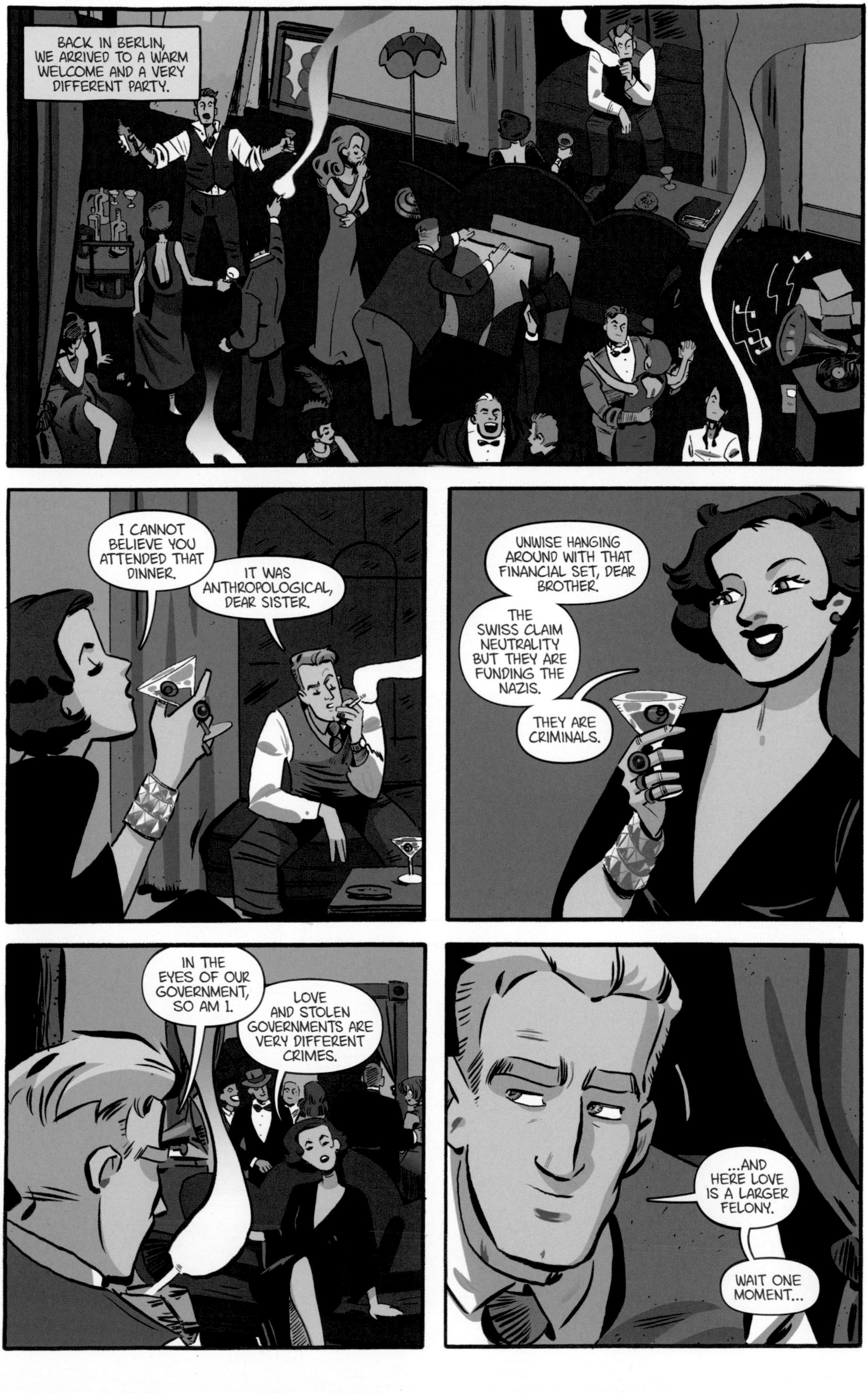
BACK IN BERLIN, WE ARRIVED TO A WARM WELCOME AND A VERY DIFFERENT PARTY.
I CANNOT BELIEVE YOU ATTENDED THAT DINNER.
IT WAS ANTHROPOLOGICAL, DEAR SISTER.
UNWISE HANGING AROUND WITH THAT FINANCIAL SET, DEAR BROTHER.
THE SWISS CLAIM NEUTRALITY BUT THEY ARE FUNDING THE NAZIS.
THEY ARE CRIMINALS.
IN THE EYES OF OUR GOVERNMENT, SO AM I.
LOVE AND STOLEN GOVERNMENTS ARE VERY DIFFERENT CRIMES.
...AND HERE LOVE IS A LARGER FELONY.
WAIT ONE MOMENT...

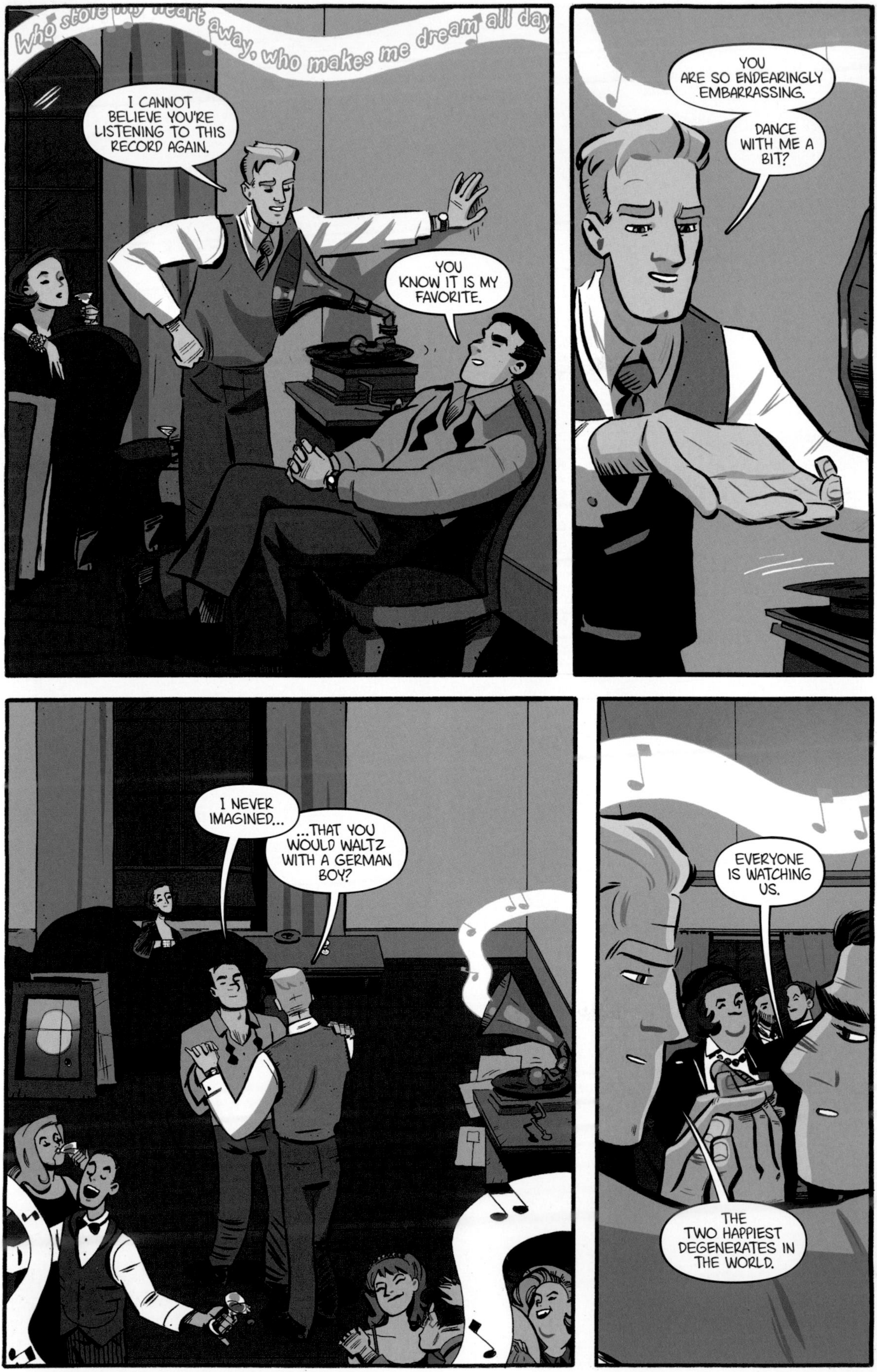
who stole my heart away, who makes me dream all day
I CANNOT BELIEVE YOU'RE LISTENING TO THIS RECORD AGAIN.
YOU KNOW IT IS MY FAVORITE.
YOU ARE SO ENDEARINGLY EMBARRASSING.
DANCE WITH ME A BIT?
I NEVER IMAGINED...
...THAT YOU WOULD WALTZ WITH A GERMAN BOY?
EVERYONE IS WATCHING US.
THE TWO HAPPIEST DEGENERATES IN THE WORLD.

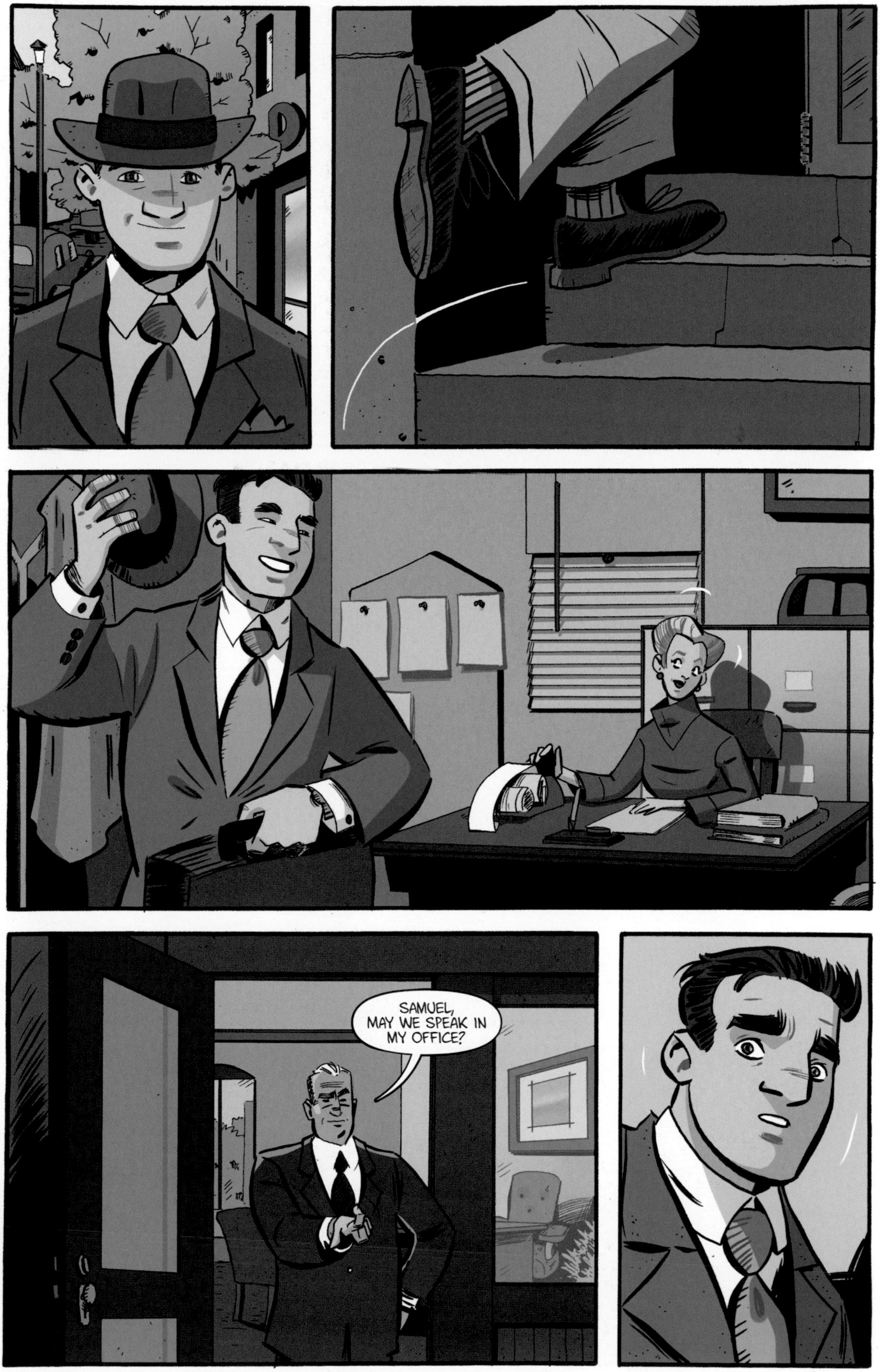
SAMUEL, MAY WE SPEAK IN MY OFFICE?

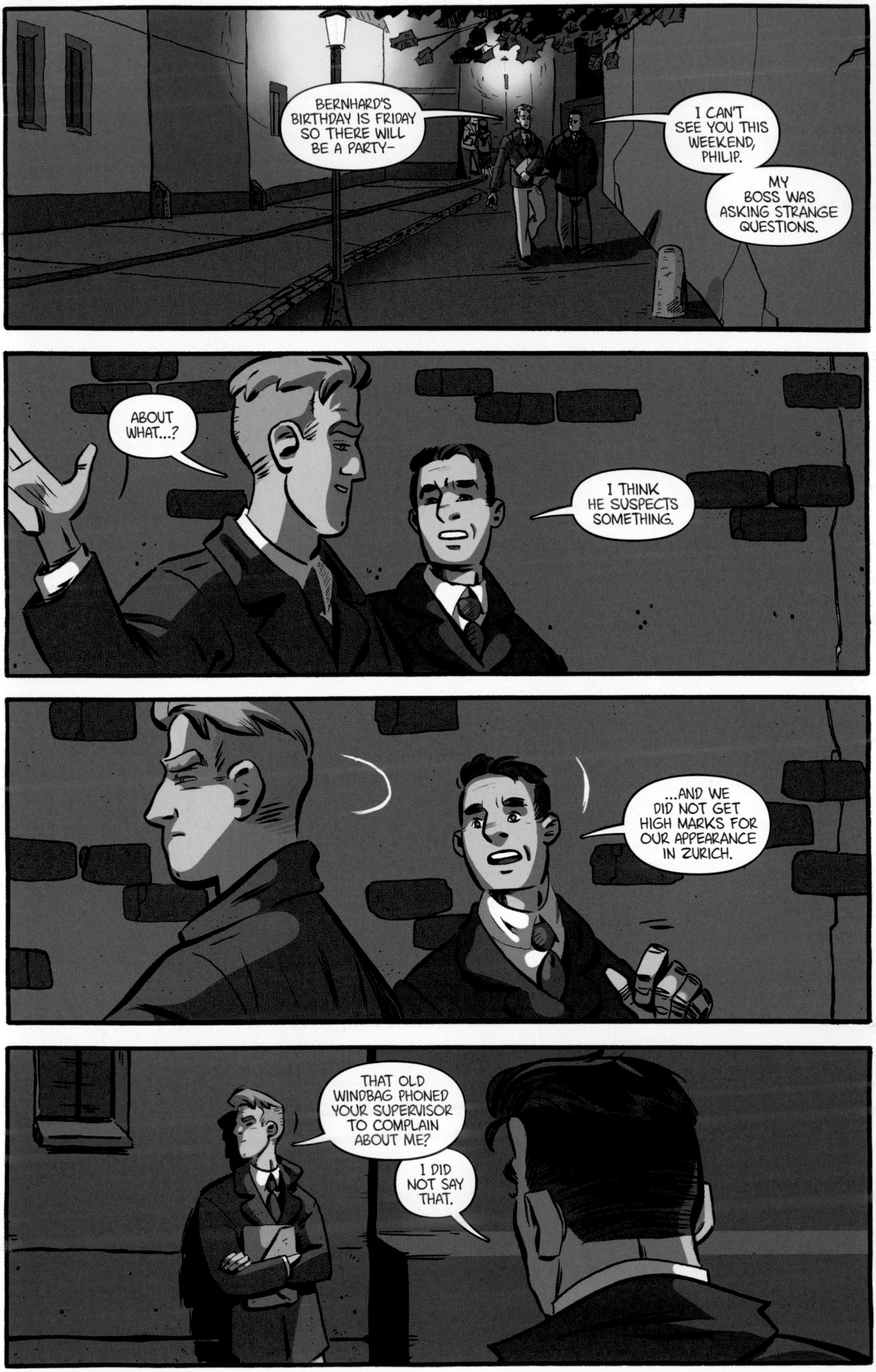
BERNHARD'S BIRTHDAY IS FRIDAY SO THERE WILL BE A PARTY-
I CAN'T SEE YOU THIS WEEKEND, PHILIP.
MY BOSS WAS ASKING STRANGE QUESTIONS.
ABOUT WHAT...?
I THINK HE SUSPECTS SOMETHING.
...AND WE DID NOT GET HIGH MARKS FOR OUR APPEARANCE IN ZURICH.
THAT OLD WINDBAG PHONED YOUR SUPERVISOR TO COMPLAIN ABOUT ME?
I DID NOT SAY THAT.

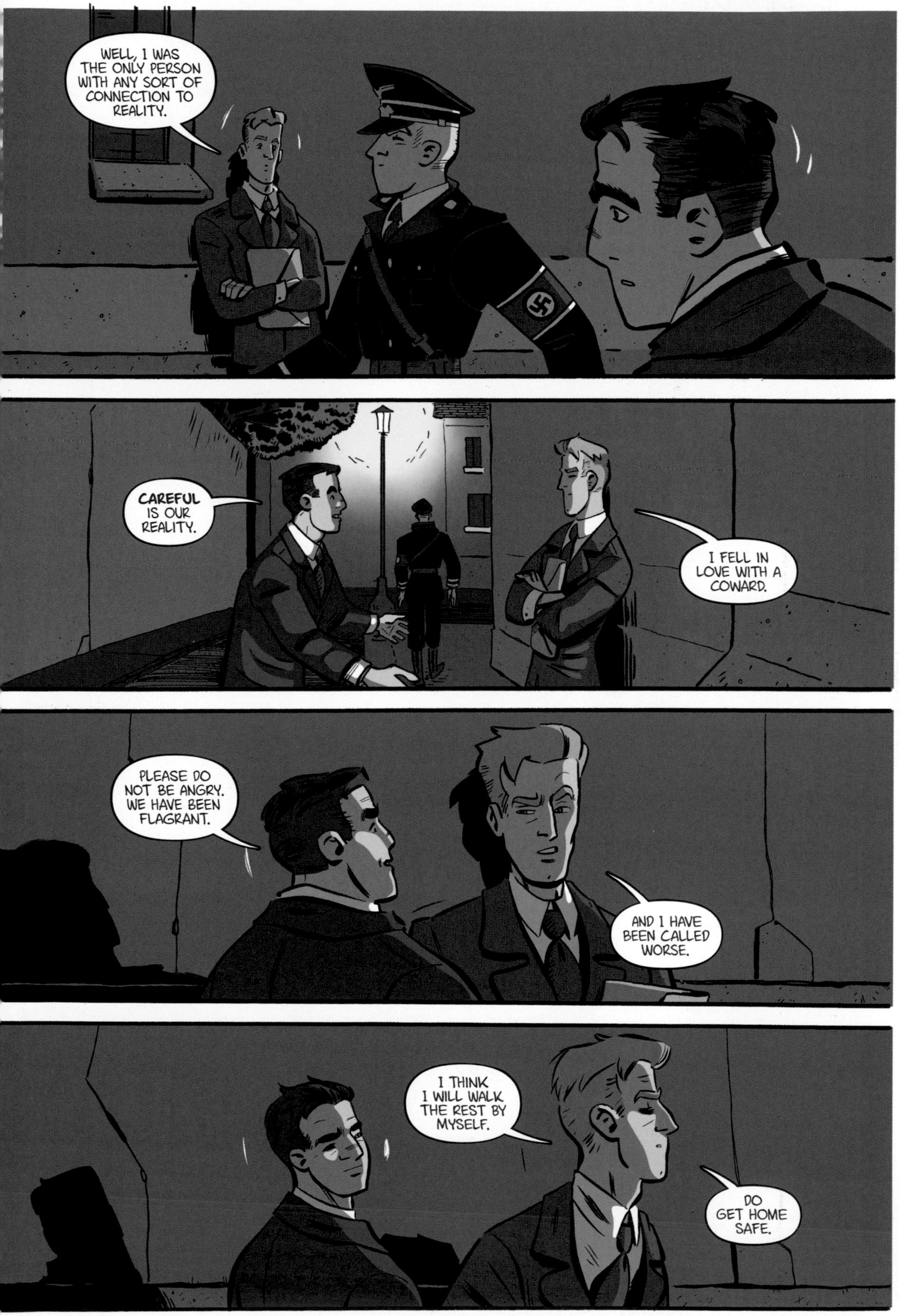
WELL, I WAS THE ONLY PERSON WITH ANY SORT OF CONNECTION TO REALITY.
CAREFUL IS OUR REALITY.
I FELL IN LOVE WITH A COWARD.
PLEASE DO NOT BE ANGRY. WE HAVE BEEN FLAGRANT.
AND I HAVE BEEN CALLED WORSE.
I THINK I WILL WALK THE REST BY MYSELF.
DO GET HOME SAFE.

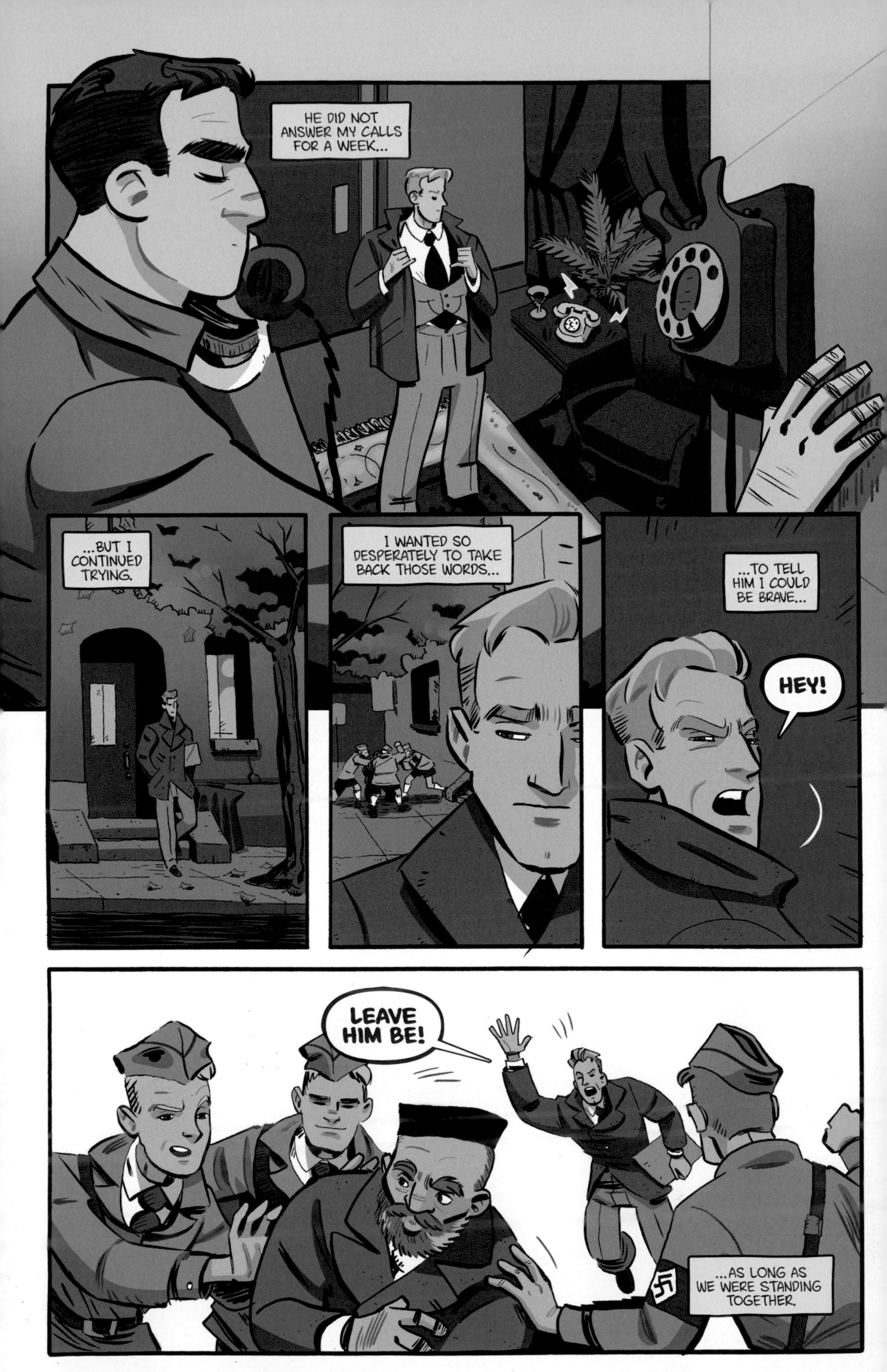
HE DID NOT ANSWER MY CALLS FOR A WEEK...
...BUT I CONTINUED TRYING.
I WANTED SO DESPERATELY TO TAKE BACK THOSE WORDS...
...TO TELL HIM I COULD BE BRAVE...
HEY!
LEAVE HIM BE!
...AS LONG AS WE WERE STANDING TOGETHER.

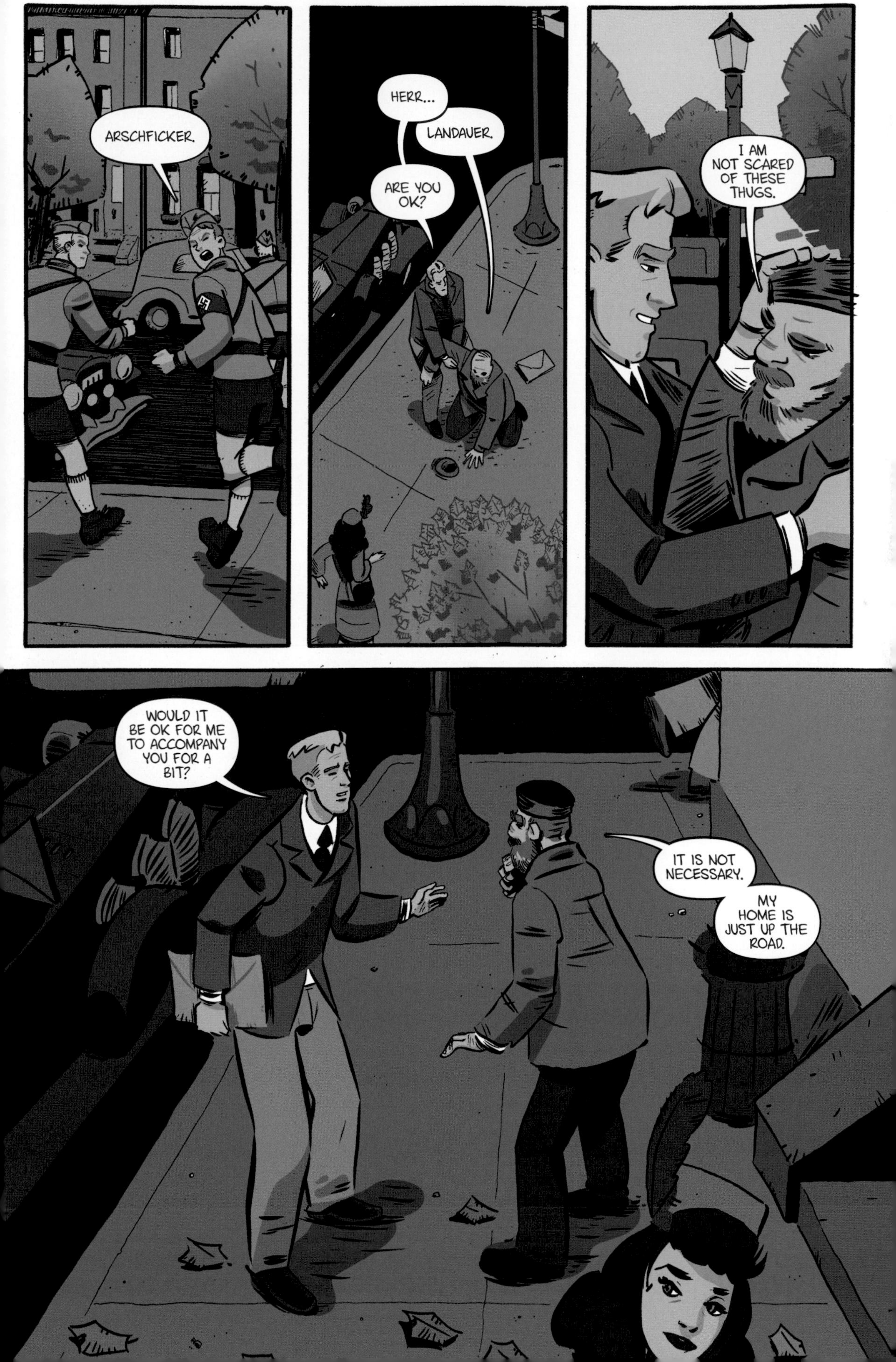
ARSCHFICKER.
HERR...
LANDAUER.
ARE YOU OK?
I AM NOT SCARED OF THESE THUGS.
WOULD IT BE OK FOR ME TO ACCOMPANY YOU FOR A BIT?
IT IS NOT NECESSARY.
MY HOME IS JUST UP THE ROAD.

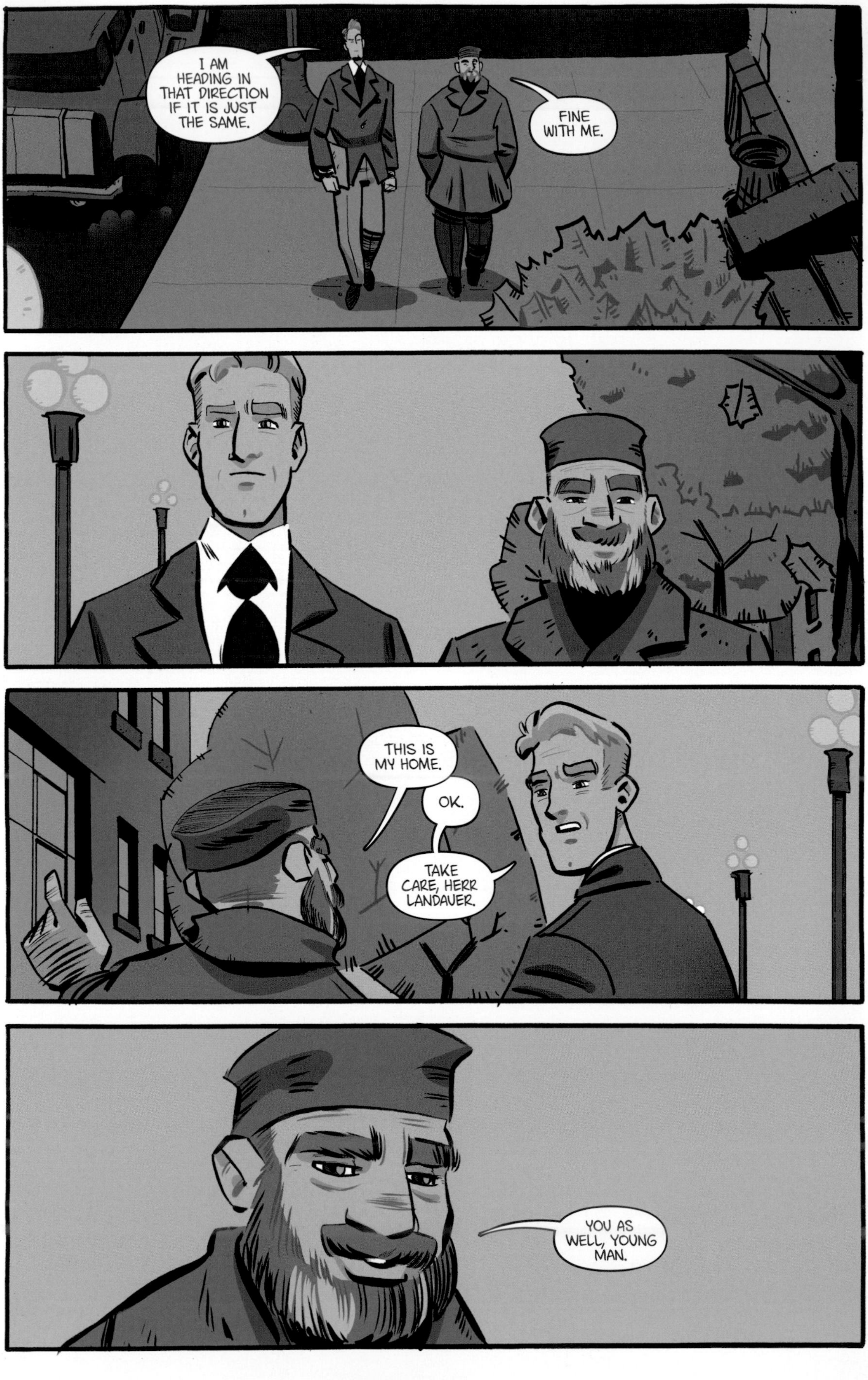
I AM HEADING IN THAT DIRECTION IF IT IS JUST THE SAME.
FINE WITH ME.
THIS IS MY HOME.
OK.
TAKE CARE, HERR LANDAUER.
YOU AS WELL, YOUNG MAN.

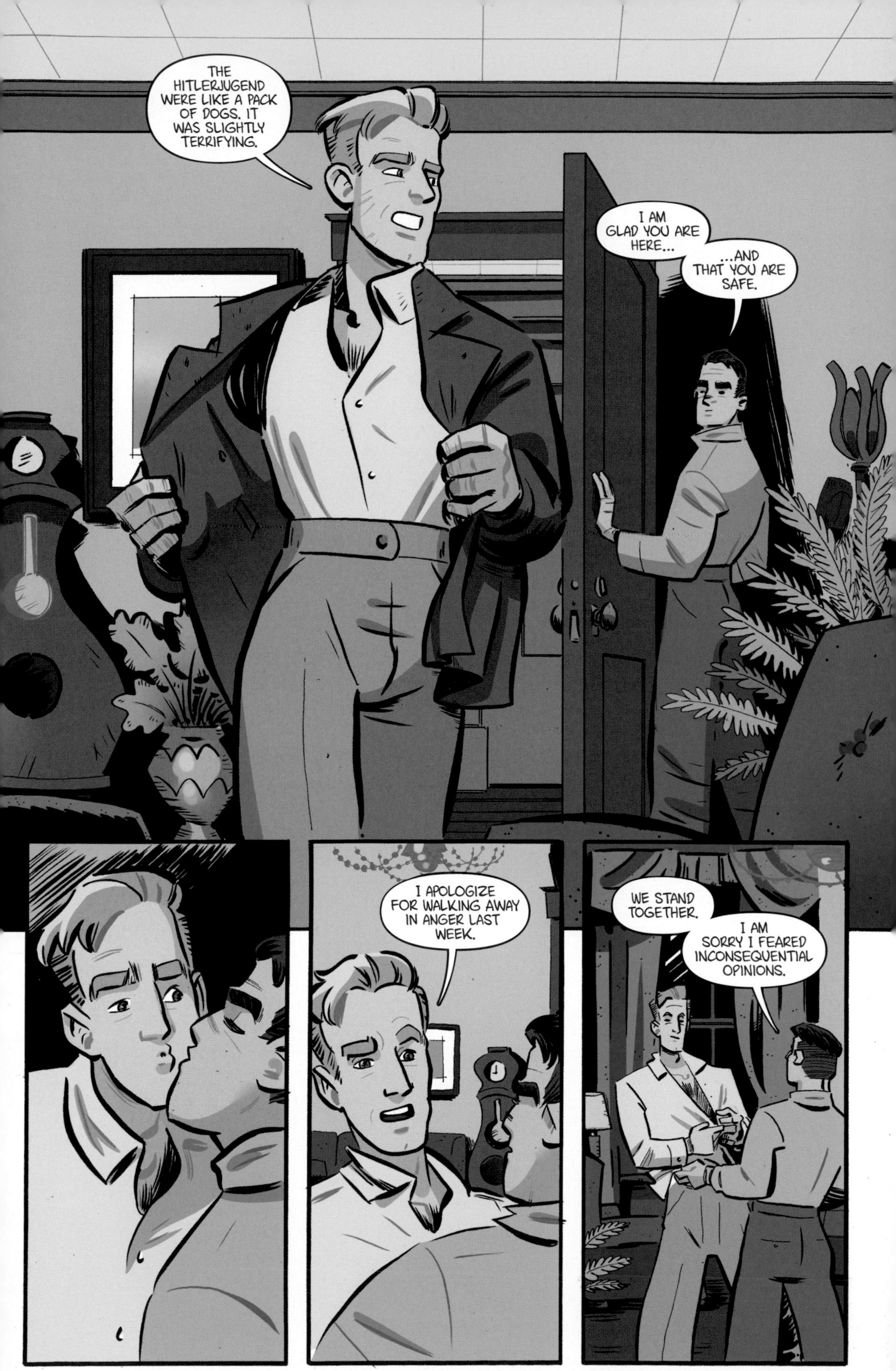
THE HITLERJUGEND WERE LIKE A PACK OF DOGS. IT WAS SLIGHTLY TERRIFYING.
I AM GLAD YOU ARE HERE...
...AND THAT YOU ARE SAFE.
I APOLOGIZE FOR WALKING AWAY IN ANGER LAST WEEK.
WE STAND TOGETHER.
I AM SORRY I FEARED INCONSEQUENTIAL OPINIONS.

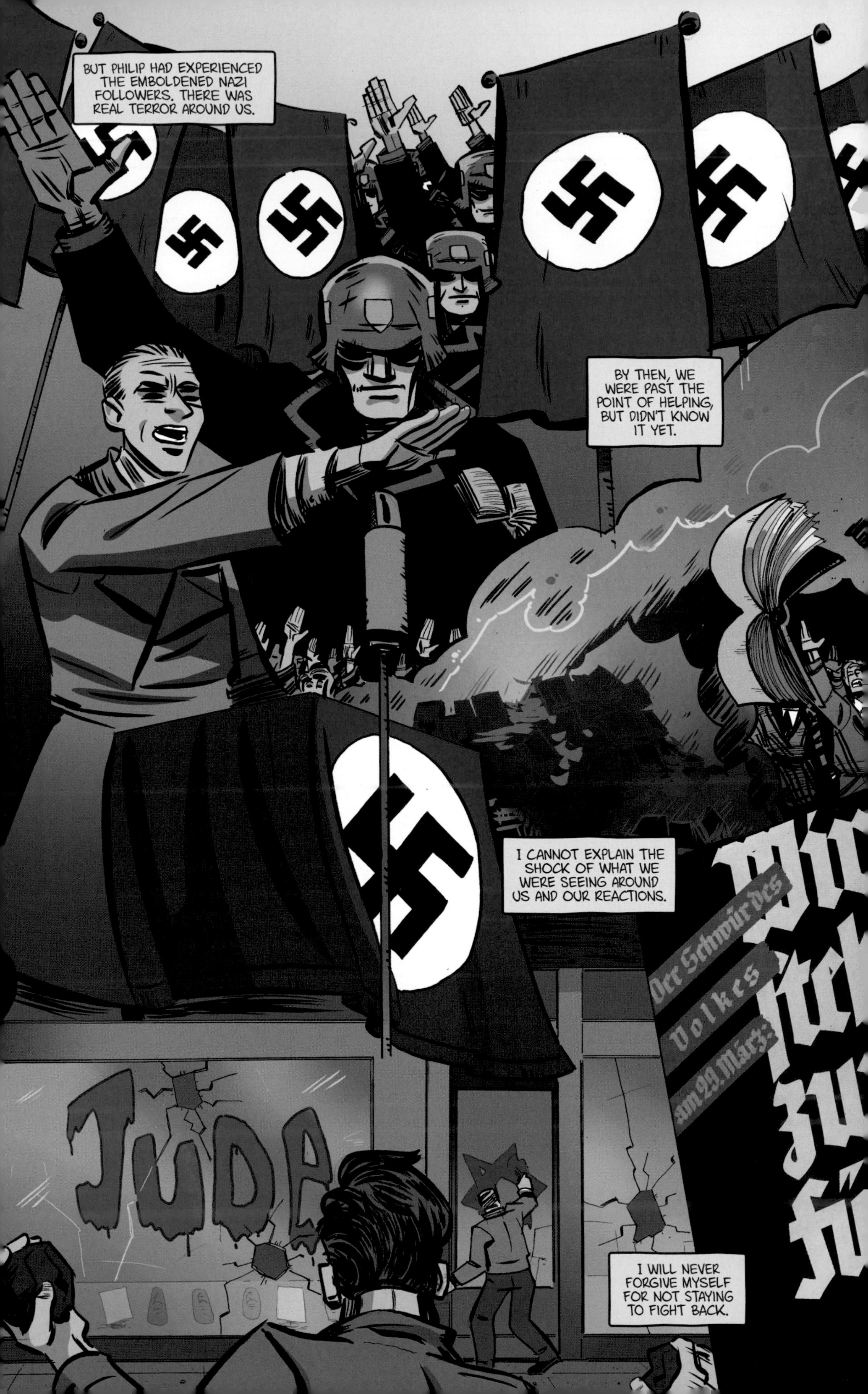
BUT PHILIP HAD EXPERIENCED THE EMBOLDENED NAZI FOLLOWERS. THERE WAS REAL TERROR AROUND US.
BY THEN, WE WERE PAST THE POINT OF HELPING, BUT DIDN'T KNOW IT YET.
I CANNOT EXPLAIN THE SHOCK OF WHAT WE WERE SEEING AROUND US AND OUR REACTIONS.
Der Schwur des Volkes am 29. März:
I WILL NEVER FORGIVE MYSELF FOR NOT STAYING TO FIGHT BACK.

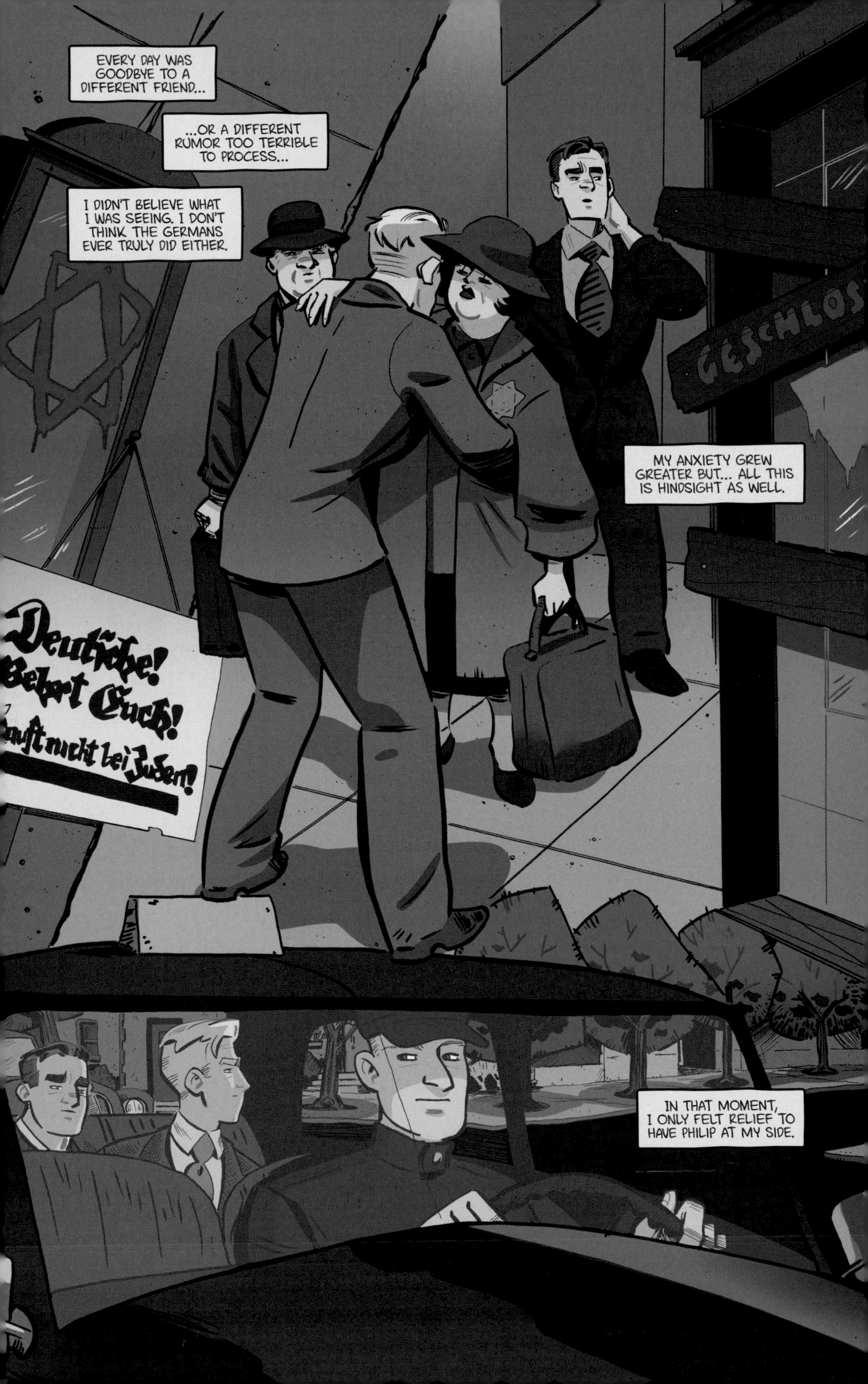
EVERY DAY WAS GOODBYE TO A DIFFERENT FRIEND...
...OR A DIFFERENT RUMOR TOO TERRIBLE TO PROCESS...
I DIDN'T BELIEVE WHAT I WAS SEEING. I DON'T THINK THE GERMANS EVER TRULY DID EITHER.
Deutsche!
ehrt Euch!
auft nicht bei Juden!
GESCHLOS
MY ANXIETY GREW GREATER BUT... ALL THIS IS HINDSIGHT AS WELL.
IN THAT MOMENT, I ONLY FELT RELIEF TO HAVE PHILIP AT MY SIDE.

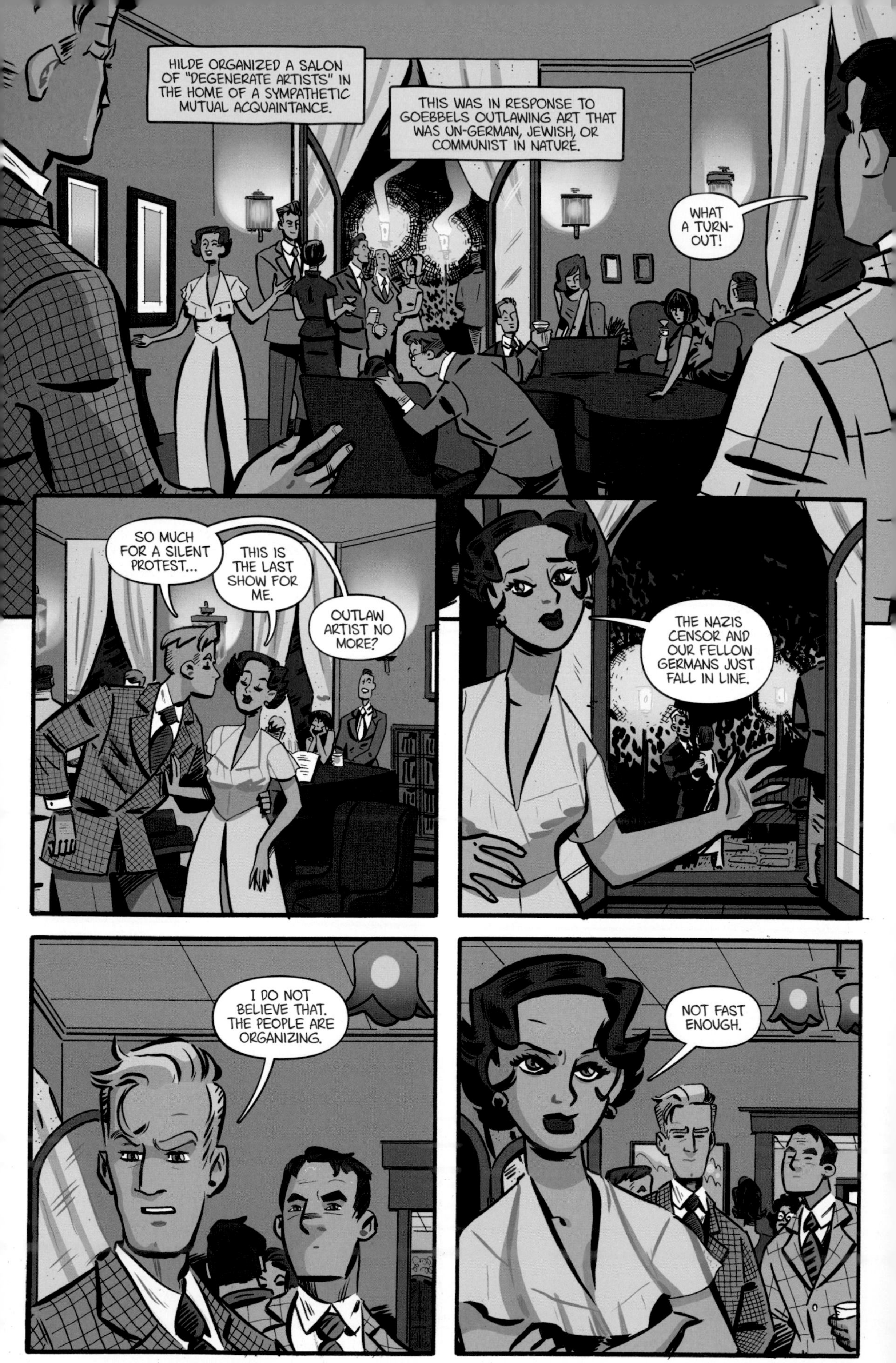
HILDE ORGANIZED A SALON OF "DEGENERATE ARTISTS" IN THE HOME OF A SYMPATHETIC MUTUAL ACQUAINTANCE.
THIS WAS IN RESPONSE TO GOEBBELS OUTLAWING ART THAT WAS UN-GERMAN, JEWISH, OR COMMUNIST IN NATURE.
WHAT A TURN-OUT!
SO MUCH FOR A SILENT PROTEST...
THIS IS THE LAST SHOW FOR ME.
OUTLAW ARTIST NO MORE?
THE NAZIS CENSOR AND OUR FELLOW GERMANS JUST FALL IN LINE.
I DO NOT BELIEVE THAT. THE PEOPLE ARE ORGANIZING.
NOT FAST ENOUGH.

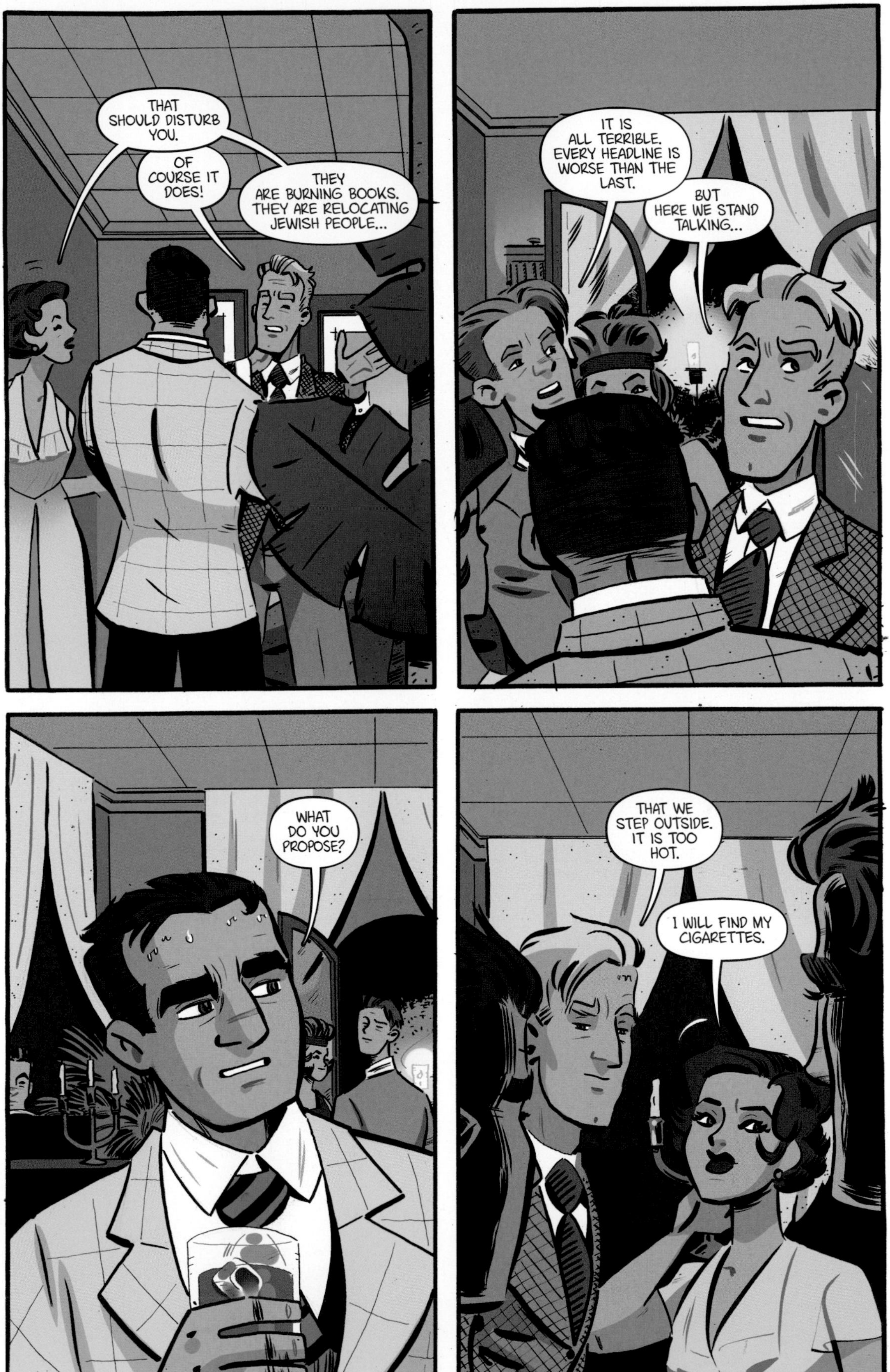
THAT SHOULD DISTURB YOU.
OF COURSE IT DOES!
THEY ARE BURNING BOOKS. THEY ARE RELOCATING JEWISH PEOPLE...
IT IS ALL TERRIBLE. EVERY HEADLINE IS WORSE THAN THE LAST.
BUT HERE WE STAND TALKING...
WHAT DO YOU PROPOSE?
THAT WE STEP OUTSIDE. IT IS TOO HOT.
I WILL FIND MY CIGARETTES.

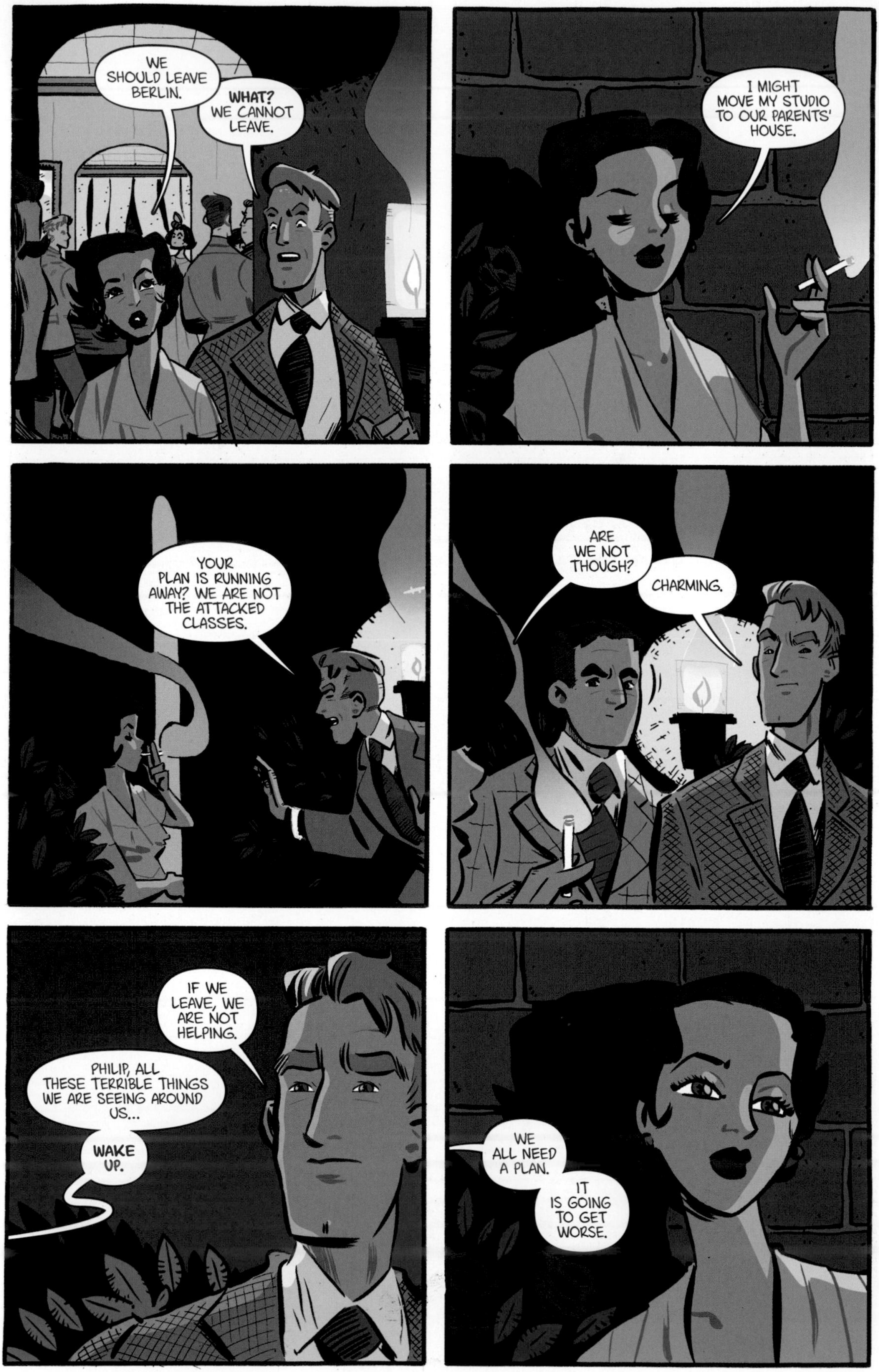
WE SHOULD LEAVE BERLIN.
WHAT? WE CANNOT LEAVE.
I MIGHT MOVE MY STUDIO TO OUR PARENTS' HOUSE.
YOUR PLAN IS RUNNING AWAY? WE ARE NOT THE ATTACKED CLASSES.
ARE WE NOT THOUGH?
CHARMING.
IF WE LEAVE, WE ARE NOT HELPING.
PHILIP, ALL THESE TERRIBLE THINGS WE ARE SEEING AROUND US...
WAKE UP.
WE ALL NEED A PLAN.
IT IS GOING TO GET WORSE.

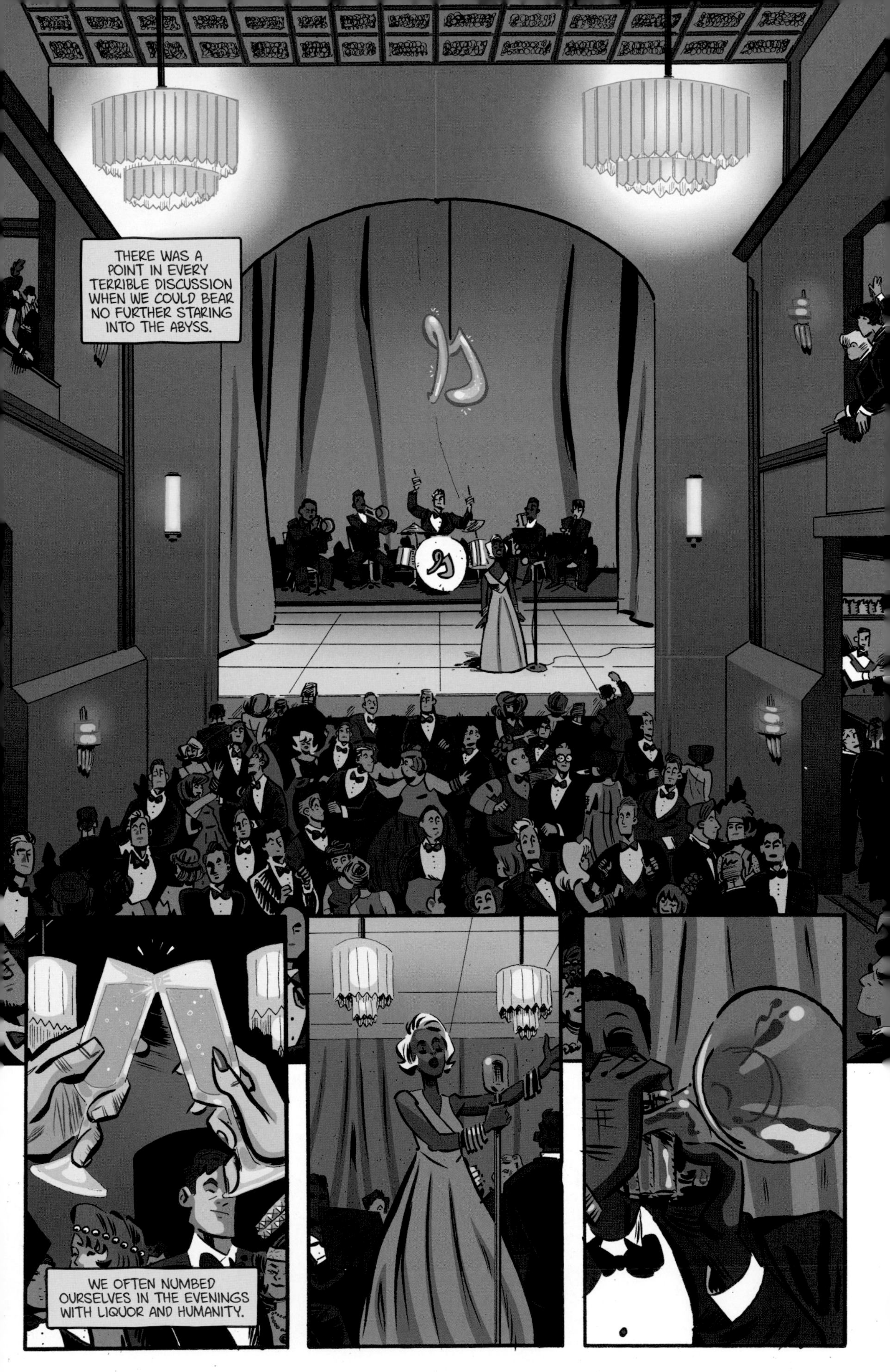
THERE WAS A POINT IN EVERY TERRIBLE DISCUSSION WHEN WE COULD BEAR NO FURTHER STARING INTO THE ABYSS.
WE OFTEN NUMBED OURSELVES IN THE EVENINGS WITH LIQUOR AND HUMANITY.

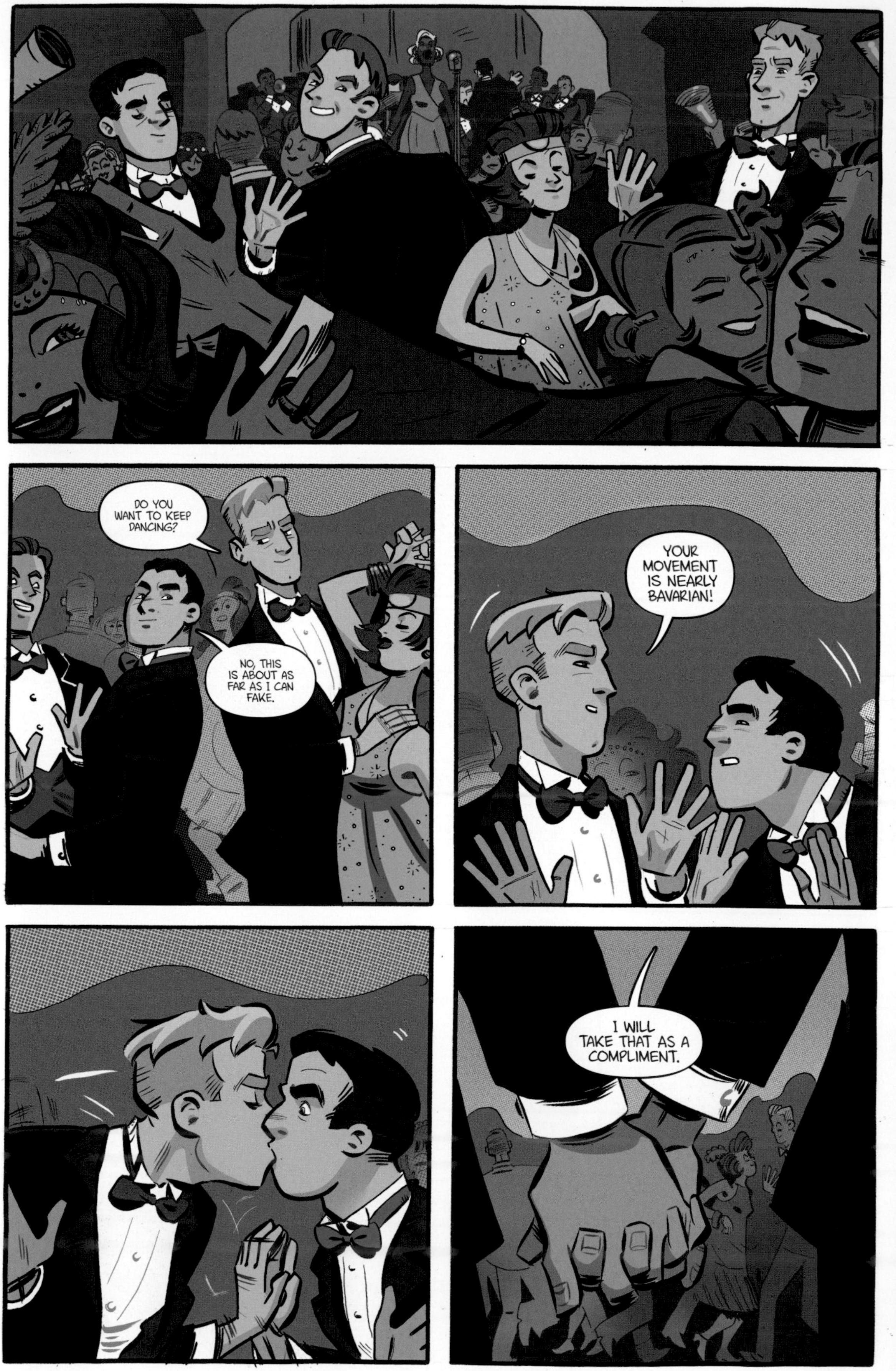
DO YOU WANT TO KEEP DANCING?
NO, THIS IS ABOUT AS FAR AS I CAN FAKE.
YOUR MOVEMENT IS NEARLY BAVARIAN!
I WILL TAKE THAT AS A COMPLIMENT.

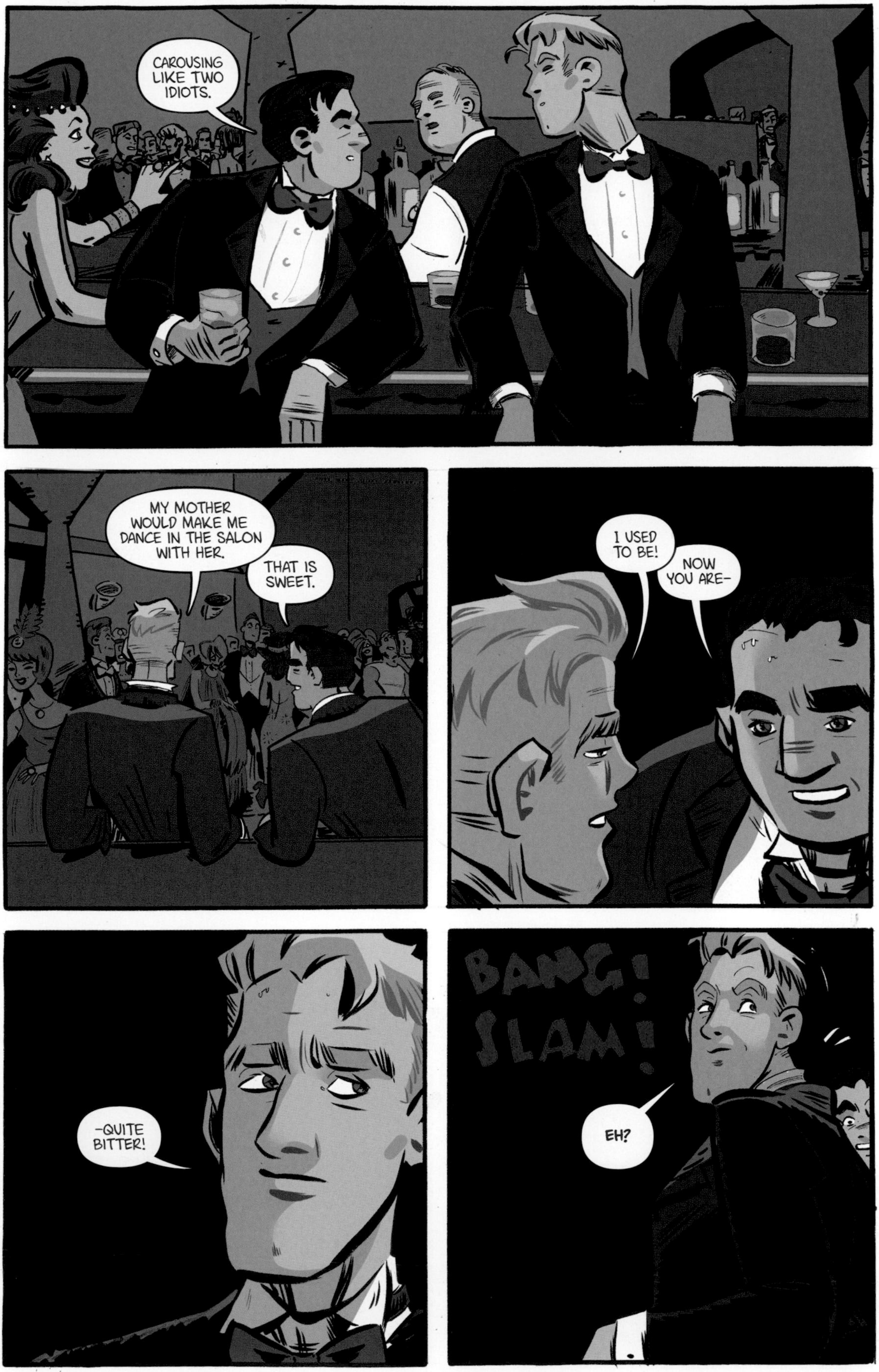
CAROUSING LIKE TWO IDIOTS.
MY MOTHER WOULD MAKE ME DANCE IN THE SALON WITH HER.
THAT IS SWEET.
I USED TO BE!
NOW YOU ARE–
–QUITE BITTER!
BANG! SLAM!
EH?

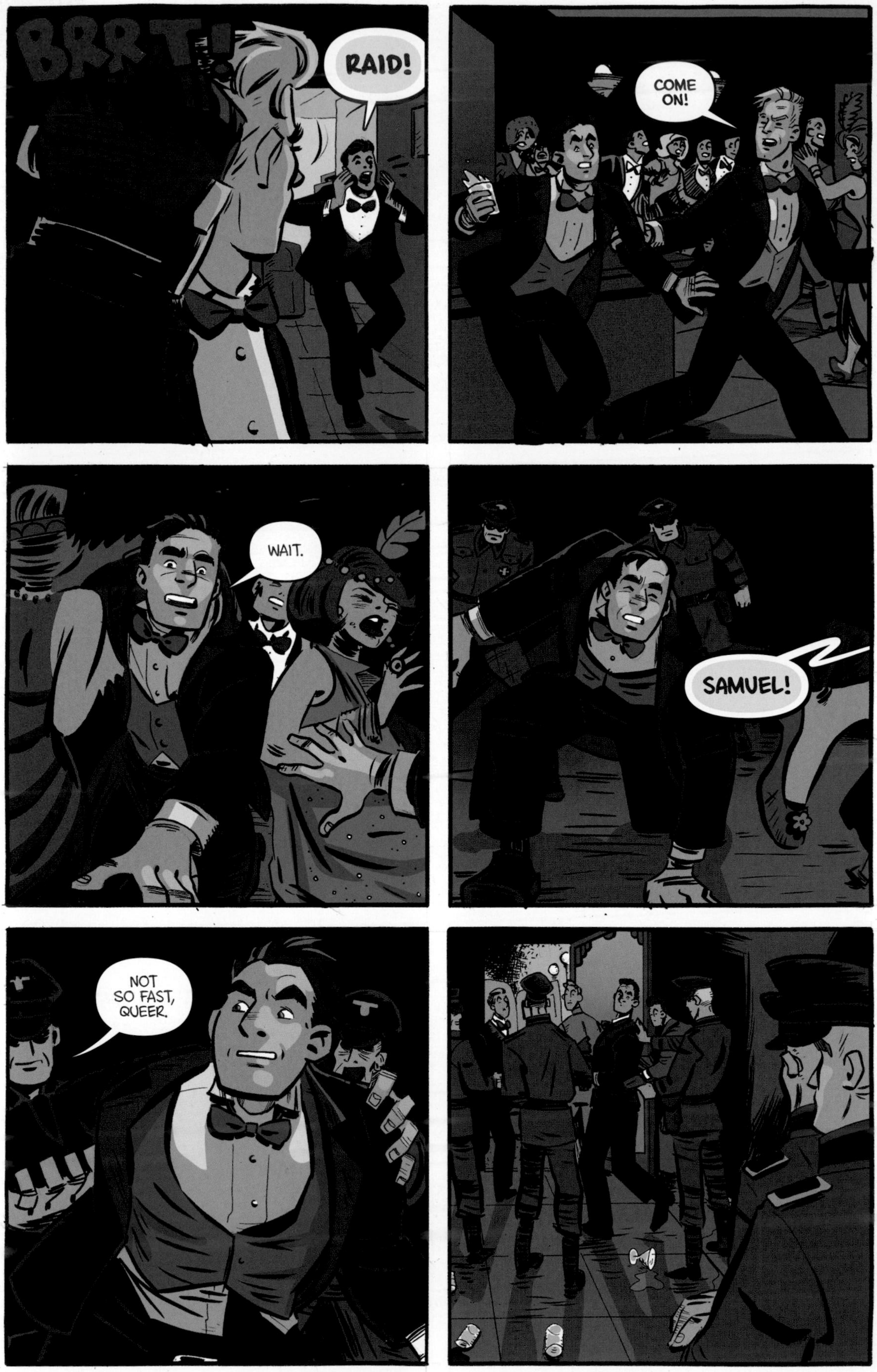
BRRT!
RAID!
COME ON!
WAIT.
SAMUEL!
NOT SO FAST, QUEER.

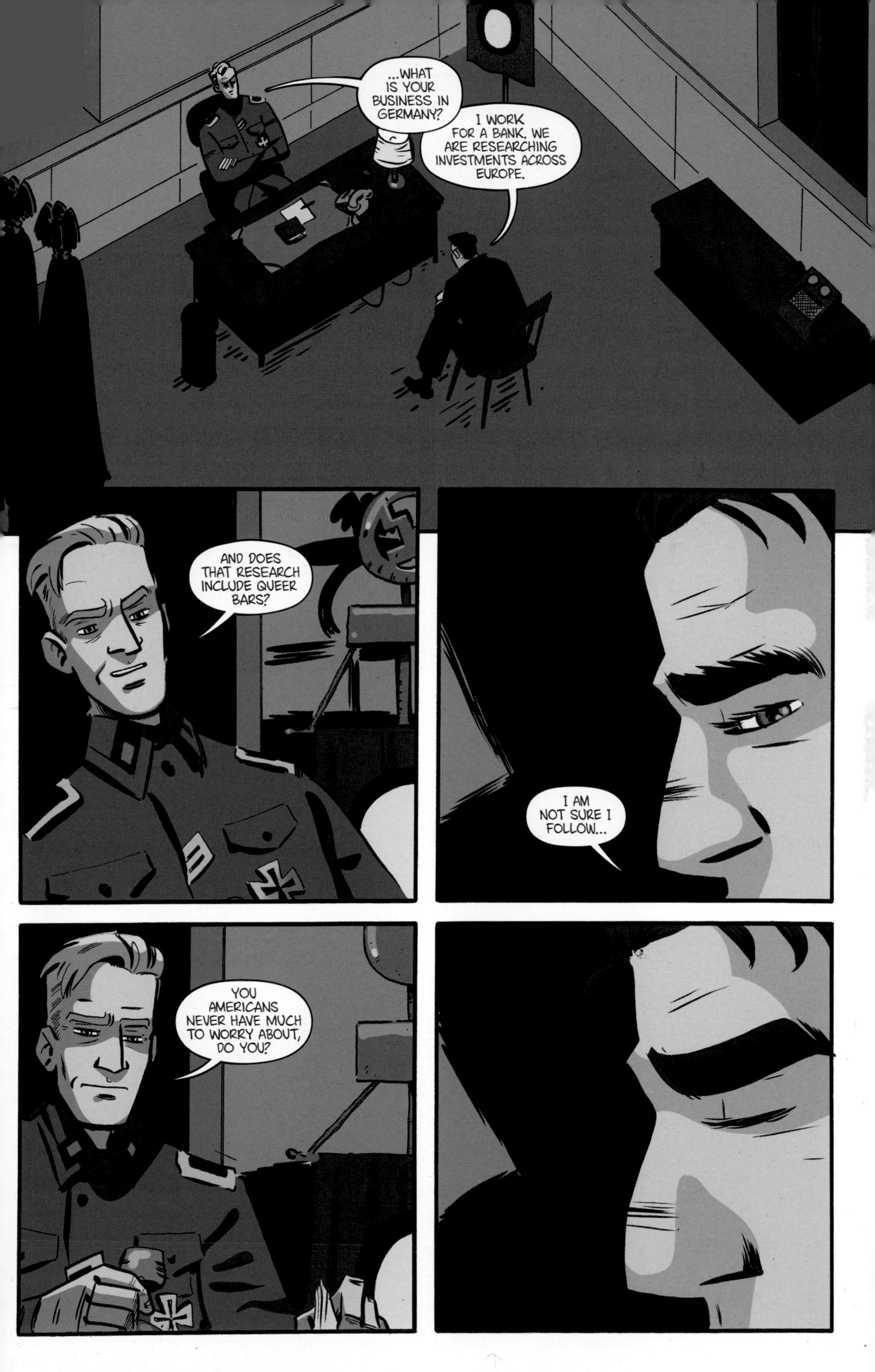
...WHAT IS YOUR BUSINESS IN GERMANY?
I WORK FOR A BANK. WE ARE RESEARCHING INVESTMENTS ACROSS EUROPE.
AND DOES THAT RESEARCH INCLUDE QUEER BARS?
I AM NOT SURE I FOLLOW...
YOU AMERICANS NEVER HAVE MUCH TO WORRY ABOUT, DO YOU?

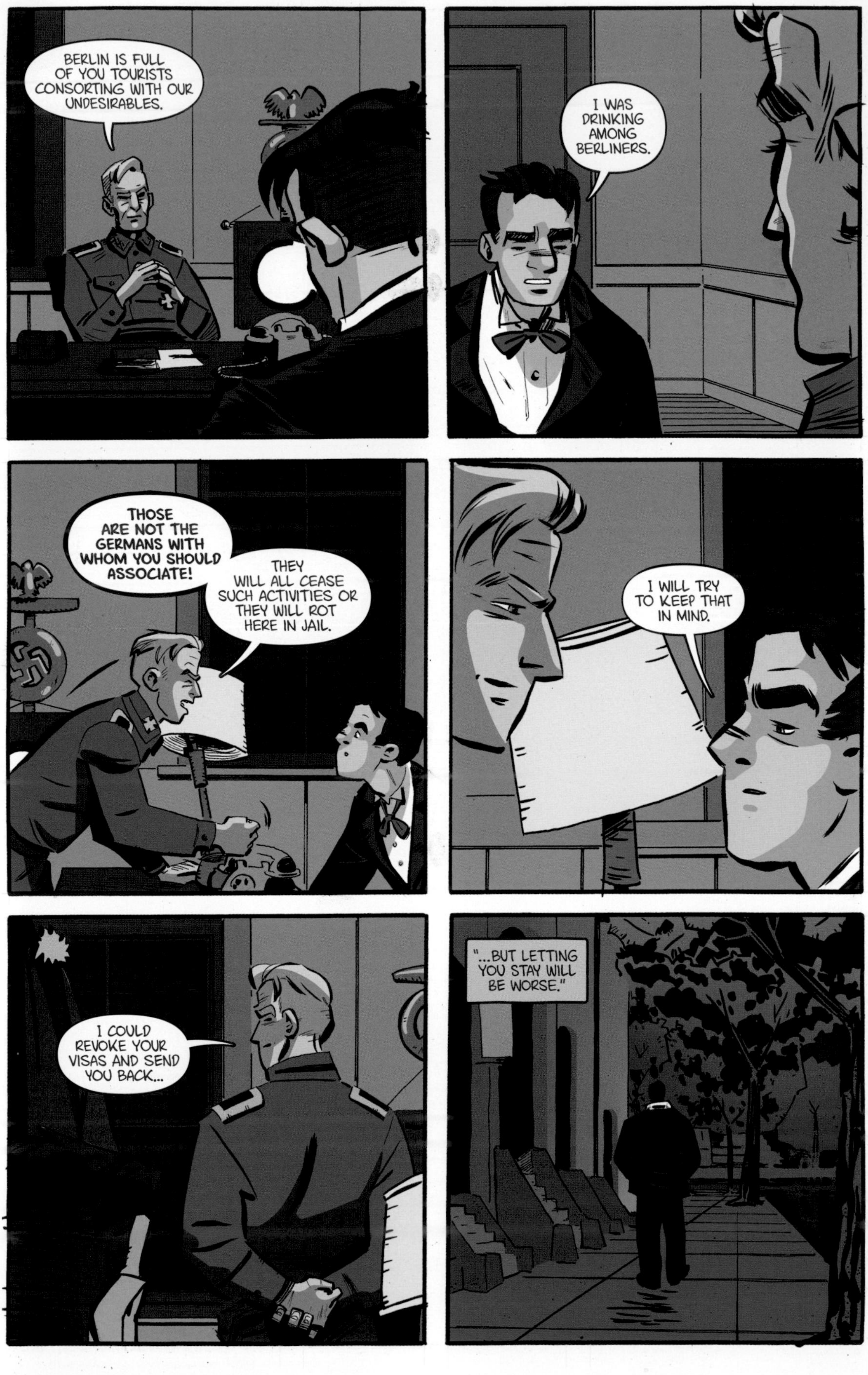
BERLIN IS FULL OF YOU TOURISTS CONSORTING WITH OUR UNDESIRABLES.
I WAS DRINKING AMONG BERLINERS.
THOSE ARE NOT THE GERMANS WITH WHOM YOU SHOULD ASSOCIATE!
THEY WILL ALL CEASE SUCH ACTIVITIES OR THEY WILL ROT HERE IN JAIL.
I WILL TRY TO KEEP THAT IN MIND.
I COULD REVOKE YOUR VISAS AND SEND YOU BACK...
"...BUT LETTING YOU STAY WILL BE WORSE."

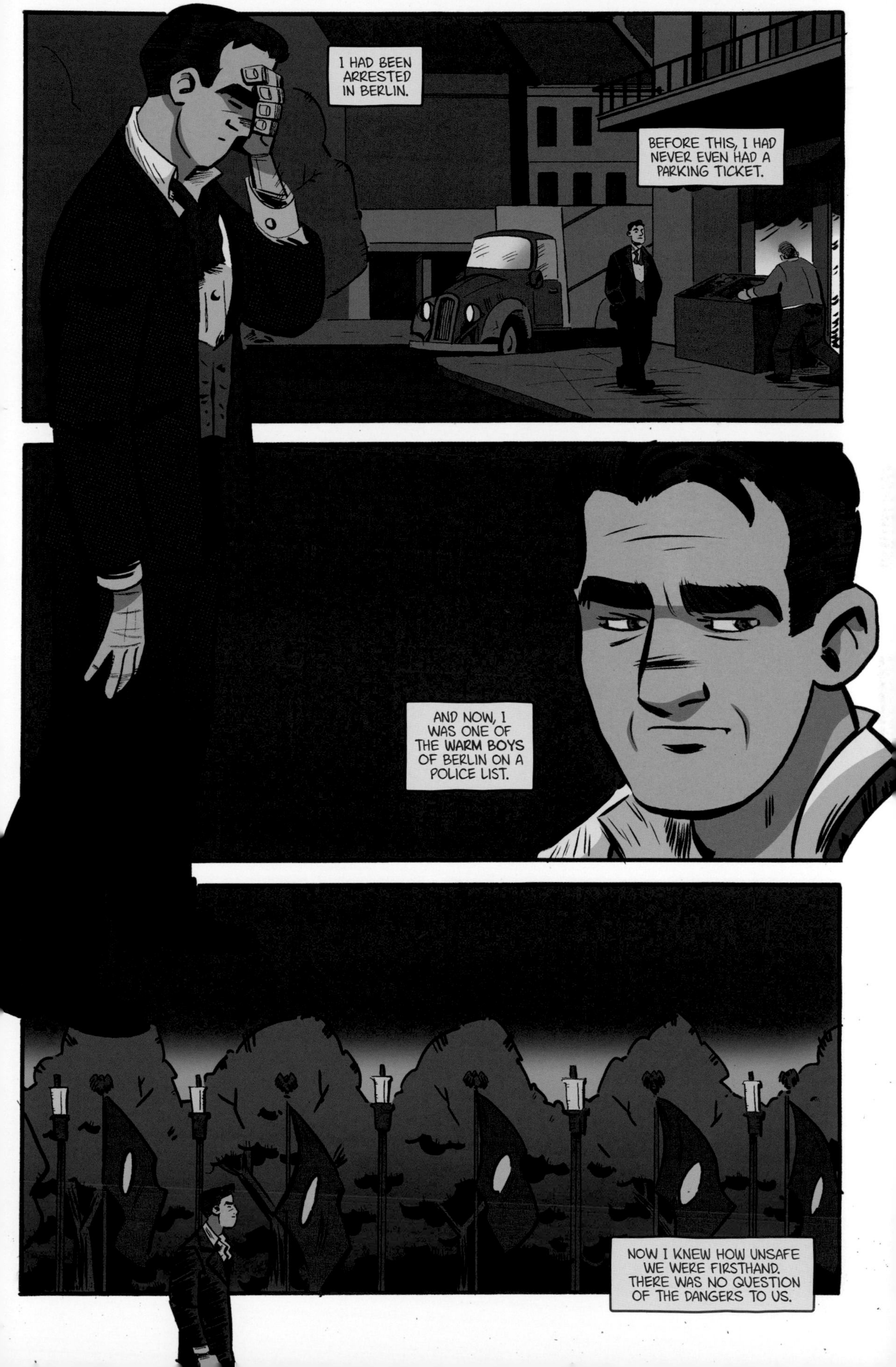
I HAD BEEN ARRESTED IN BERLIN.
BEFORE THIS, I HAD NEVER EVEN HAD A PARKING TICKET.
AND NOW, I WAS ONE OF THE WARM BOYS OF BERLIN ON A POLICE LIST.
NOW I KNEW HOW UNSAFE WE WERE FIRSTHAND. THERE WAS NO QUESTION OF THE DANGERS TO US.

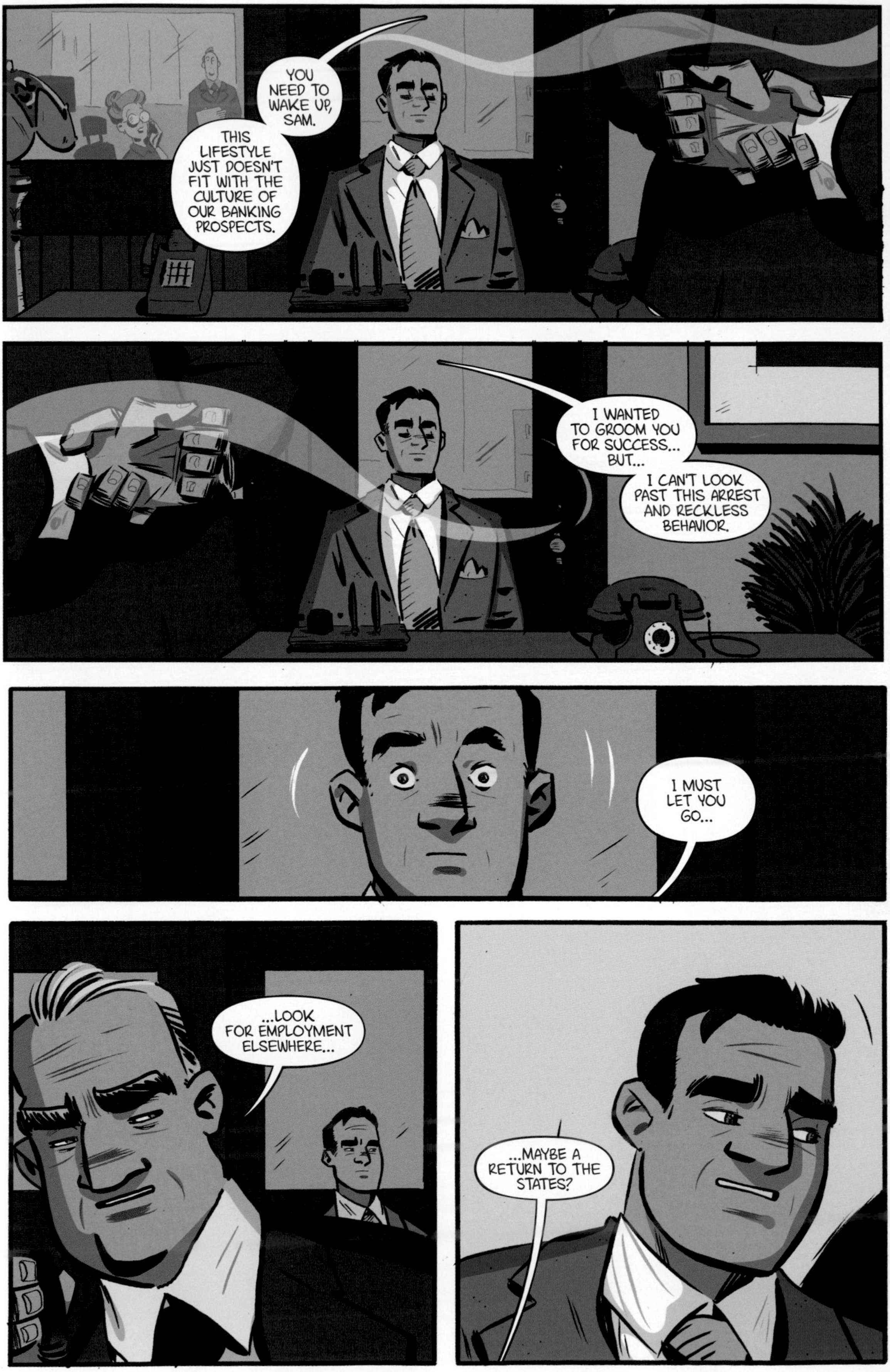
YOU NEED TO WAKE UP, SAM.
THIS LIFESTYLE JUST DOESN'T FIT WITH THE CULTURE OF OUR BANKING PROSPECTS.
I WANTED TO GROOM YOU FOR SUCCESS... BUT...
I CAN'T LOOK PAST THIS ARREST AND RECKLESS BEHAVIOR.
I MUST LET YOU GO...
...LOOK FOR EMPLOYMENT ELSEWHERE...
...MAYBE A RETURN TO THE STATES?

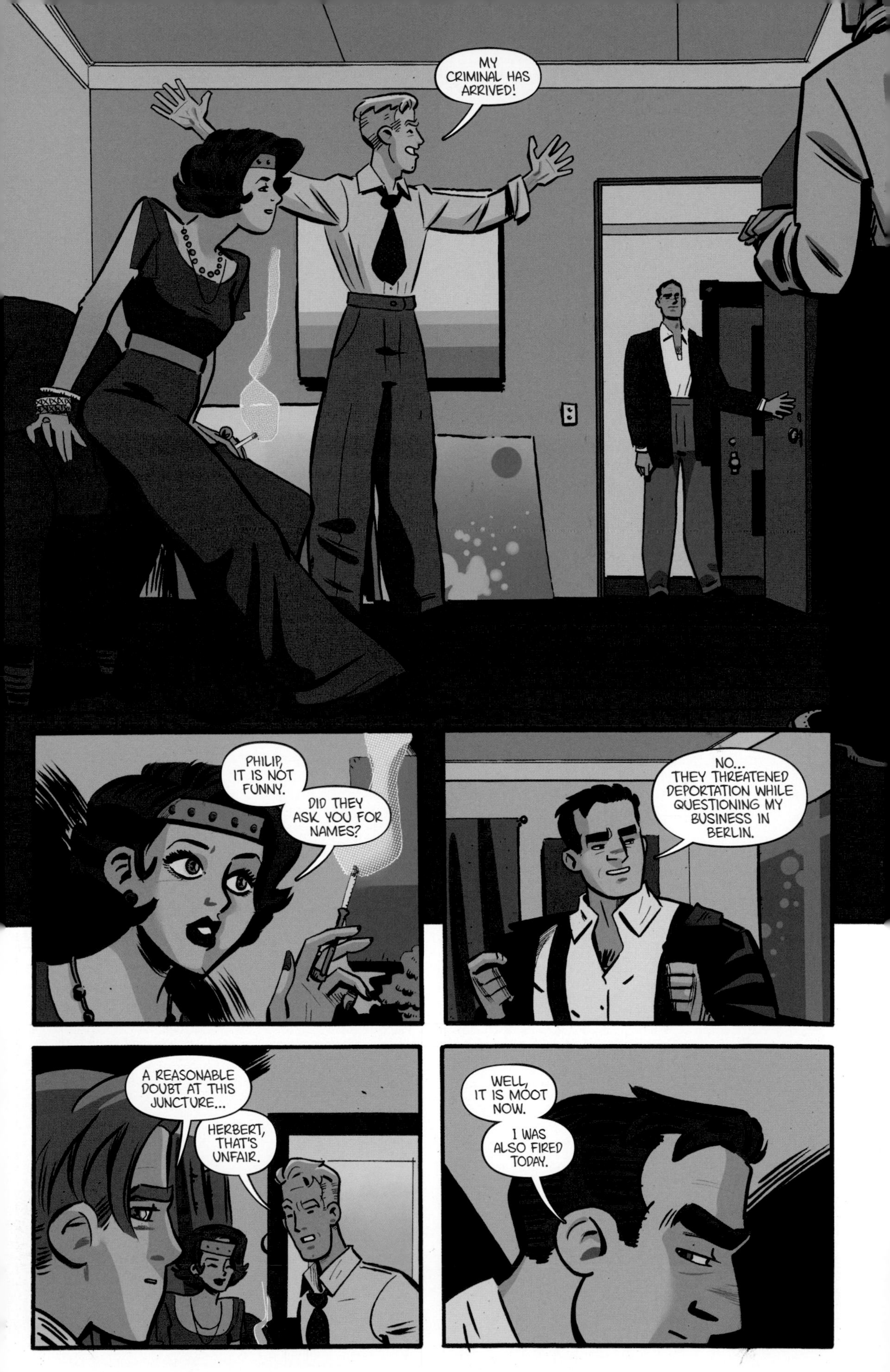
MY CRIMINAL HAS ARRIVED!
PHILIP, IT IS NOT FUNNY.
DID THEY ASK YOU FOR NAMES?
NO... THEY THREATENED DEPORTATION WHILE QUESTIONING MY BUSINESS IN BERLIN.
A REASONABLE DOUBT AT THIS JUNCTURE...
HERBERT, THAT'S UNFAIR.
WELL, IT IS MOOT NOW.
I WAS ALSO FIRED TODAY.

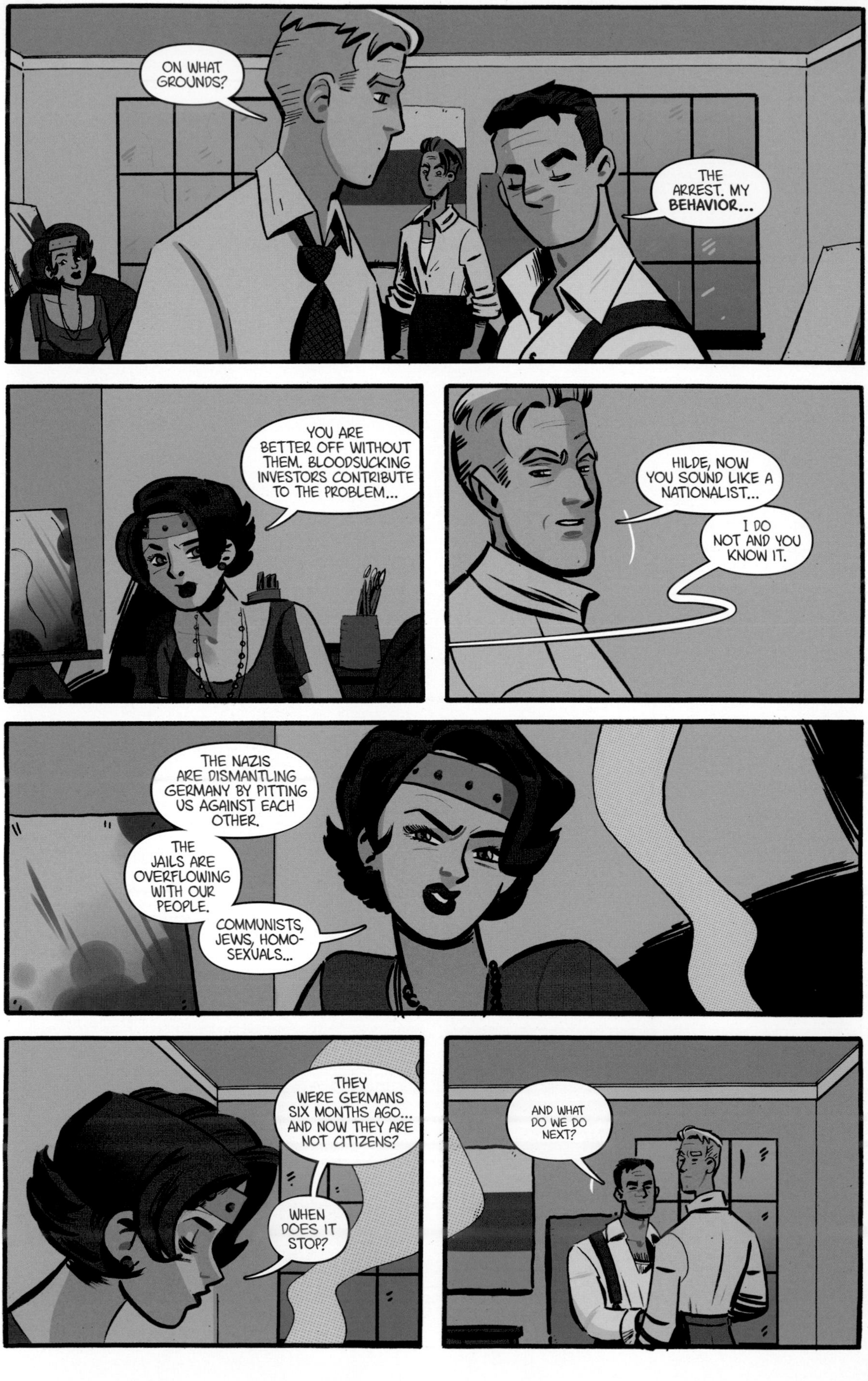
ON WHAT GROUNDS?
THE ARREST. MY **BEHAVIOR...**
YOU ARE BETTER OFF WITHOUT THEM. BLOODSUCKING INVESTORS CONTRIBUTE TO THE PROBLEM...
HILDE, NOW YOU SOUND LIKE A NATIONALIST...
I DO NOT AND YOU KNOW IT.
THE NAZIS ARE DISMANTLING GERMANY BY PITTING US AGAINST EACH OTHER.
THE JAILS ARE OVERFLOWING WITH OUR PEOPLE.
COMMUNISTS, JEWS, HOMO-SEXUALS...
THEY WERE GERMANS SIX MONTHS AGO... AND NOW THEY ARE NOT CITIZENS?
WHEN DOES IT STOP?
AND WHAT DO WE DO NEXT?

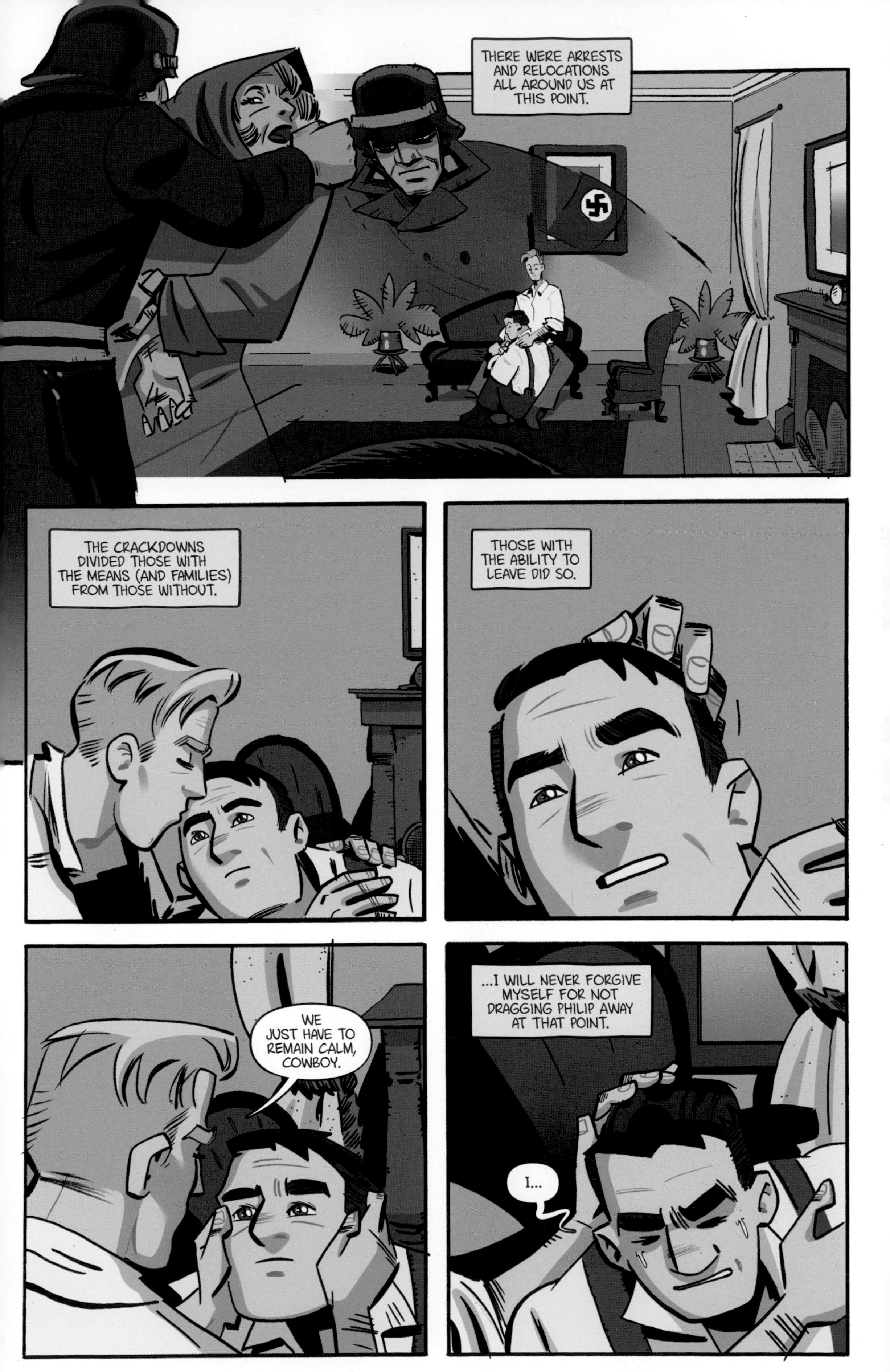
THERE WERE ARRESTS AND RELOCATIONS ALL AROUND US AT THIS POINT.
THE CRACKDOWNS DIVIDED THOSE WITH THE MEANS (AND FAMILIES) FROM THOSE WITHOUT.
THOSE WITH THE ABILITY TO LEAVE DID SO.
WE JUST HAVE TO REMAIN CALM, COWBOY.
...I WILL NEVER FORGIVE MYSELF FOR NOT DRAGGING PHILIP AWAY AT THAT POINT.
I...

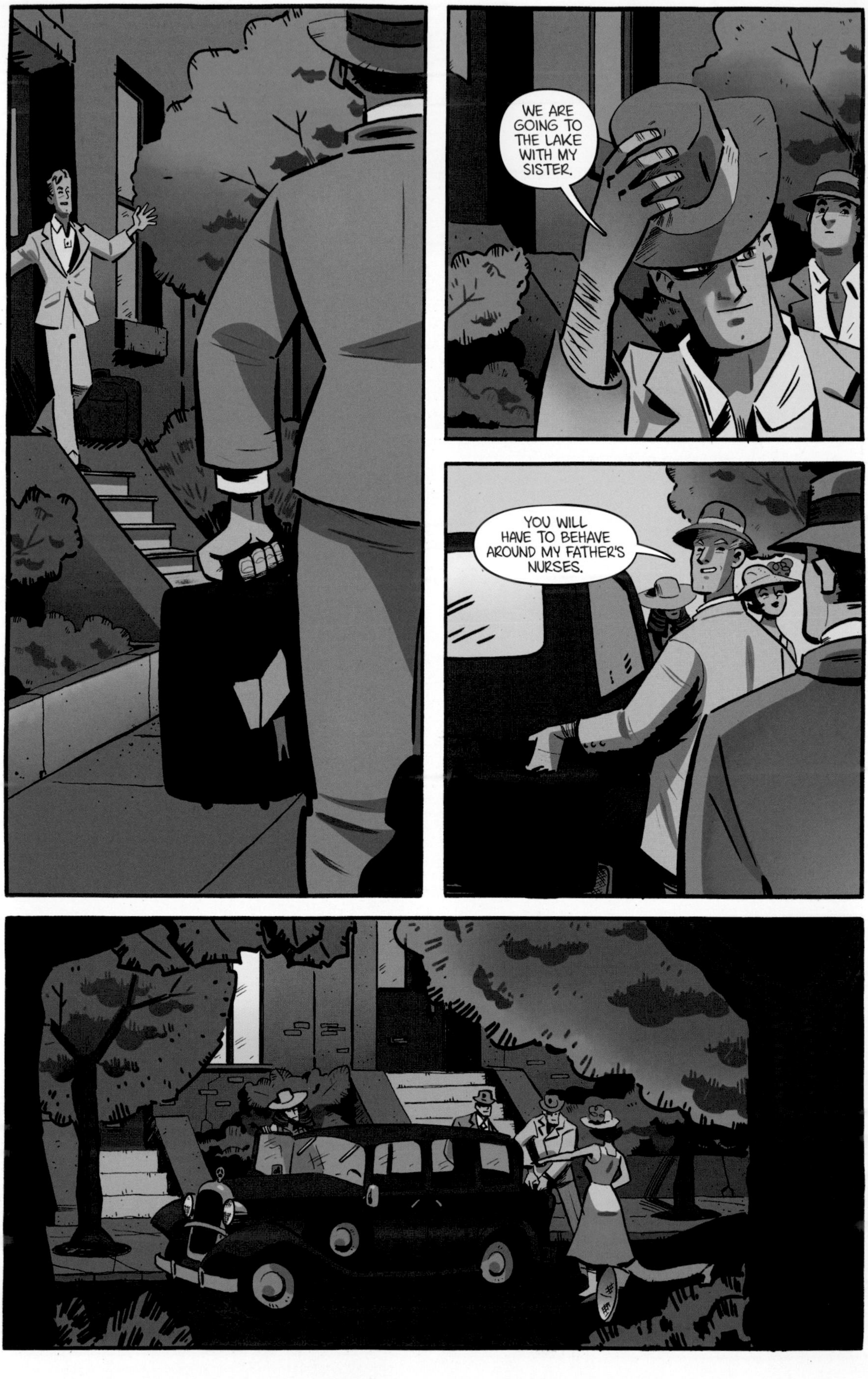
WE ARE GOING TO THE LAKE WITH MY SISTER.
YOU WILL HAVE TO BEHAVE AROUND MY FATHER'S NURSES.

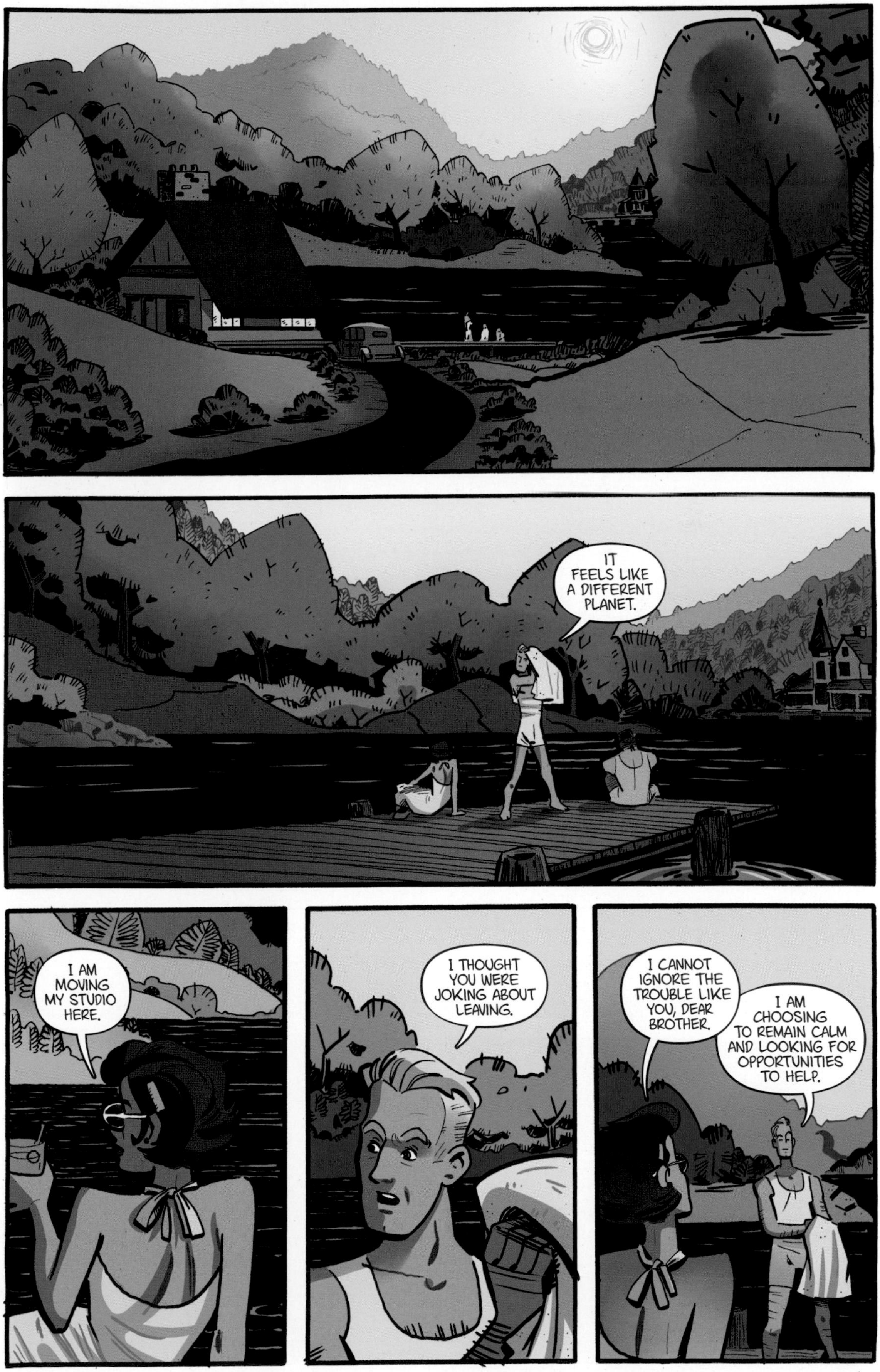
IT FEELS LIKE A DIFFERENT PLANET.
I AM MOVING MY STUDIO HERE.
I THOUGHT YOU WERE JOKING ABOUT LEAVING.
I CANNOT IGNORE THE TROUBLE LIKE YOU, DEAR BROTHER.
I AM CHOOSING TO REMAIN CALM AND LOOKING FOR OPPORTUNITIES TO HELP.

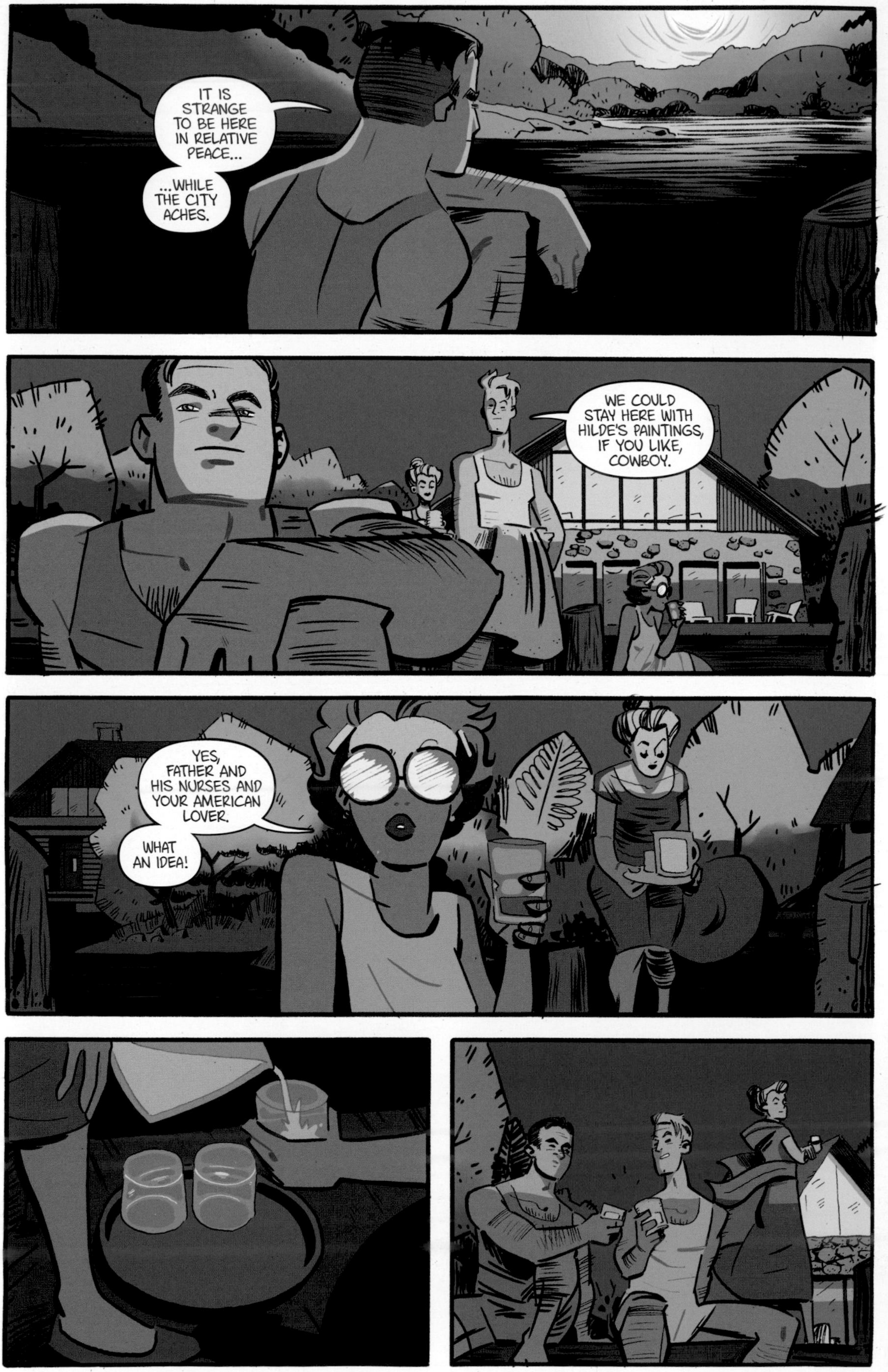
IT IS STRANGE TO BE HERE IN RELATIVE PEACE...
...WHILE THE CITY ACHES.
WE COULD STAY HERE WITH HILDE'S PAINTINGS, IF YOU LIKE, COWBOY.
YES, FATHER AND HIS NURSES AND YOUR AMERICAN LOVER.
WHAT AN IDEA!

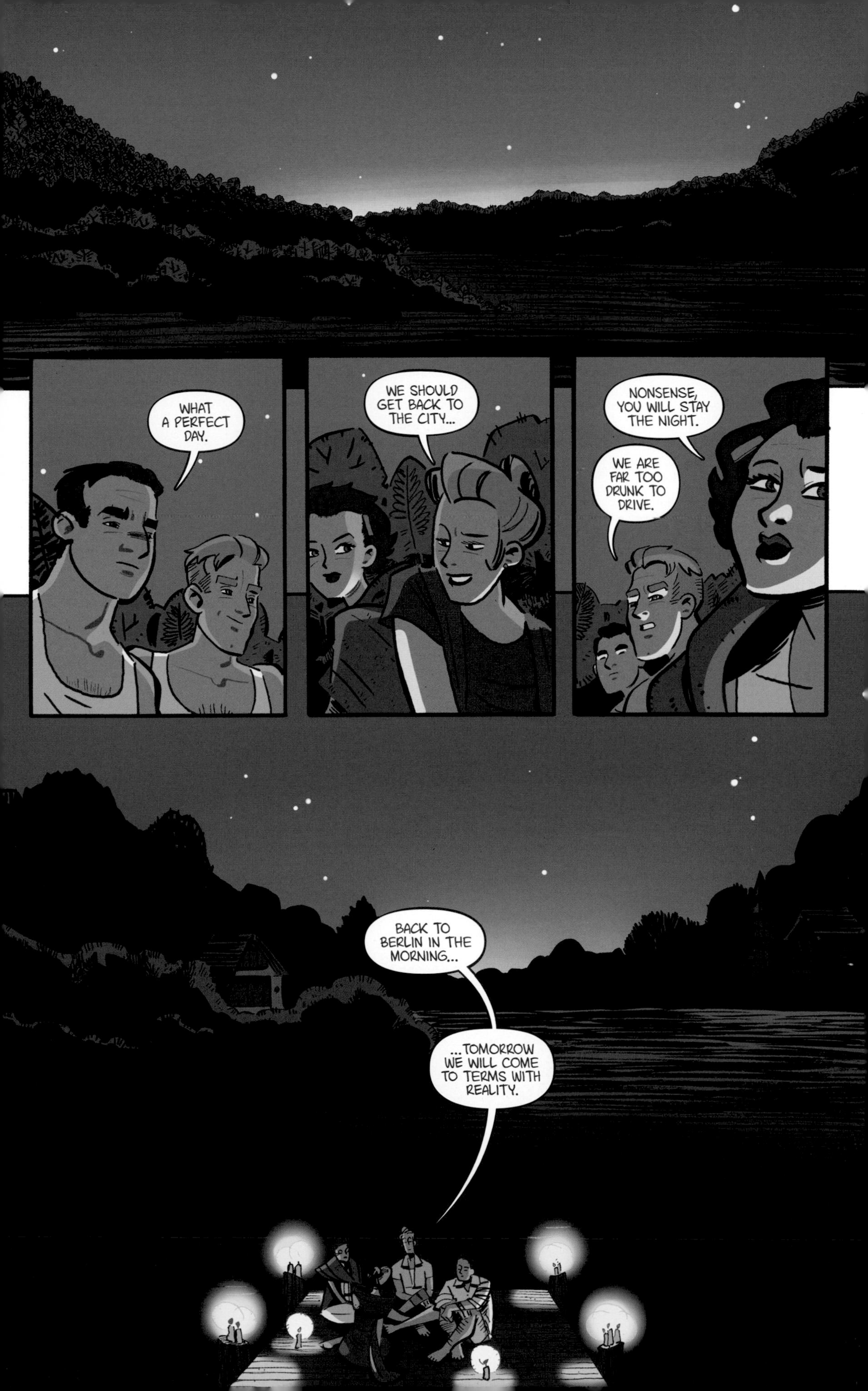
WHAT A PERFECT DAY.
WE SHOULD GET BACK TO THE CITY...
NONSENSE, YOU WILL STAY THE NIGHT.
WE ARE FAR TOO DRUNK TO DRIVE.
BACK TO BERLIN IN THE MORNING...
...TOMORROW WE WILL COME TO TERMS WITH REALITY.

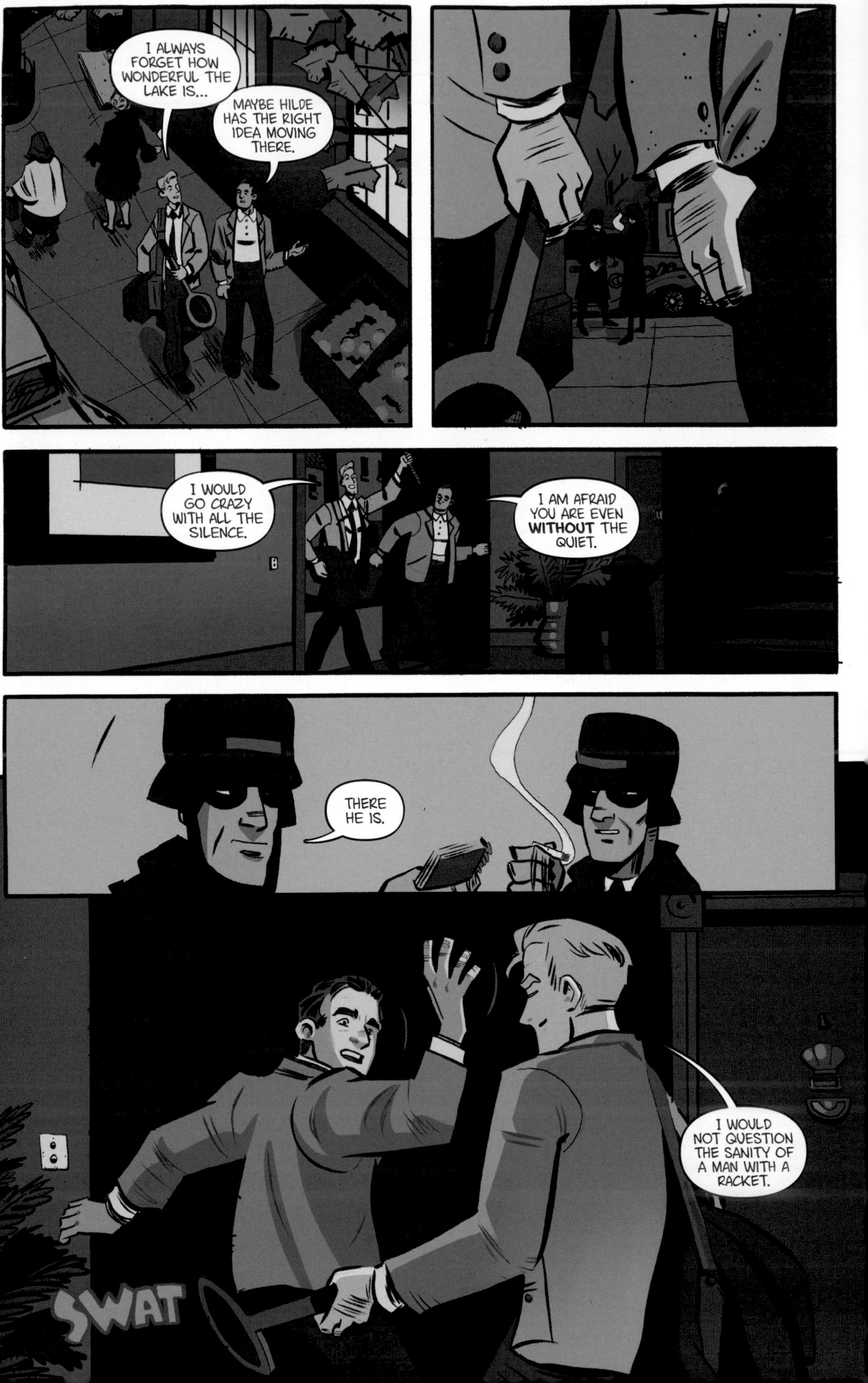
I ALWAYS FORGET HOW WONDERFUL THE LAKE IS...
MAYBE HILDE HAS THE RIGHT IDEA MOVING THERE.
I WOULD GO CRAZY WITH ALL THE SILENCE.
I AM AFRAID YOU ARE EVEN WITHOUT THE QUIET.
THERE HE IS.
I WOULD NOT QUESTION THE SANITY OF A MAN WITH A RACKET.
SWAT

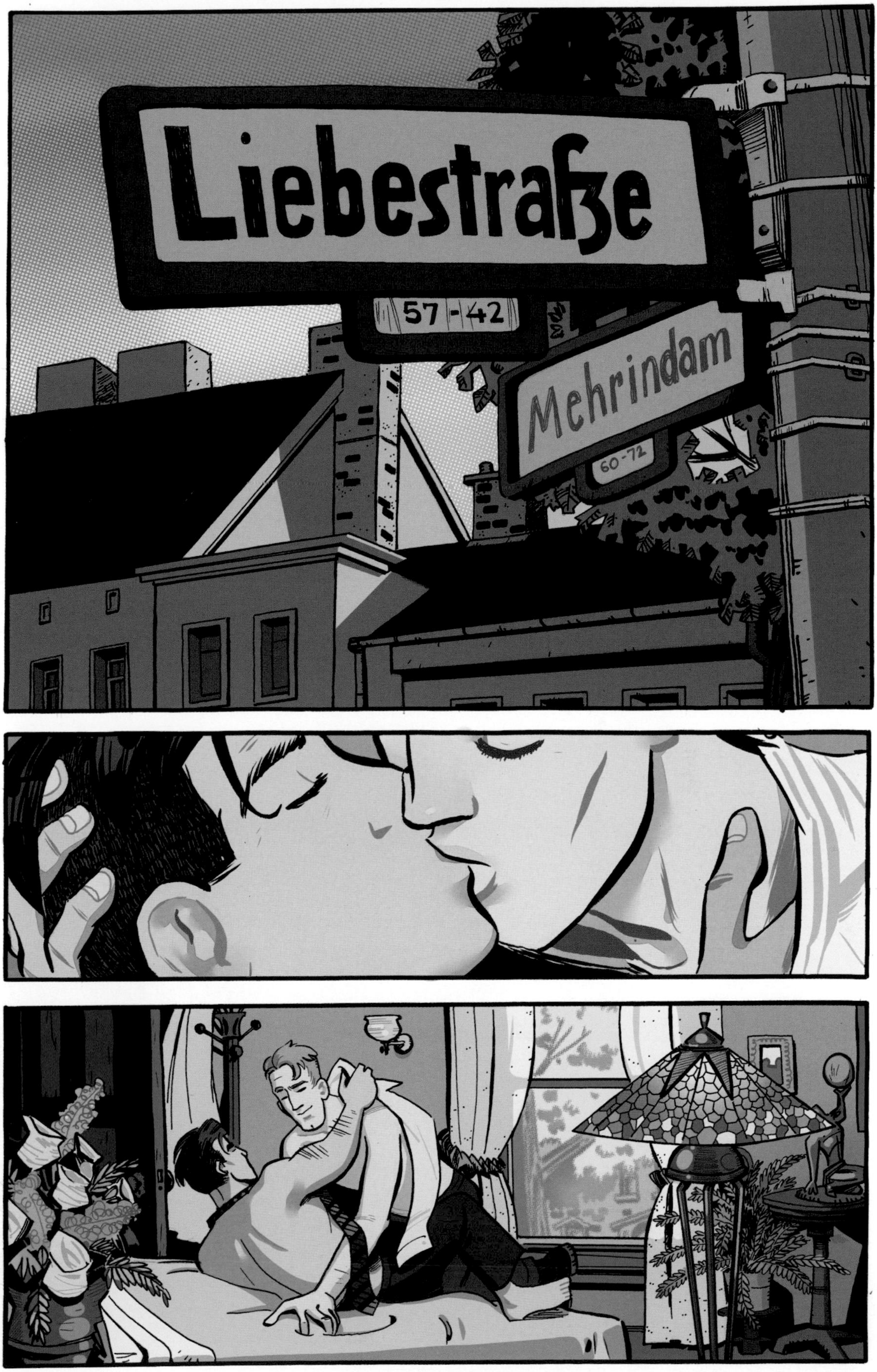
Liebestraße
57-42
Mehrindam
60-72

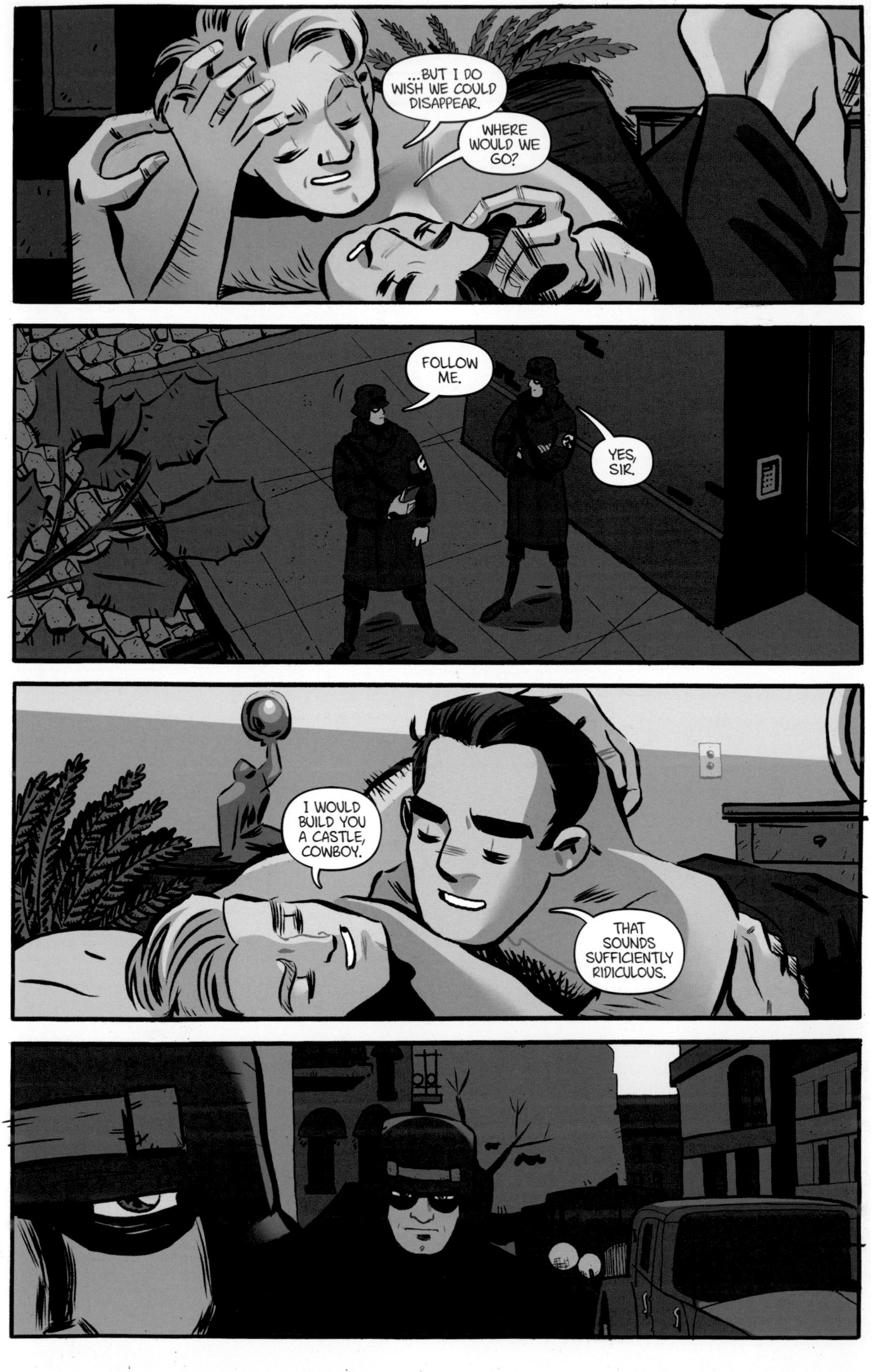
...BUT I DO WISH WE COULD DISAPPEAR.
WHERE WOULD WE GO?
FOLLOW ME.
YES, SIR.
I WOULD BUILD YOU A CASTLE, COWBOY.
THAT SOUNDS SUFFICIENTLY RIDICULOUS.

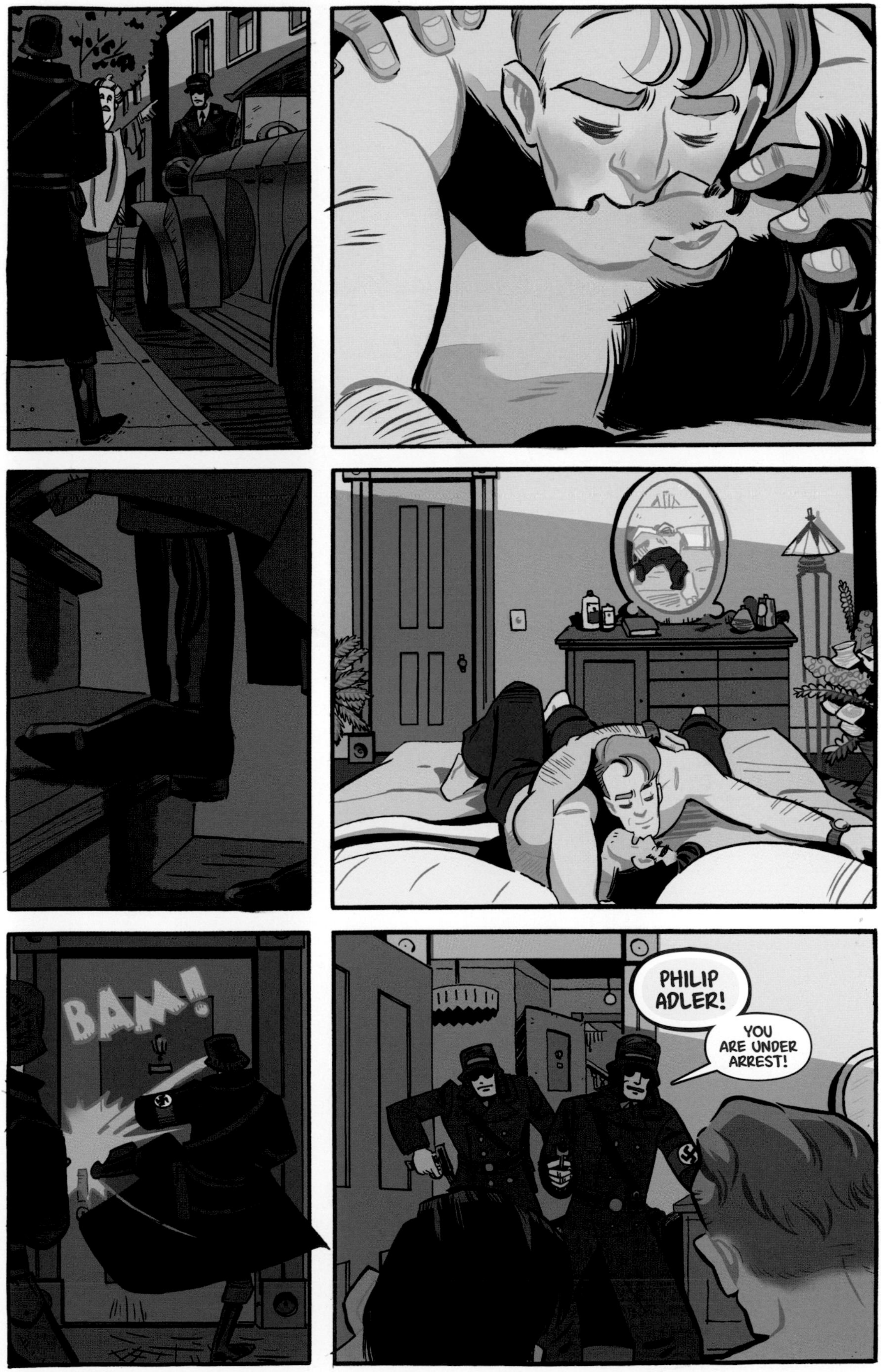
BAM!
PHILIP ADLER!
YOU ARE UNDER ARREST!

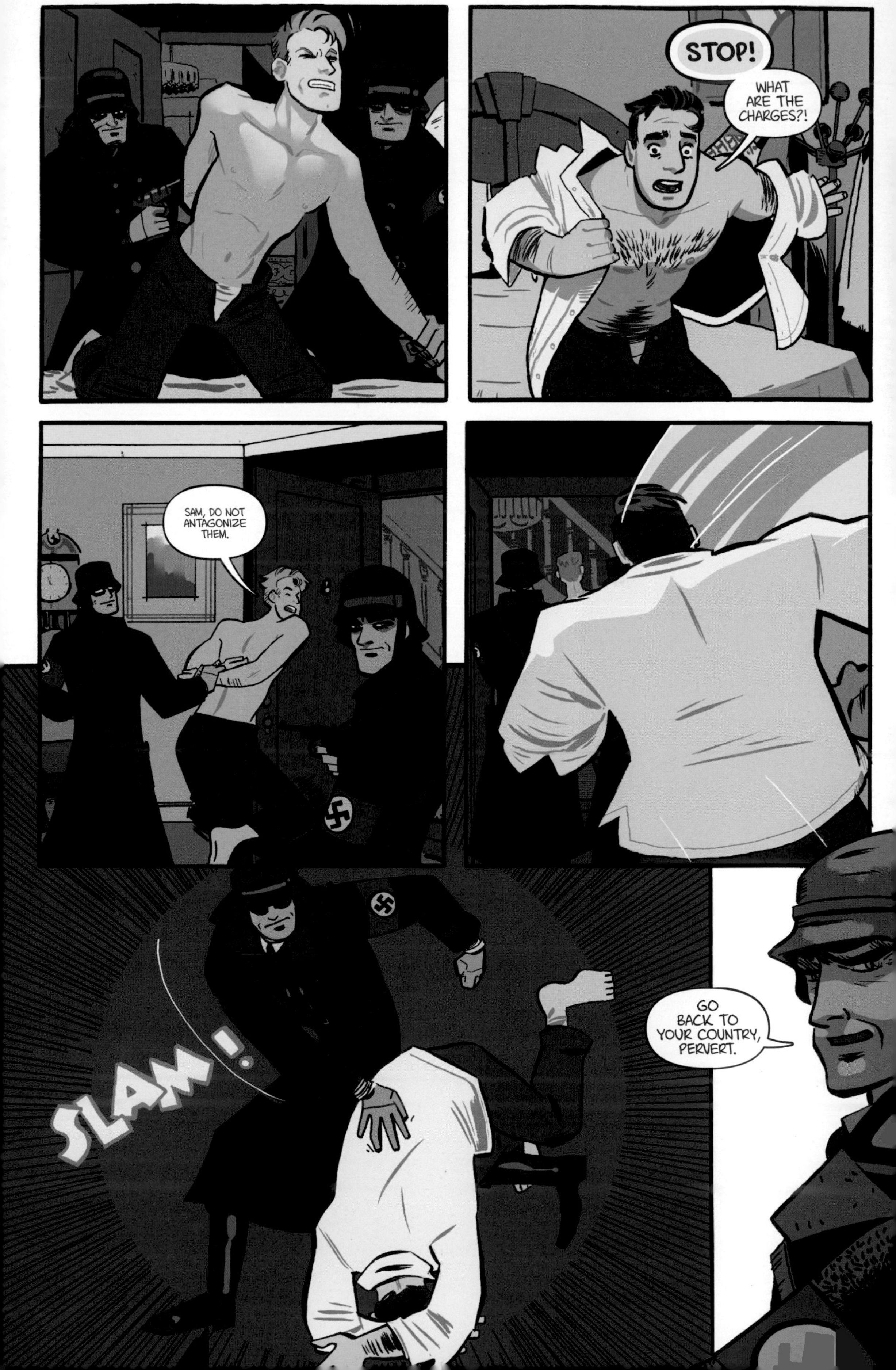
STOP!
WHAT ARE THE CHARGES?!
SAM, DO NOT ANTAGONIZE THEM.
SLAM!
GO BACK TO YOUR COUNTRY, PERVERT.

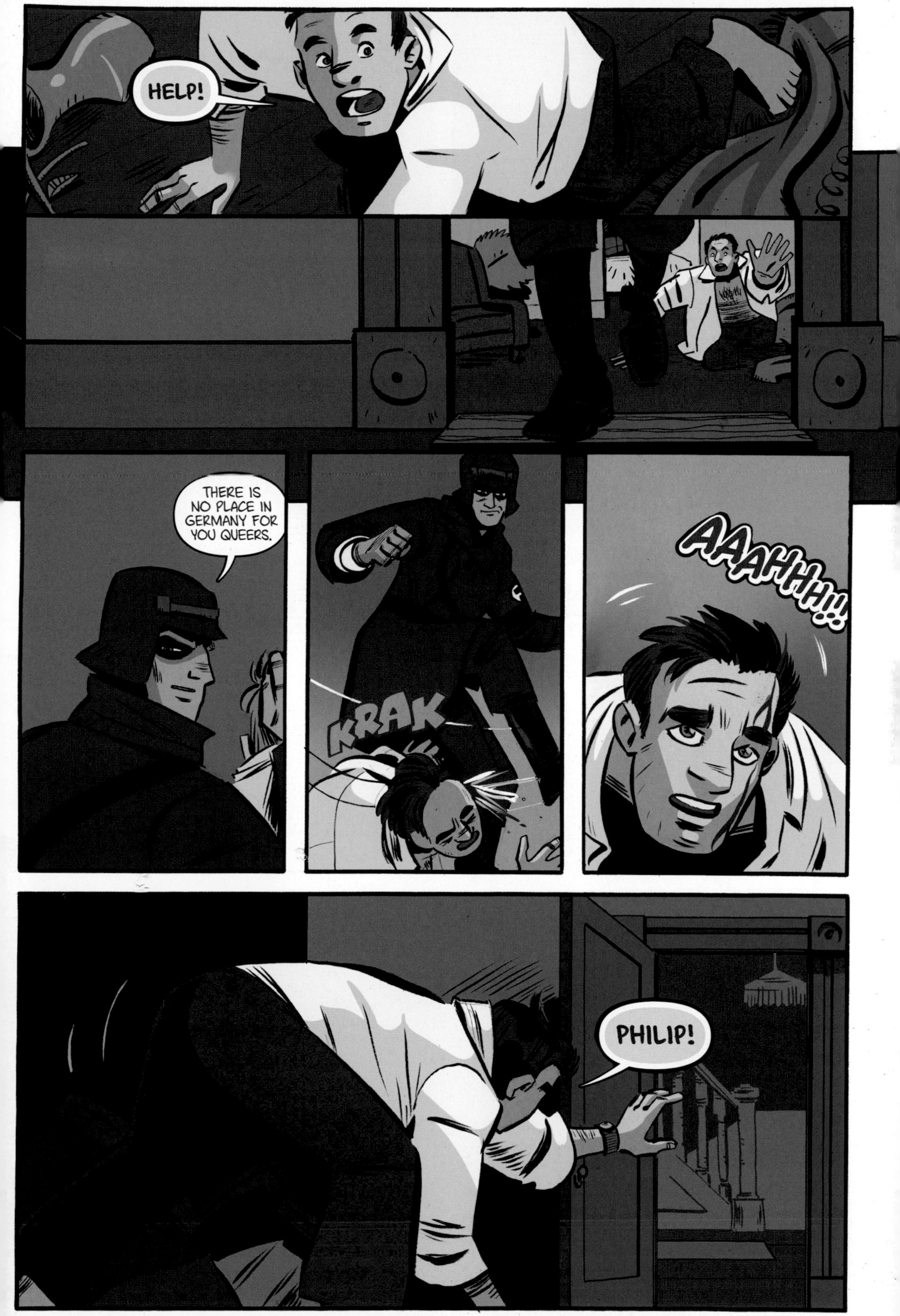
HELP!
THERE IS NO PLACE IN GERMANY FOR YOU QUEERS.
KRAK
AAAHHH!!!
PHILIP!

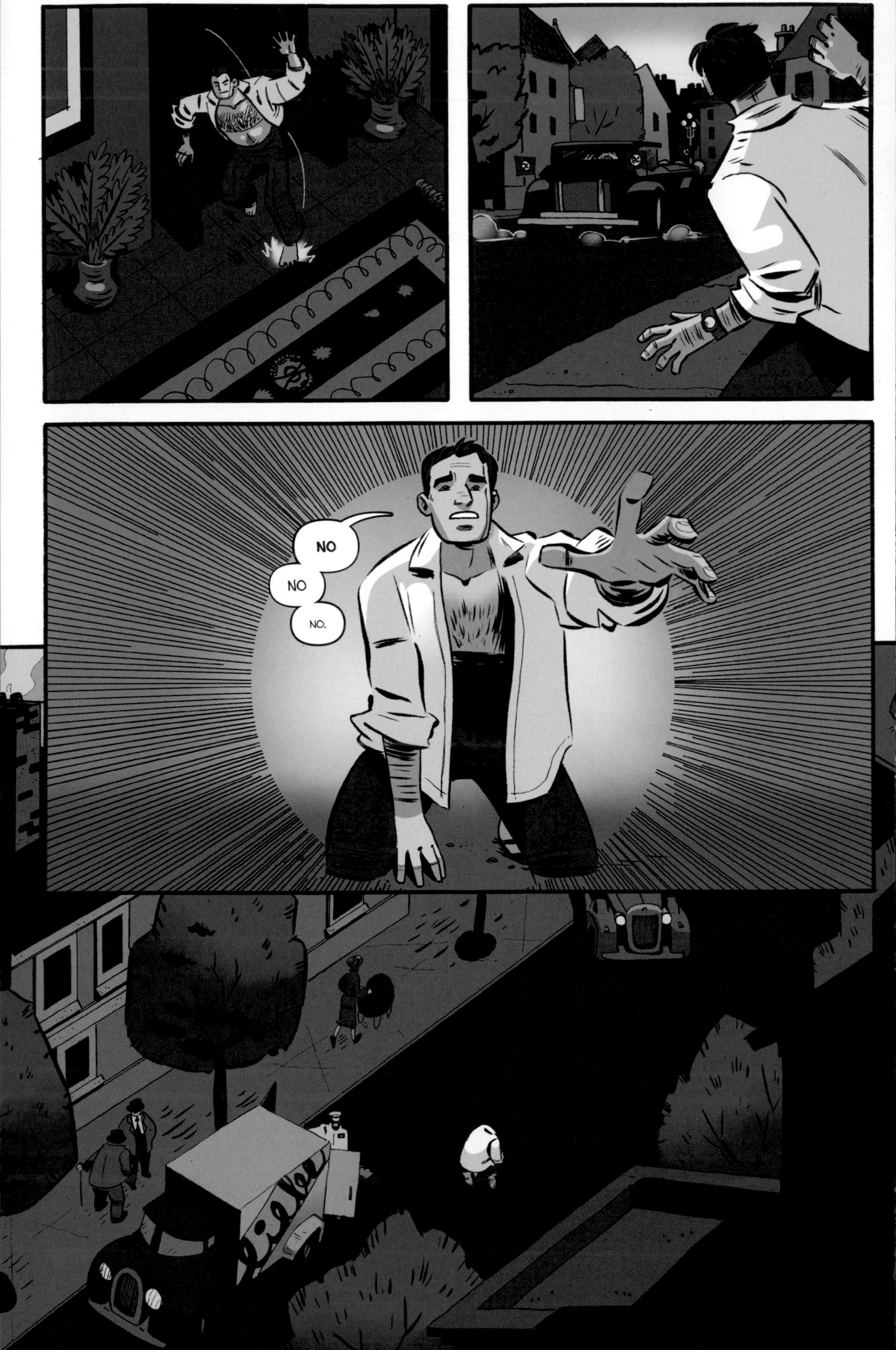
NO
NO
NO.

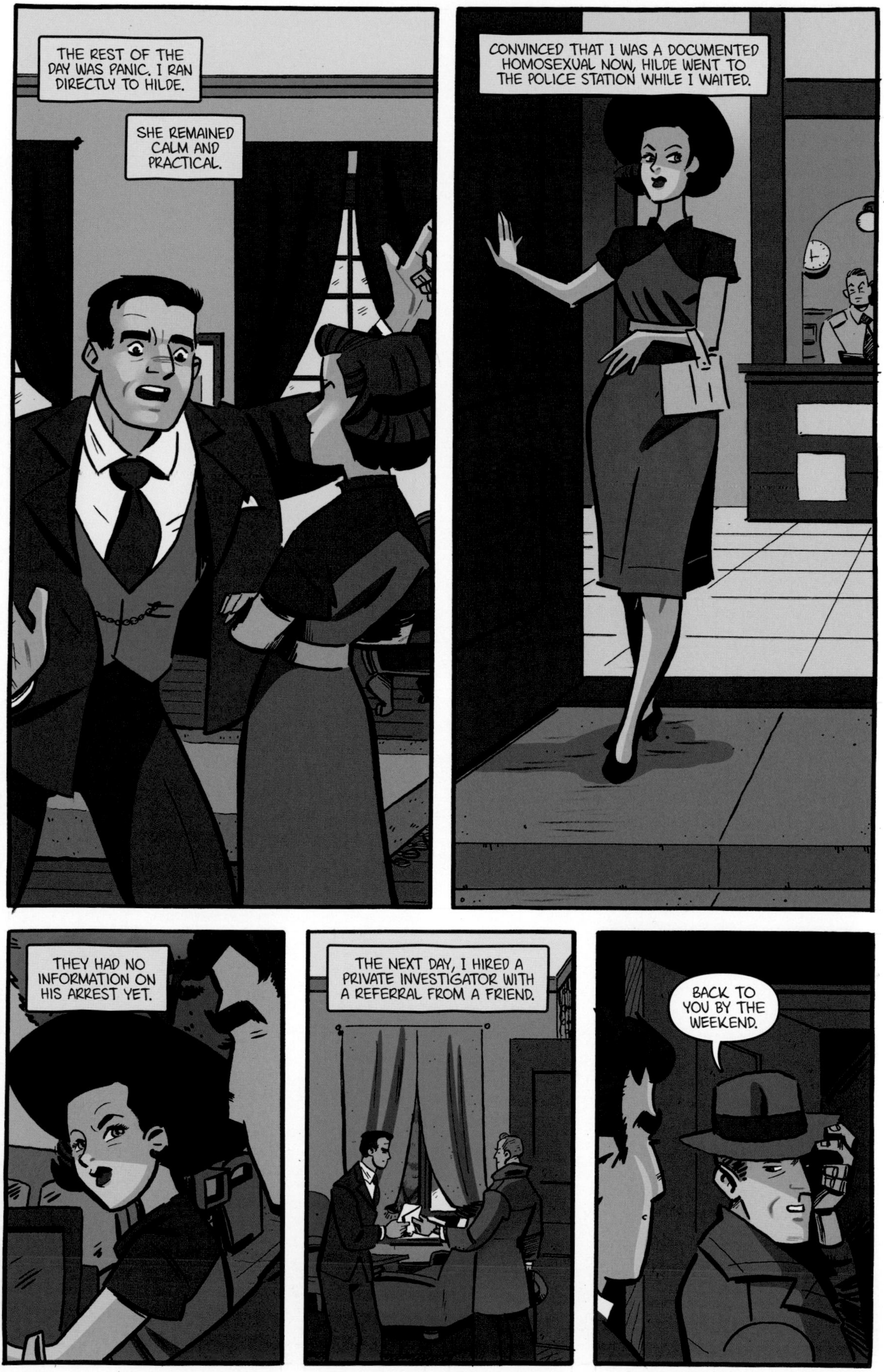
THE REST OF THE DAY WAS PANIC. I RAN DIRECTLY TO HILDE.
SHE REMAINED CALM AND PRACTICAL.
CONVINCED THAT I WAS A DOCUMENTED HOMOSEXUAL NOW, HILDE WENT TO THE POLICE STATION WHILE I WAITED.
THEY HAD NO INFORMATION ON HIS ARREST YET.
THE NEXT DAY, I HIRED A PRIVATE INVESTIGATOR WITH A REFERRAL FROM A FRIEND.
BACK TO YOU BY THE WEEKEND.

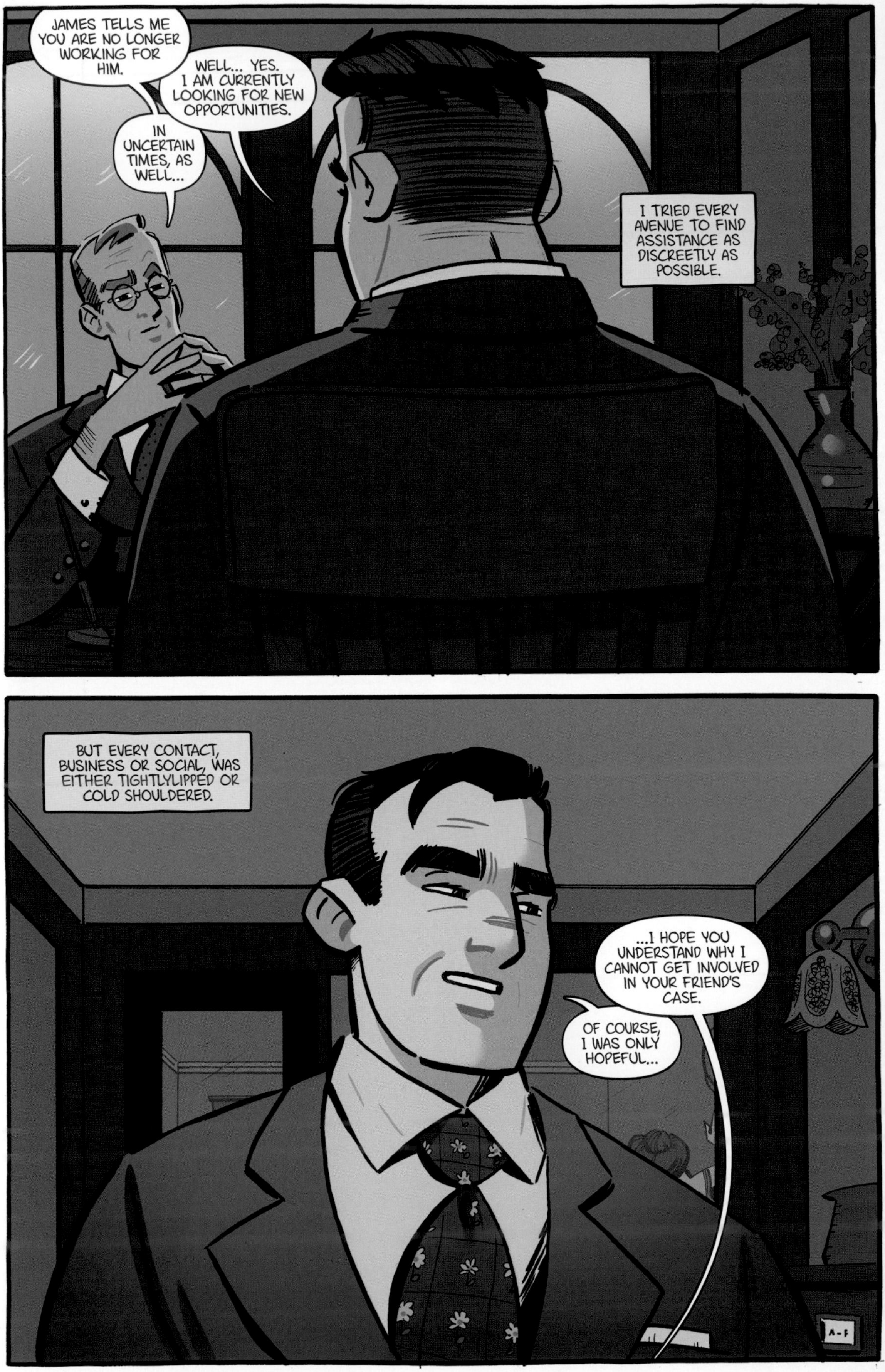
JAMES TELLS ME YOU ARE NO LONGER WORKING FOR HIM.
WELL... YES. I AM CURRENTLY LOOKING FOR NEW OPPORTUNITIES.
IN UNCERTAIN TIMES, AS WELL...
I TRIED EVERY AVENUE TO FIND ASSISTANCE AS DISCREETLY AS POSSIBLE.
BUT EVERY CONTACT, BUSINESS OR SOCIAL, WAS EITHER TIGHTLYLIPPED OR COLD SHOULDERED.
...I HOPE YOU UNDERSTAND WHY I CANNOT GET INVOLVED IN YOUR FRIEND'S CASE.
OF COURSE, I WAS ONLY HOPEFUL...

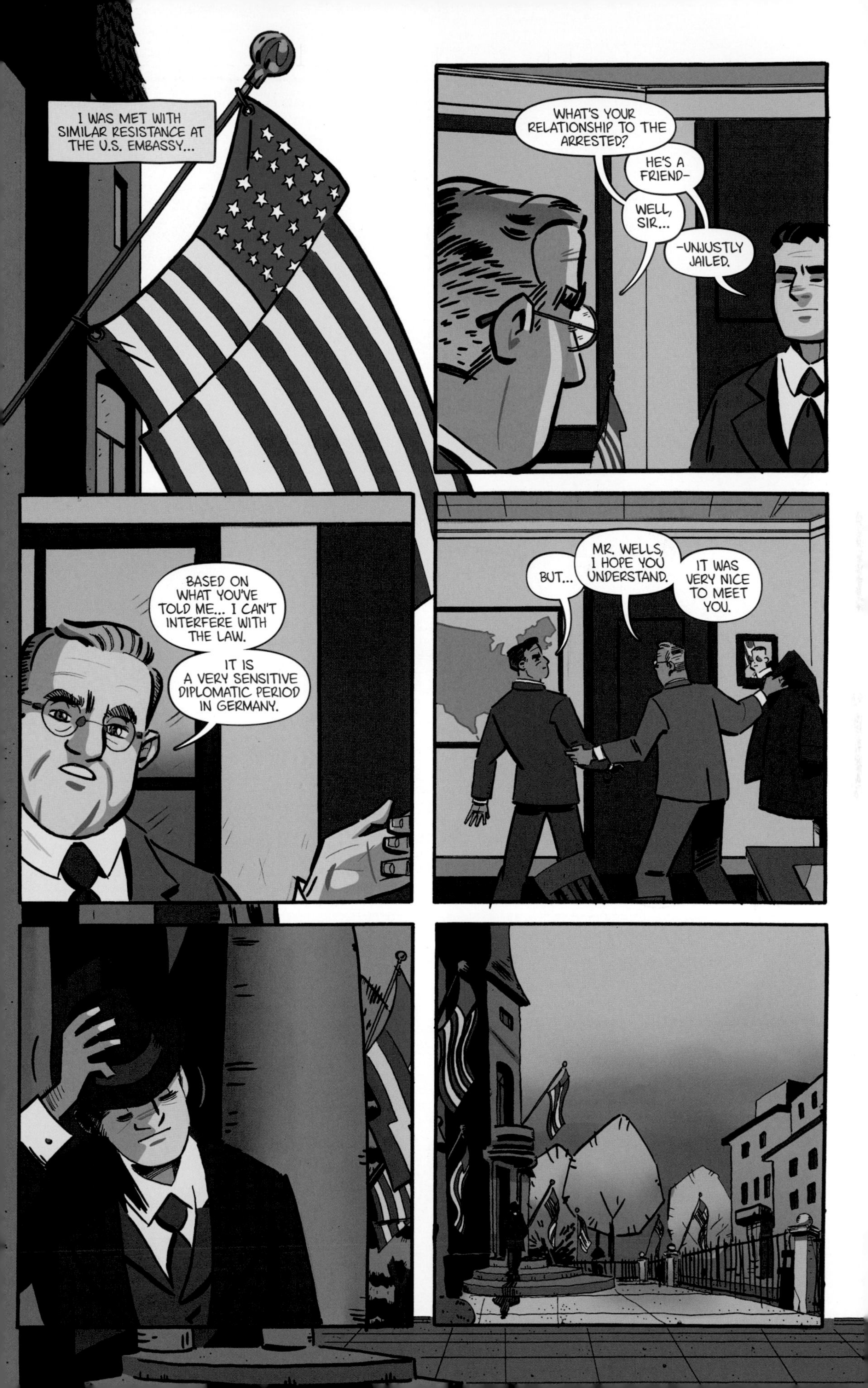
I WAS MET WITH SIMILAR RESISTANCE AT THE U.S. EMBASSY...
WHAT'S YOUR RELATIONSHIP TO THE ARRESTED?
WELL, SIR...
HE'S A FRIEND-
-UNJUSTLY JAILED.
BASED ON WHAT YOU'VE TOLD ME... I CAN'T INTERFERE WITH THE LAW.
IT IS A VERY SENSITIVE DIPLOMATIC PERIOD IN GERMANY.
BUT...
MR. WELLS, I HOPE YOU UNDERSTAND.
IT WAS VERY NICE TO MEET YOU.

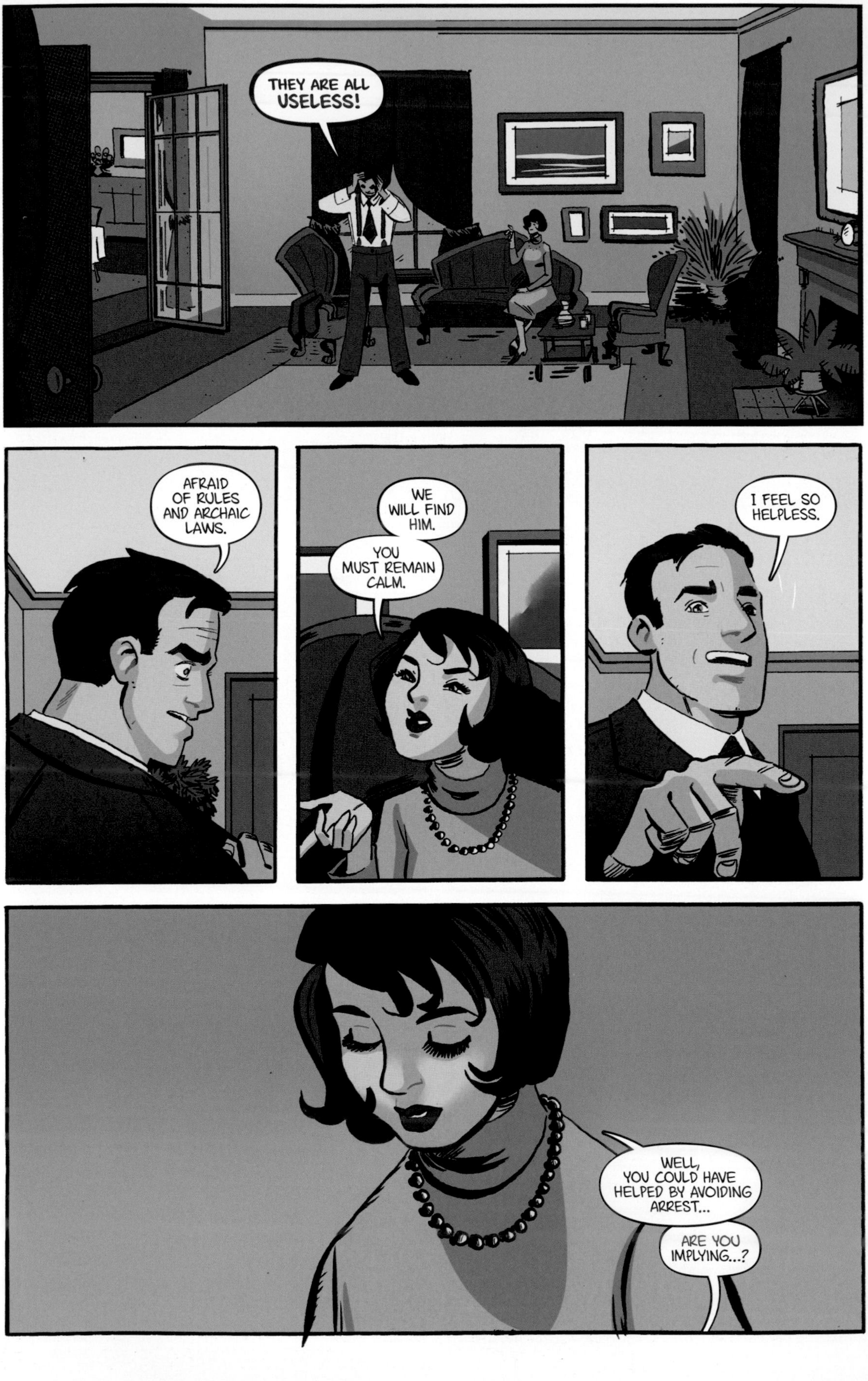
THEY ARE ALL USELESS!
AFRAID OF RULES AND ARCHAIC LAWS.
WE WILL FIND HIM.
YOU MUST REMAIN CALM.
I FEEL SO HELPLESS.
WELL, YOU COULD HAVE HELPED BY AVOIDING ARREST...
ARE YOU IMPLYING...?

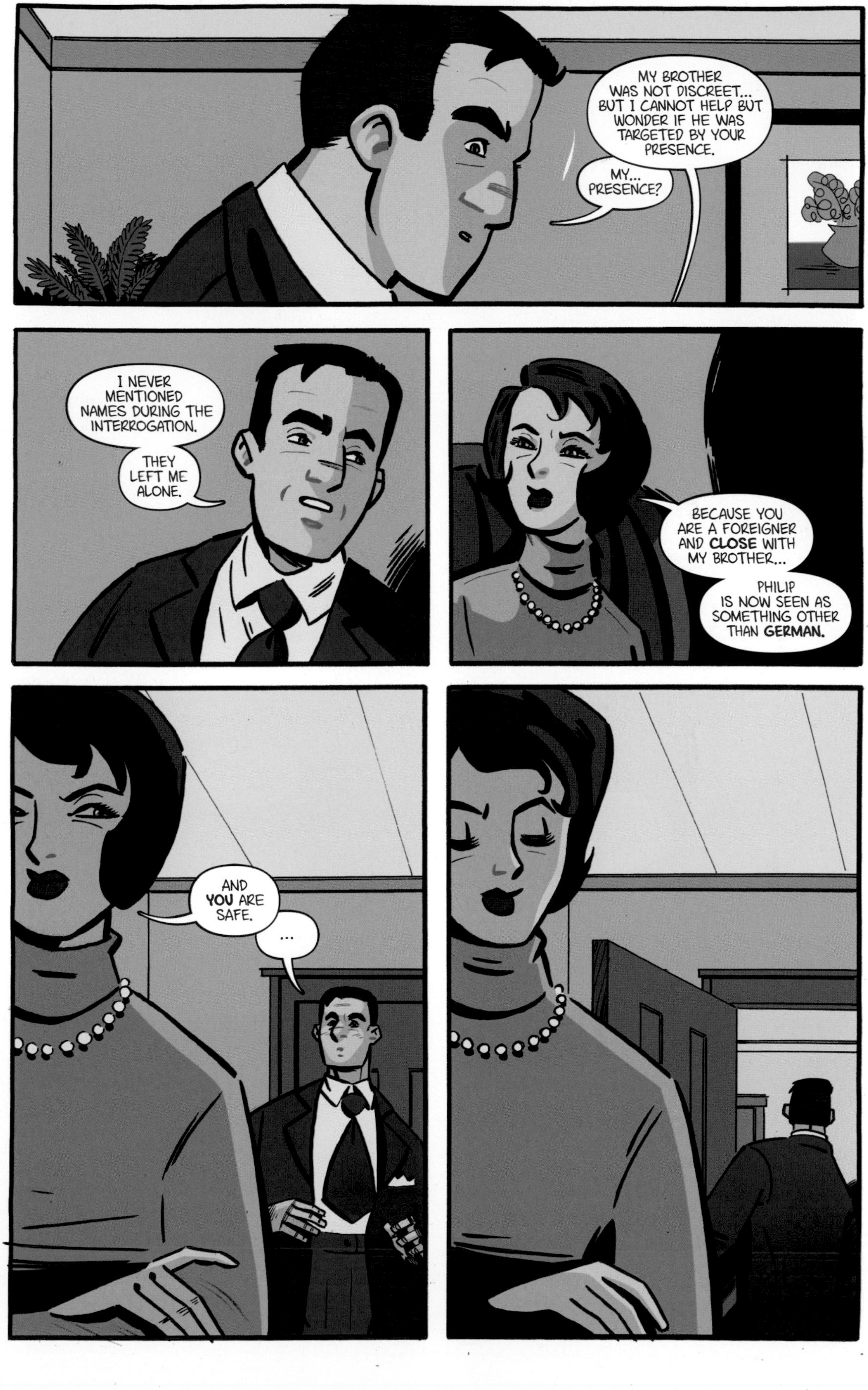
MY BROTHER WAS NOT DISCREET... BUT I CANNOT HELP BUT WONDER IF HE WAS TARGETED BY YOUR PRESENCE.
MY... PRESENCE?
I NEVER MENTIONED NAMES DURING THE INTERROGATION.
THEY LEFT ME ALONE.
BECAUSE YOU ARE A FOREIGNER AND CLOSE WITH MY BROTHER...
PHILIP IS NOW SEEN AS SOMETHING OTHER THAN GERMAN.
AND YOU ARE SAFE.
...

I FELT GUILTY LEAVING THE HOUSE...

...BUT SITTING STILL FELT USELESS ALSO.

HE WILL TURN UP SOON.

THIS IS BAD.

I CAN FEEL IT.

THEY ARE JUST TRYING TO GET NAMES OUT OF HIM...

TOO MANY OF THESE OLD SOLDIERS KNOW HIS FATHER...

...BACK TO YOU IN NO TIME.

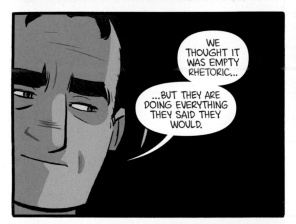

WE THOUGHT IT WAS EMPTY RHETORIC...

...BUT THEY ARE DOING EVERYTHING THEY SAID THEY WOULD.

YOU SHOULD NOT PANIC.

I AM SORRY.

ALL I CAN THINK ABOUT IS MY PANIC.

WE SHOULD LEAVE... IN CASE THERE IS NEWS.

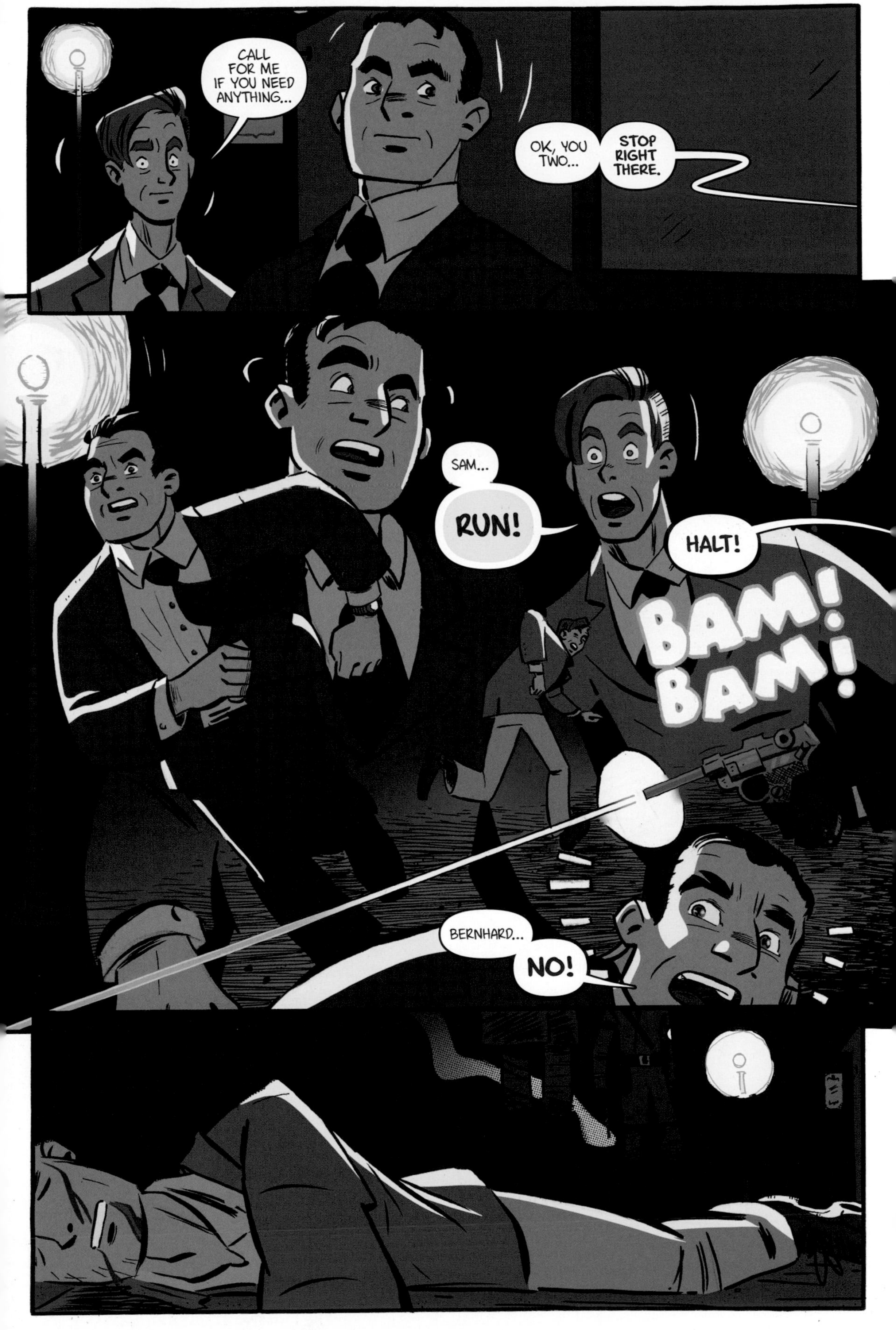
CALL FOR ME IF YOU NEED ANYTHING...
OK, YOU TWO...
STOP RIGHT THERE.
SAM...
RUN!
HALT!
BAM! BAM!
BERNHARD...
NO!

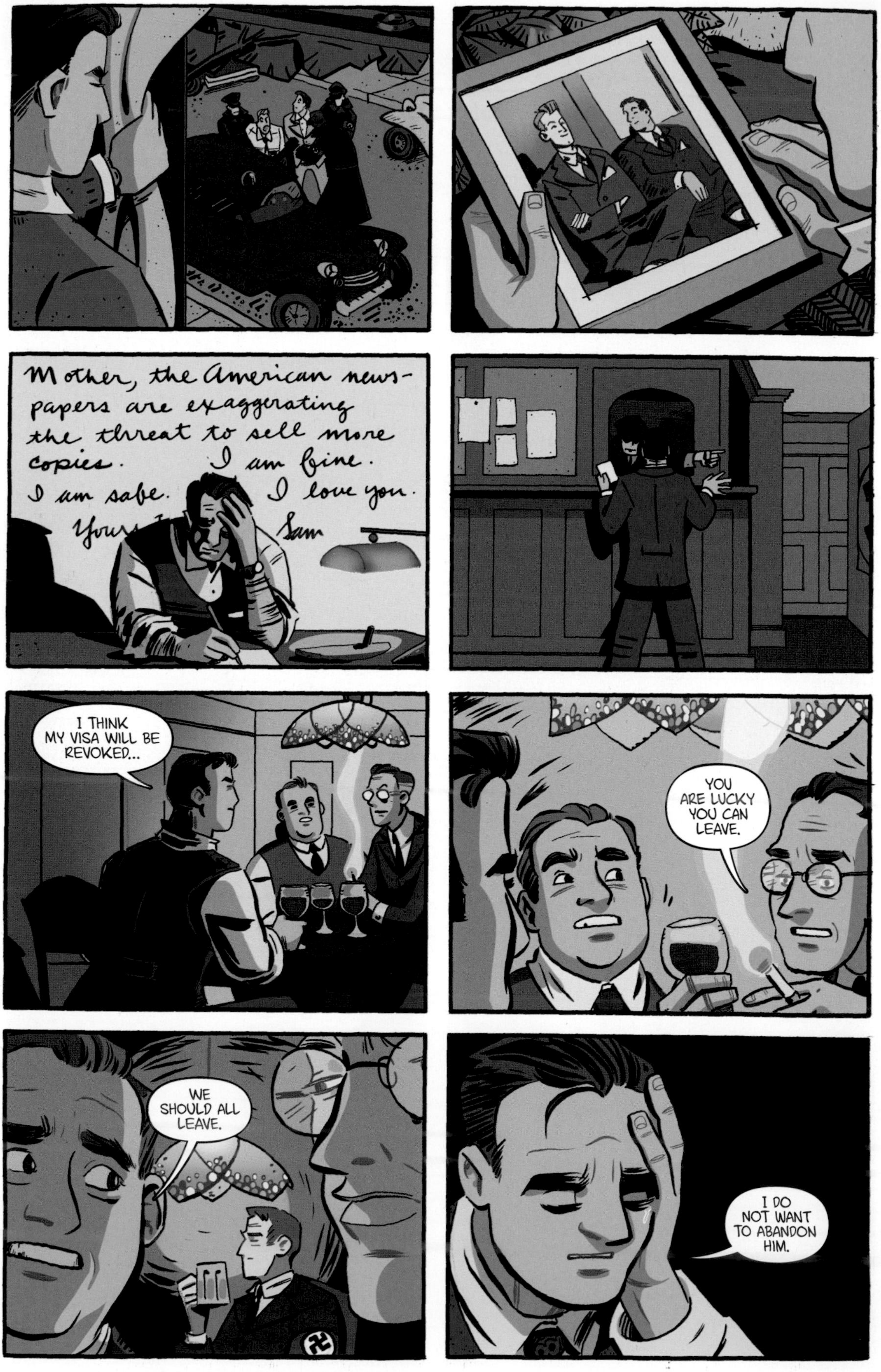
Mother, the American news-papers are exaggerating the threat to sell more copies. I am fine. I am safe. I love you.
Yours
Sam
I THINK MY VISA WILL BE REVOKED...
YOU ARE LUCKY YOU CAN LEAVE.
WE SHOULD ALL LEAVE.
I DO NOT WANT TO ABANDON HIM.

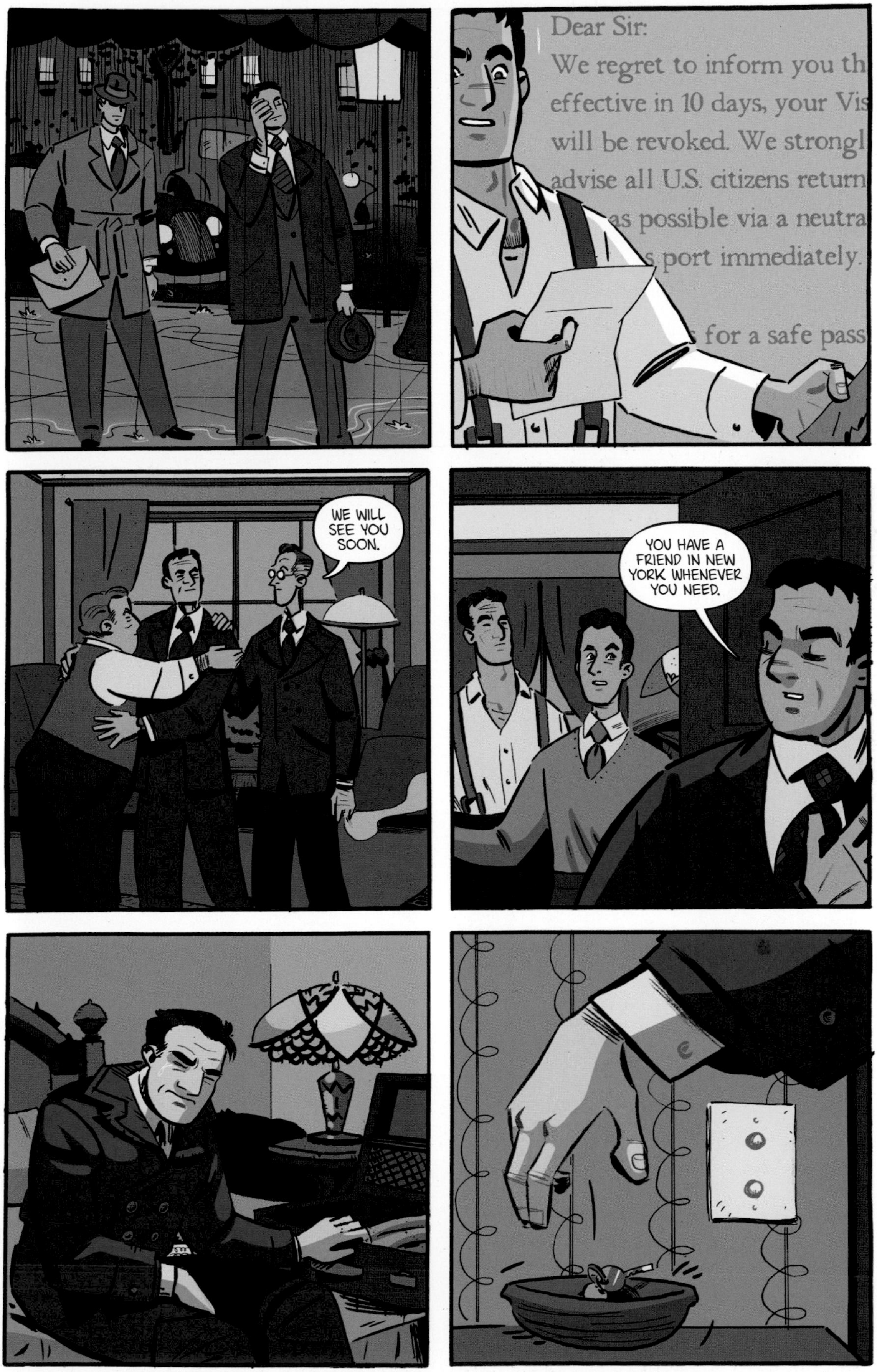
Dear Sir:
We regret to inform you th
effective in 10 days, your Vis
will be revoked. We strongl
advise all U.S. citizens return
as possible via a neutra
s port immediately.
for a safe pass
WE WILL SEE YOU SOON.
YOU HAVE A FRIEND IN NEW YORK WHENEVER YOU NEED.

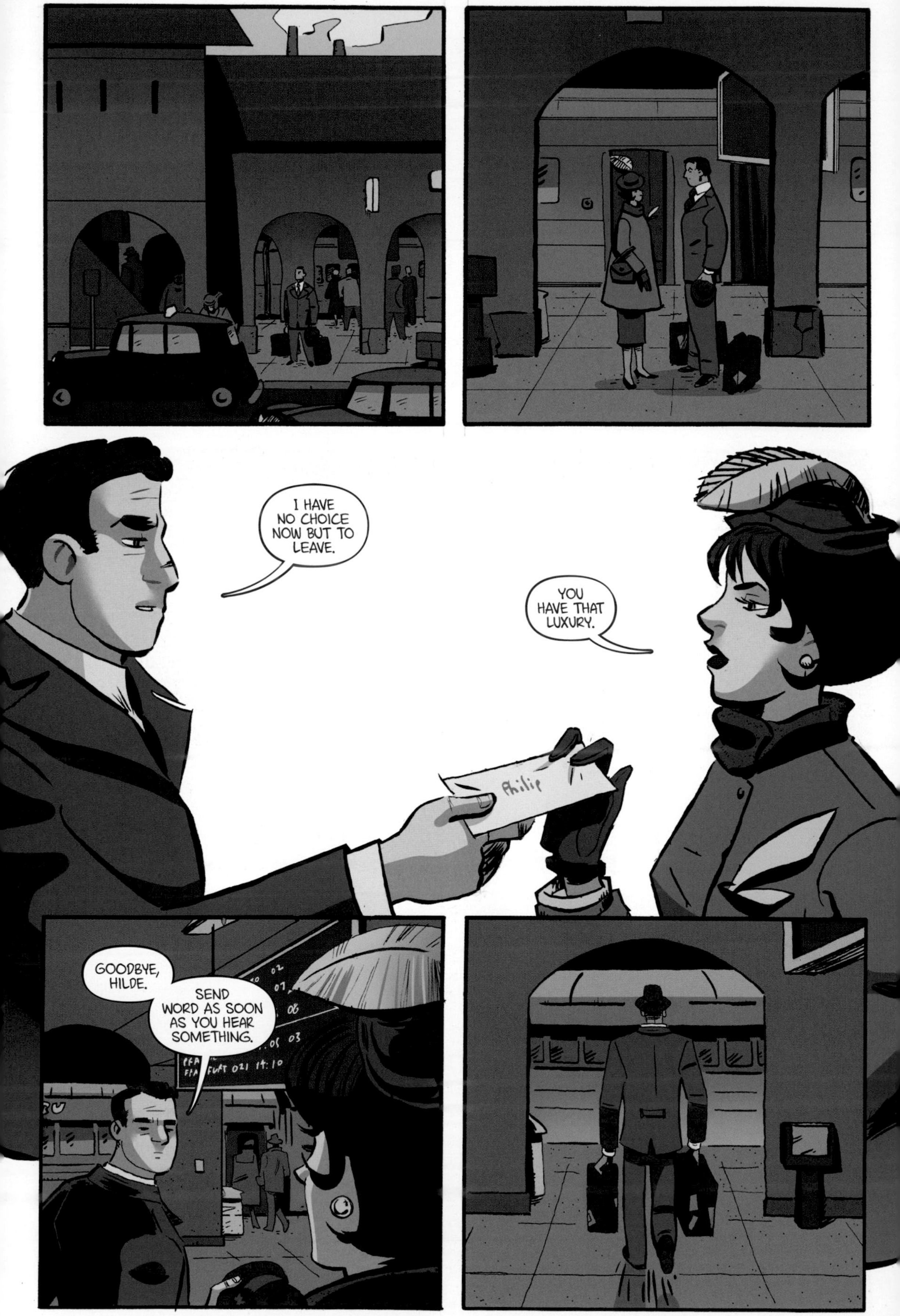
I HAVE NO CHOICE NOW BUT TO LEAVE.
YOU HAVE THAT LUXURY.
Philip
GOODBYE, HILDE.
SEND WORD AS SOON AS YOU HEAR SOMETHING.

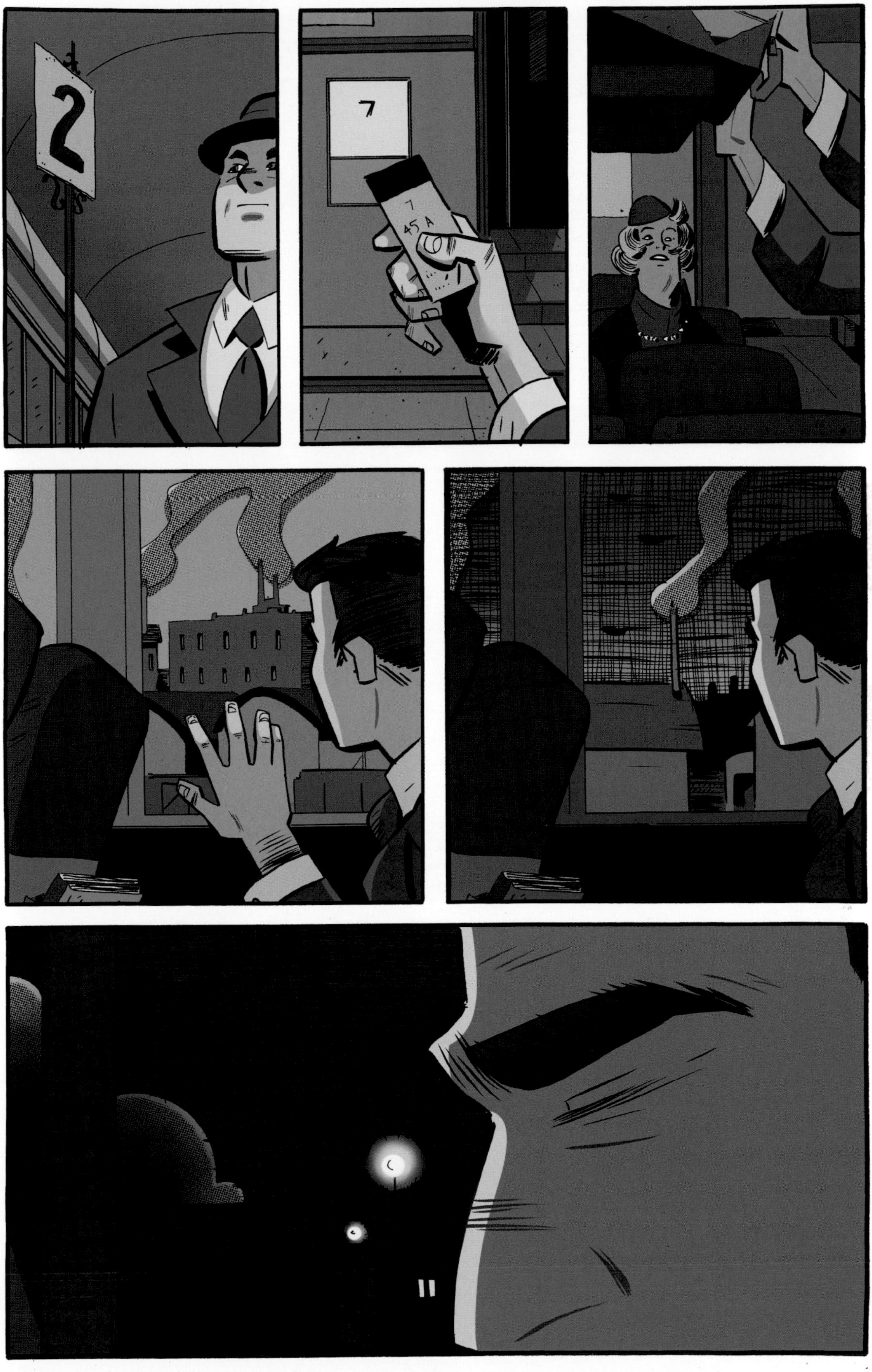
2
7
7
45 A

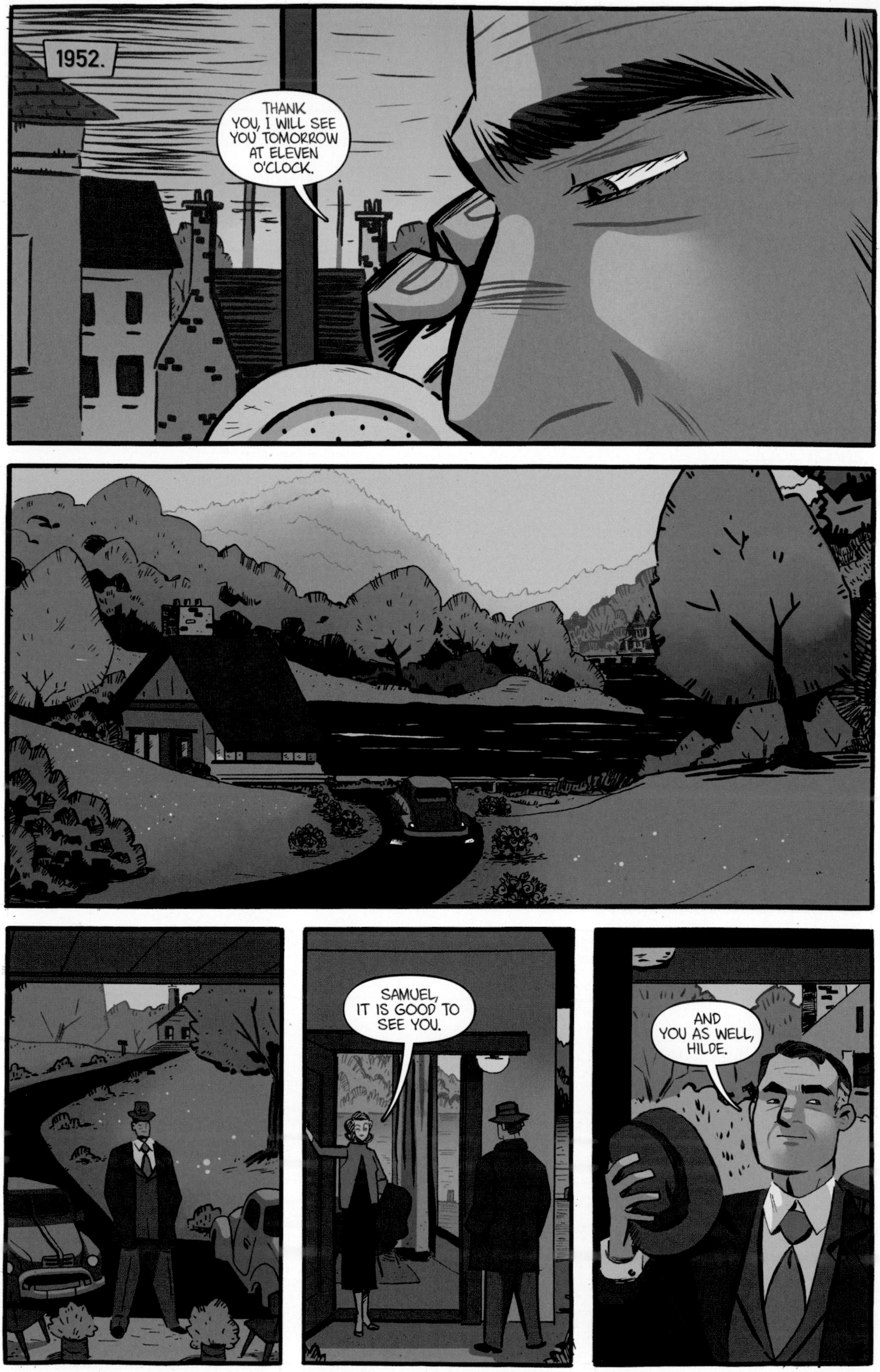
1952.
THANK YOU, I WILL SEE YOU TOMORROW AT ELEVEN O'CLOCK.
SAMUEL, IT IS GOOD TO SEE YOU.
AND YOU AS WELL, HILDE.

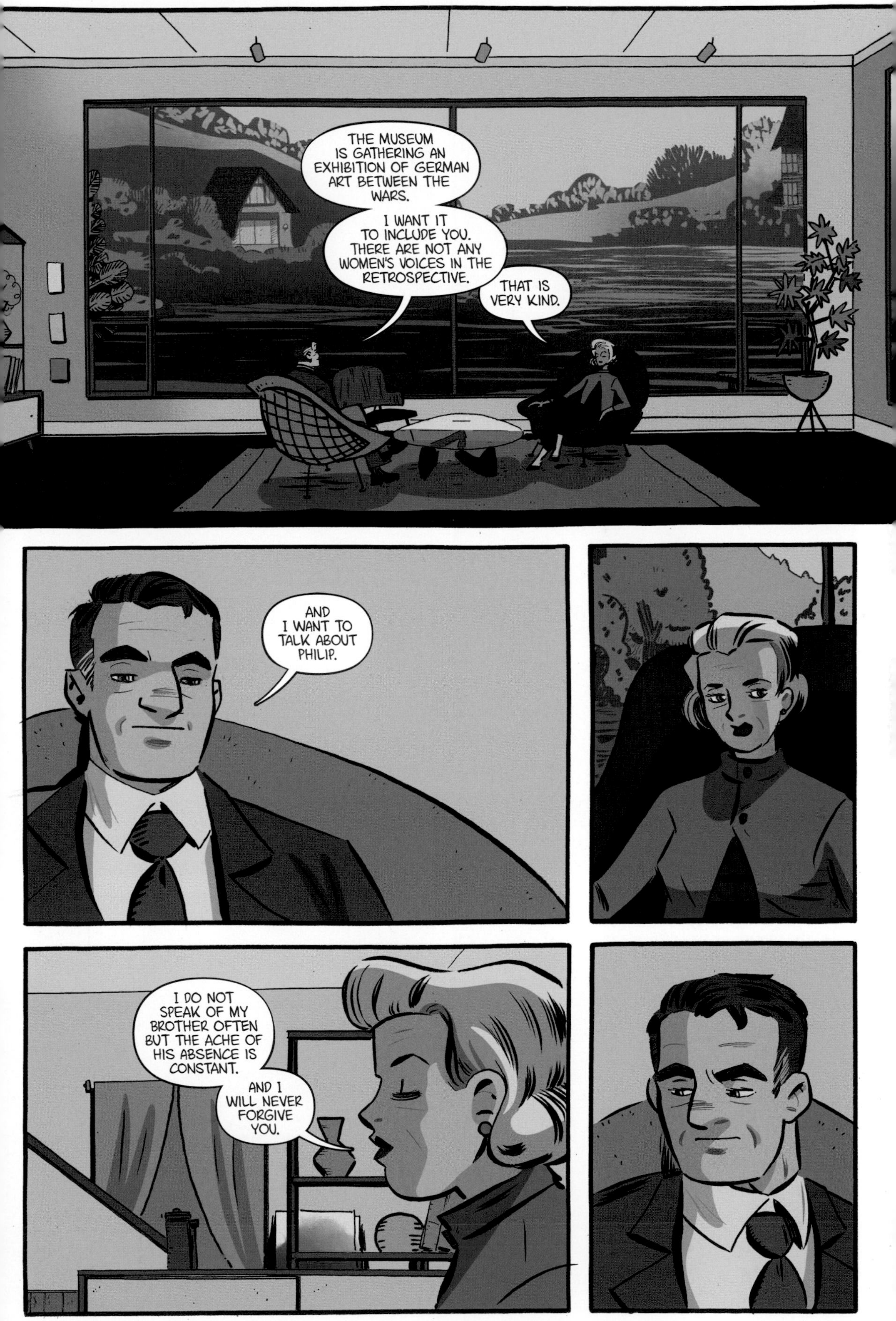
THE MUSEUM IS GATHERING AN EXHIBITION OF GERMAN ART BETWEEN THE WARS.
I WANT IT TO INCLUDE YOU. THERE ARE NOT ANY WOMEN'S VOICES IN THE RETROSPECTIVE.
THAT IS VERY KIND.
AND I WANT TO TALK ABOUT PHILIP.
I DO NOT SPEAK OF MY BROTHER OFTEN BUT THE ACHE OF HIS ABSENCE IS CONSTANT.
AND I WILL NEVER FORGIVE YOU.

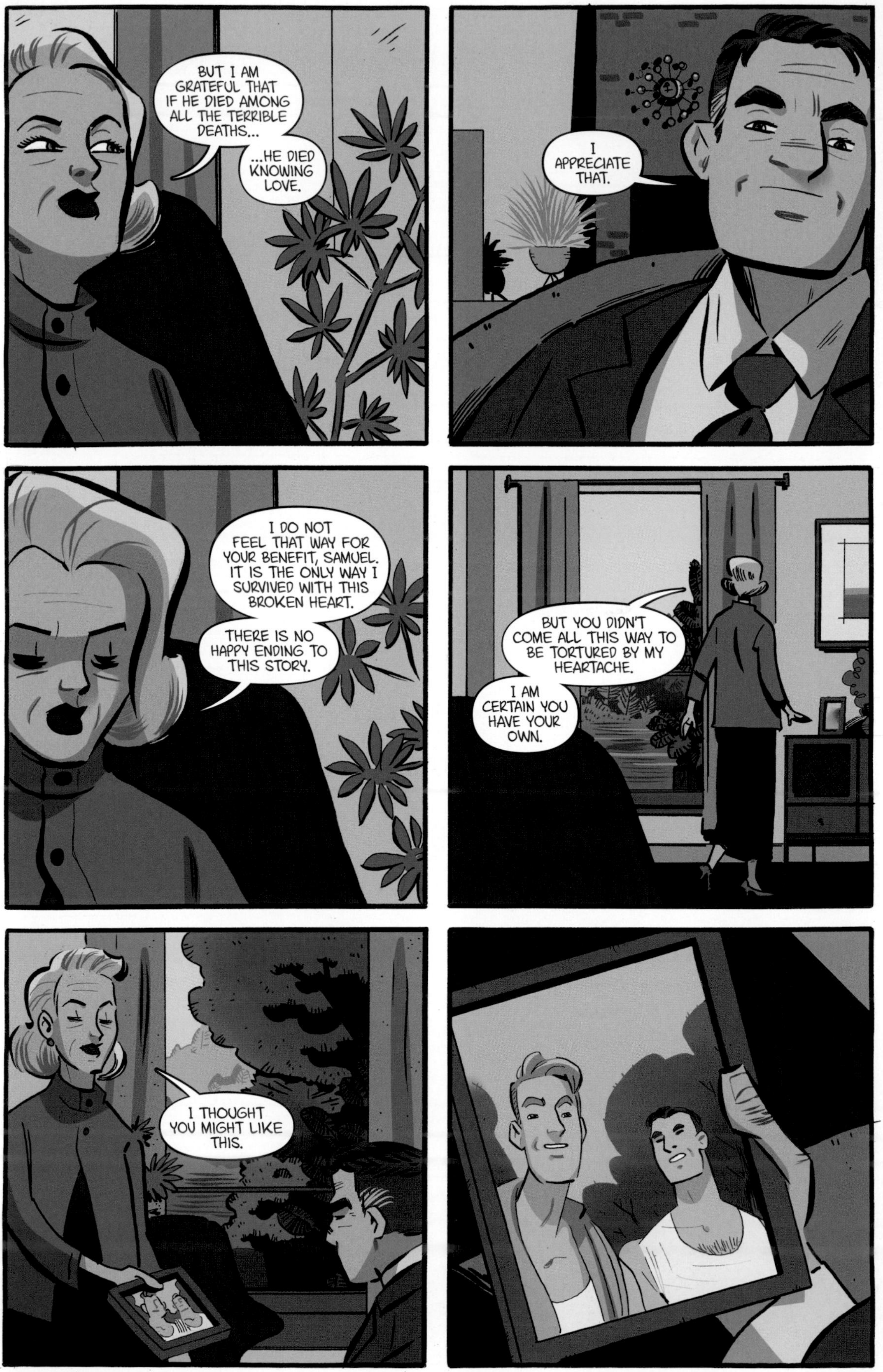

BUT I AM GRATEFUL THAT IF HE DIED AMONG ALL THE TERRIBLE DEATHS...
...HE DIED KNOWING LOVE.
I APPRECIATE THAT.
I DO NOT FEEL THAT WAY FOR YOUR BENEFIT, SAMUEL. IT IS THE ONLY WAY I SURVIVED WITH THIS BROKEN HEART.
THERE IS NO HAPPY ENDING TO THIS STORY.
BUT YOU DIDN'T COME ALL THIS WAY TO BE TORTURED BY MY HEARTACHE.
I AM CERTAIN YOU HAVE YOUR OWN.
I THOUGHT YOU MIGHT LIKE THIS.

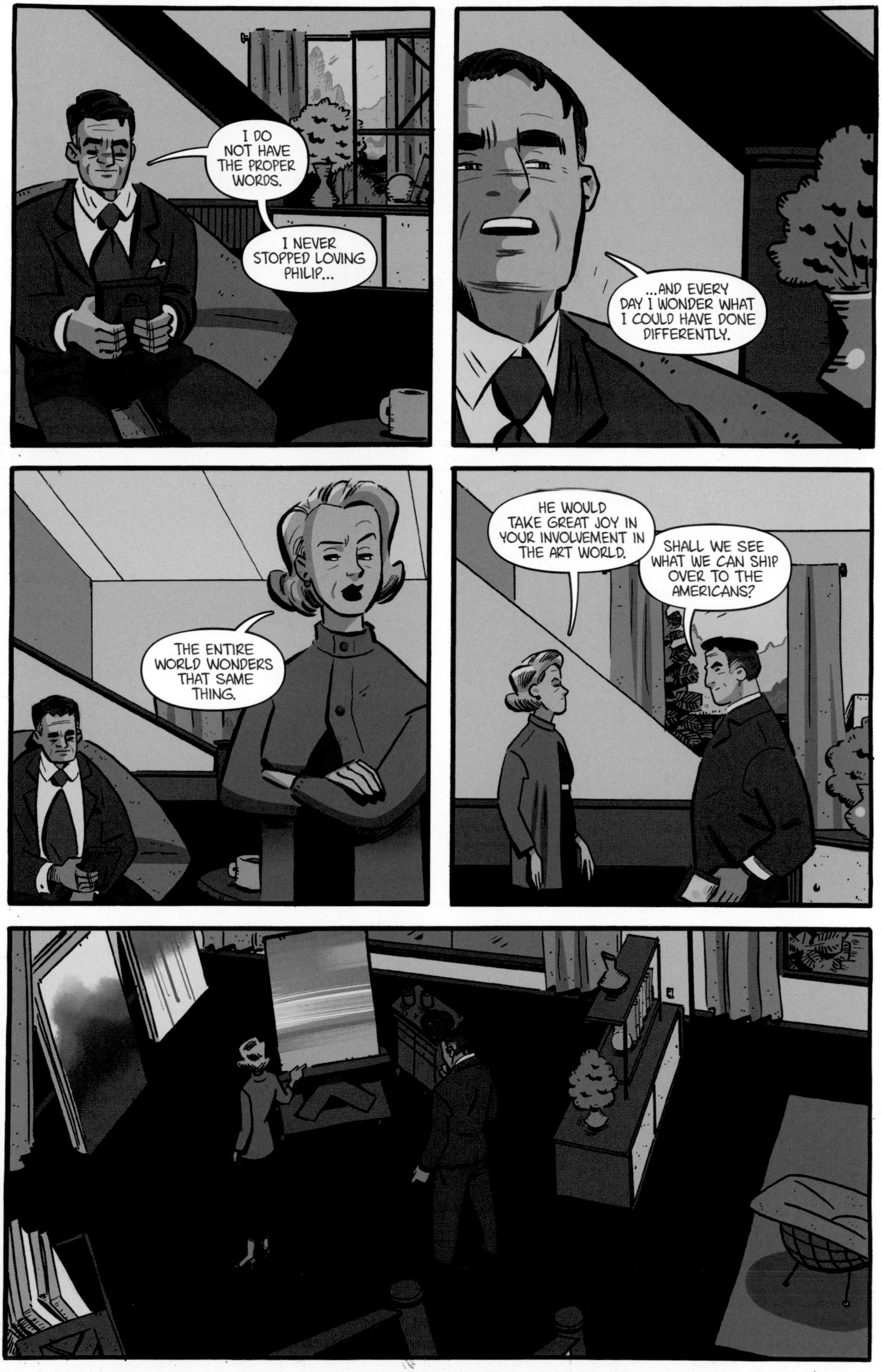
I DO NOT HAVE THE PROPER WORDS.
I NEVER STOPPED LOVING PHILIP...
...AND EVERY DAY I WONDER WHAT I COULD HAVE DONE DIFFERENTLY.
THE ENTIRE WORLD WONDERS THAT SAME THING.
HE WOULD TAKE GREAT JOY IN YOUR INVOLVEMENT IN THE ART WORLD.
SHALL WE SEE WHAT WE CAN SHIP OVER TO THE AMERICANS?

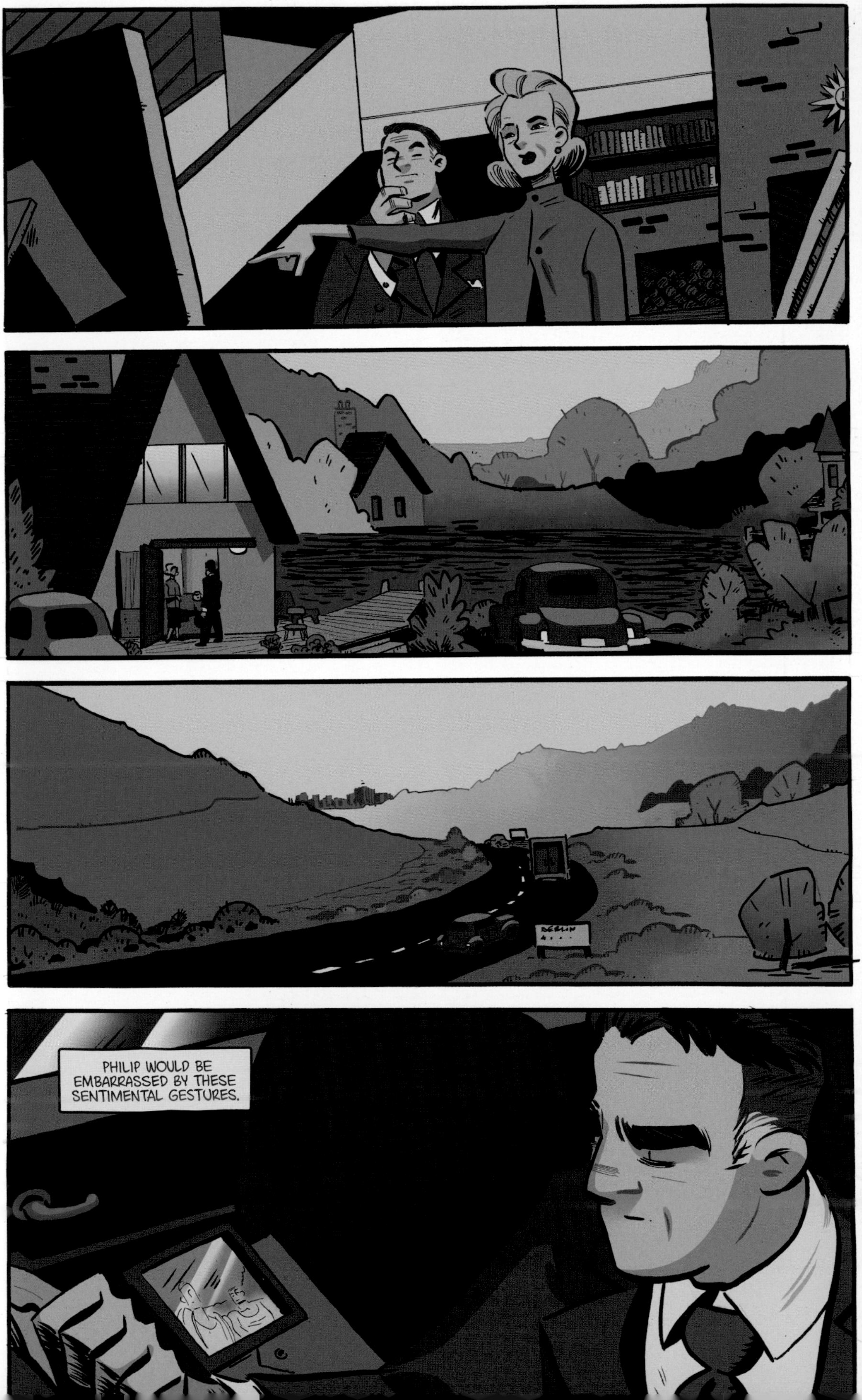
BERLIN
PHILIP WOULD BE EMBARRASSED BY THESE SENTIMENTAL GESTURES.

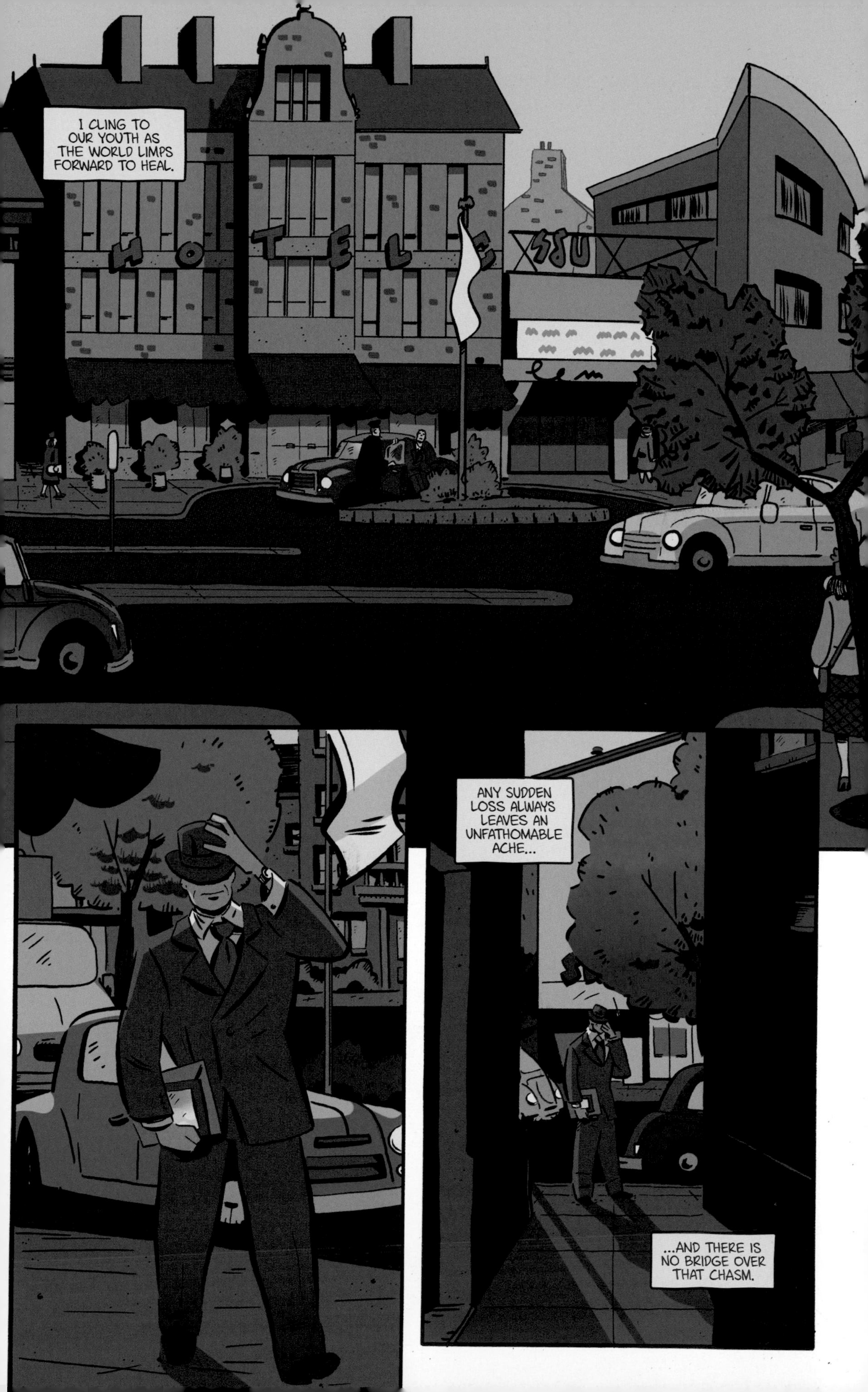

I CLING TO OUR YOUTH AS THE WORLD LIMPS FORWARD TO HEAL.
HOTEL
ANY SUDDEN LOSS ALWAYS LEAVES AN UNFATHOMABLE ACHE...
...AND THERE IS NO BRIDGE OVER THAT CHASM.

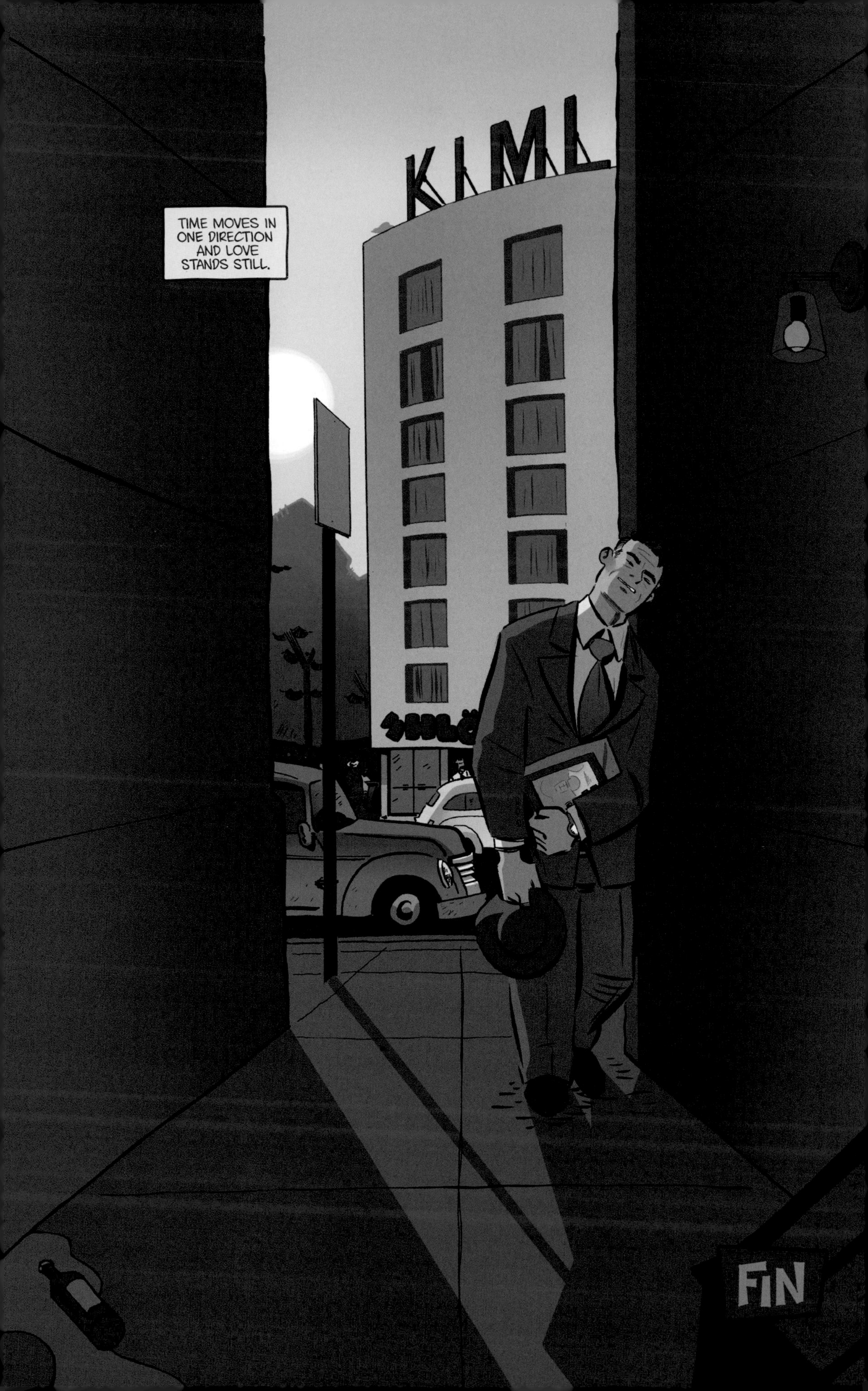

KIML
TIME MOVES IN ONE DIRECTION AND LOVE STANDS STILL.
FIN

Creating Liebestrasse

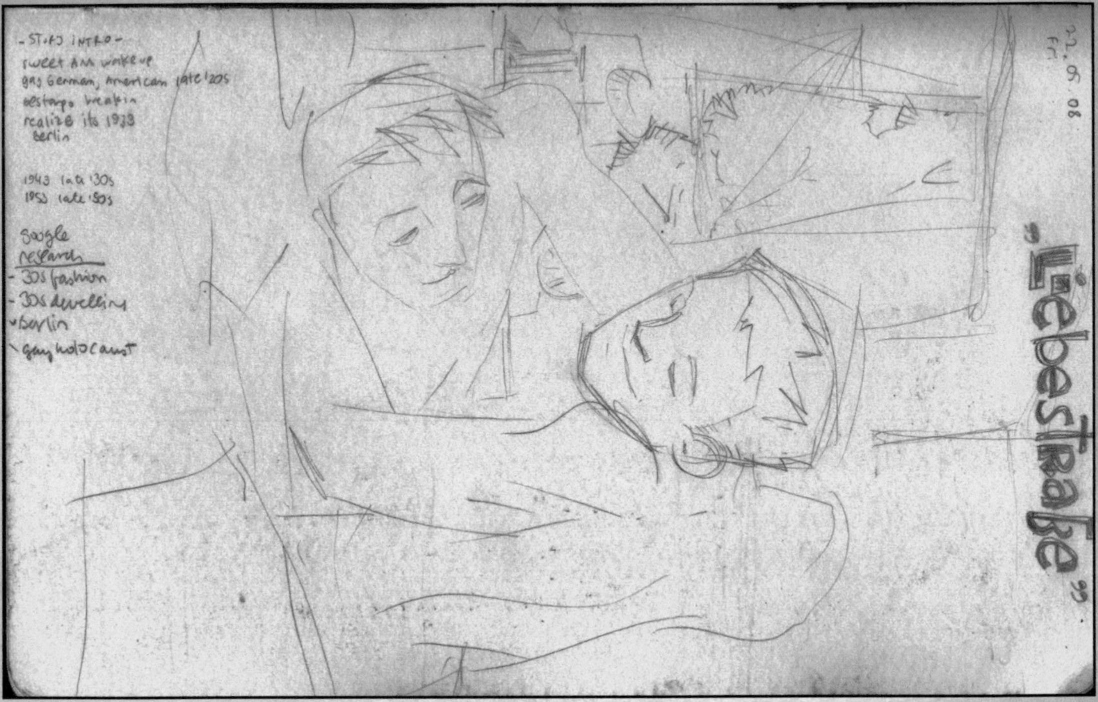
"Liebestraße"
Google research
- 30s fashion
- 30s dwelling
Berlin
gay holocaust

Liebestrasse had a very long development from an image by Tim Fish to the complete graphic novel. The following pages represent the process that brought ***Liebestrasse*** together with commentary from the creative team.

Tim Fish:

The image that inspired the entire story came to me during a month-long trip that started in Berlin and snaked its way to Poland in 2008. It's difficult to put into words the feeling I had, sitting in the park that rings the medieval walls of Kraków. The anonymous horror of Auschwitz juxtaposed with the extensive personal stories recorded at Theresienstadt. I couldn't help but think of what it would have been like to be experiencing a morning like any other, then suddenly your house is stormed. Specifically, I thought of a couple, and drew them in my sketchbook with the caption "Liebestraße." The idea sat there for years, until I challenged Greg to write a short story for me to draw—with only that premise and one scene in mind. That, and a request that Greg incorporate a car scene . . . I love drawing old cars.

Greg Lockard:

Tim mentioned the image of the couple falling into bed and it was just too wonderfully romantic to deny. We began in 2016 after we tabled at Thought Bubble and were brainstorming ideas for another short story collaboration. Tim gave me the three-panel opening page and we went back and forth until the characters cemented enough in my head for the story to start taking shape.

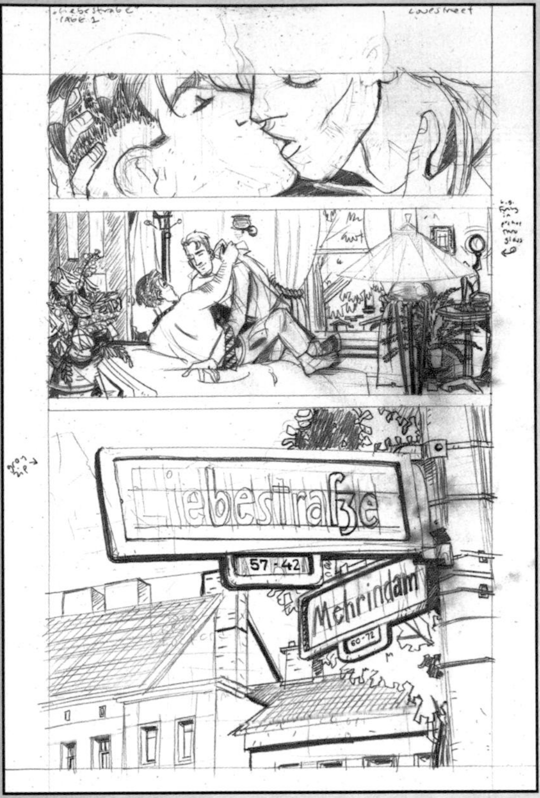
Liebestraße
57-42
Mehrindam
60-72

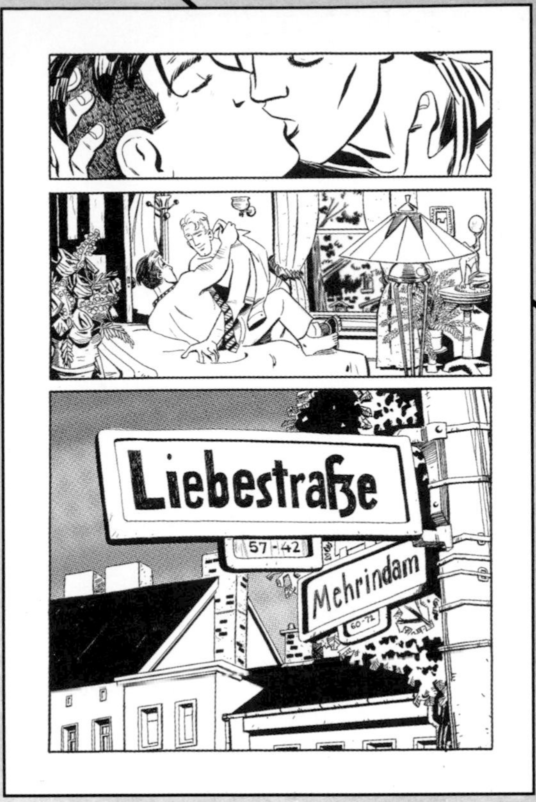
Liebestraße
57-42
Mehrindam
60-72

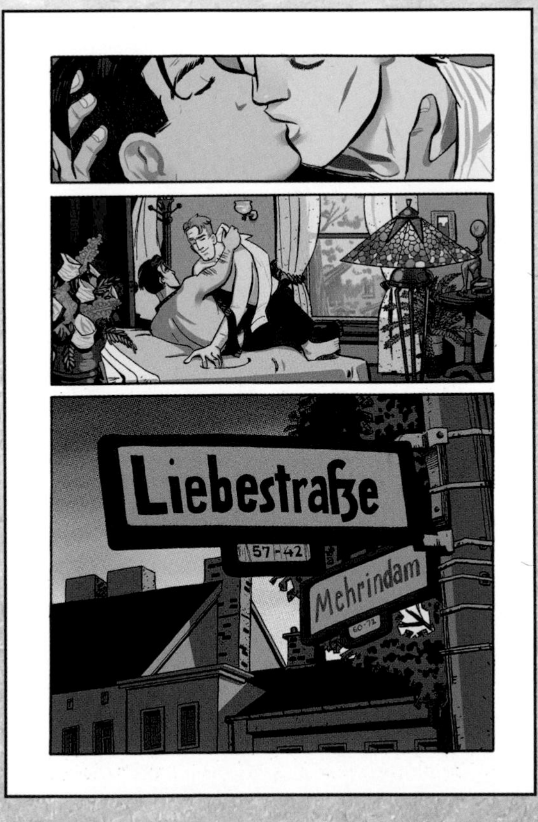
Liebestraße
57-42
Mehrindam
60-72

After we finalized a script and Tim started drawing, I asked him if I could print the short story as a zine to bring with us to Thought Bubble. Not only was it a story I was very proud of but it would give me an excuse to table at the show alongside him and Monica Gallagher. That's when we asked Héctor Barros to color Tim's line art.

After a few years of development, we finished creating a zine of the short story to bring to Thought Bubble in 2018. We showed the short story to Will Dennis, my friend and former colleague, for an opinion on whether the story merited an expanded version. Luckily, Will thought the story was great and we had enough material to expand on it.

At Thought Bubble, Will sent Chip Mosher, comiXology publisher, to my table to check out our zine and we had a chat about the possibility of publishing an expanded version with comiXology Originals. Shortly after the convention, we pitched the project with an expanded outline and were given a green light to develop a graphic novel.

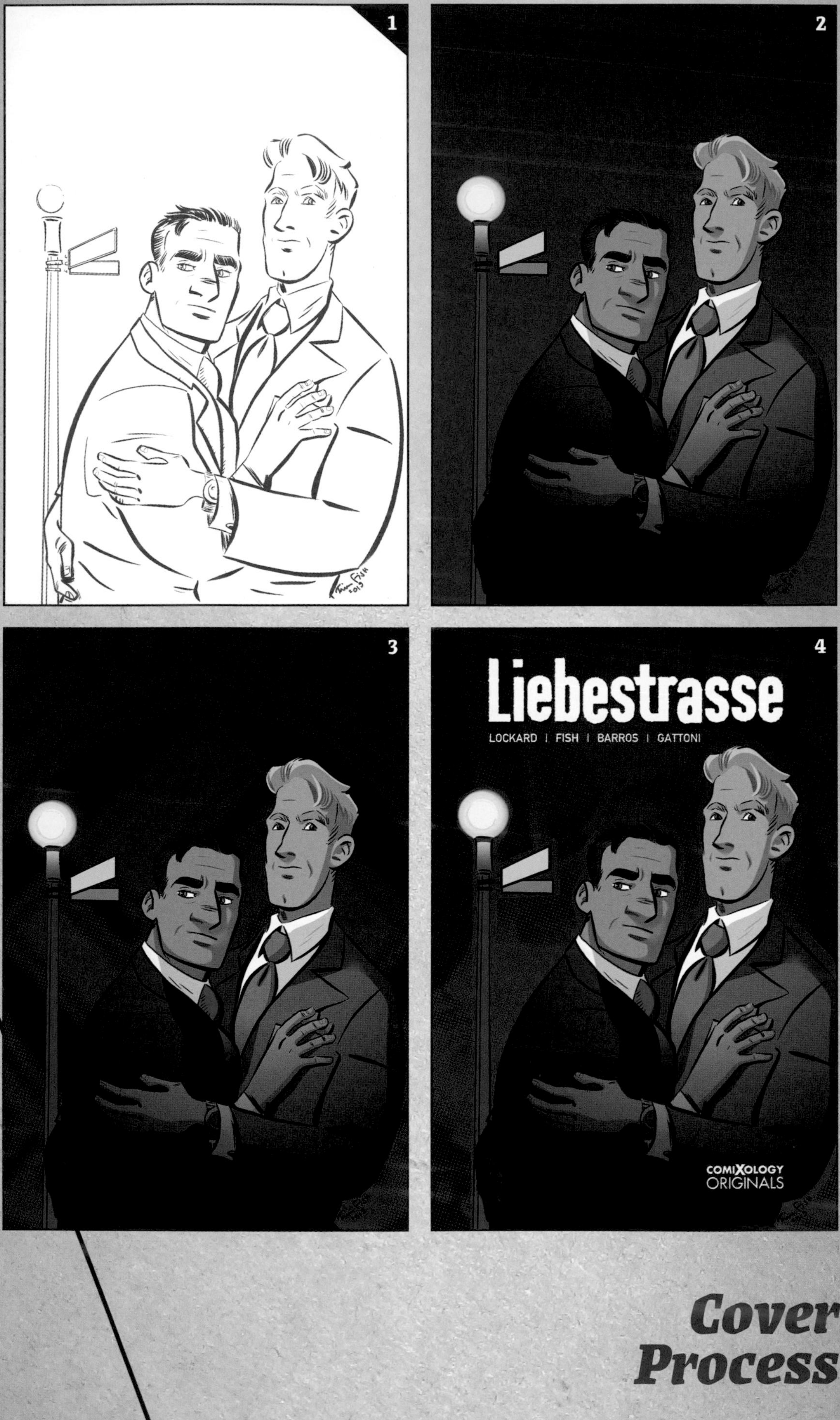
1
2
3
4
Liebestrasse
LOCKARD | FISH | BARROS | GATTONI
comiXology
ORIGINALS

Cover Process

Tim:

As the zine was produced, we had the opportunity to run the short story version (translated by Xavier Lancel) in the beautiful French magazine *La Revue* LGBT BD No. 8.

La Revue is an anthology series featuring work by queer artists telling queer stories. It was a real treat to see this in the large A4 format.

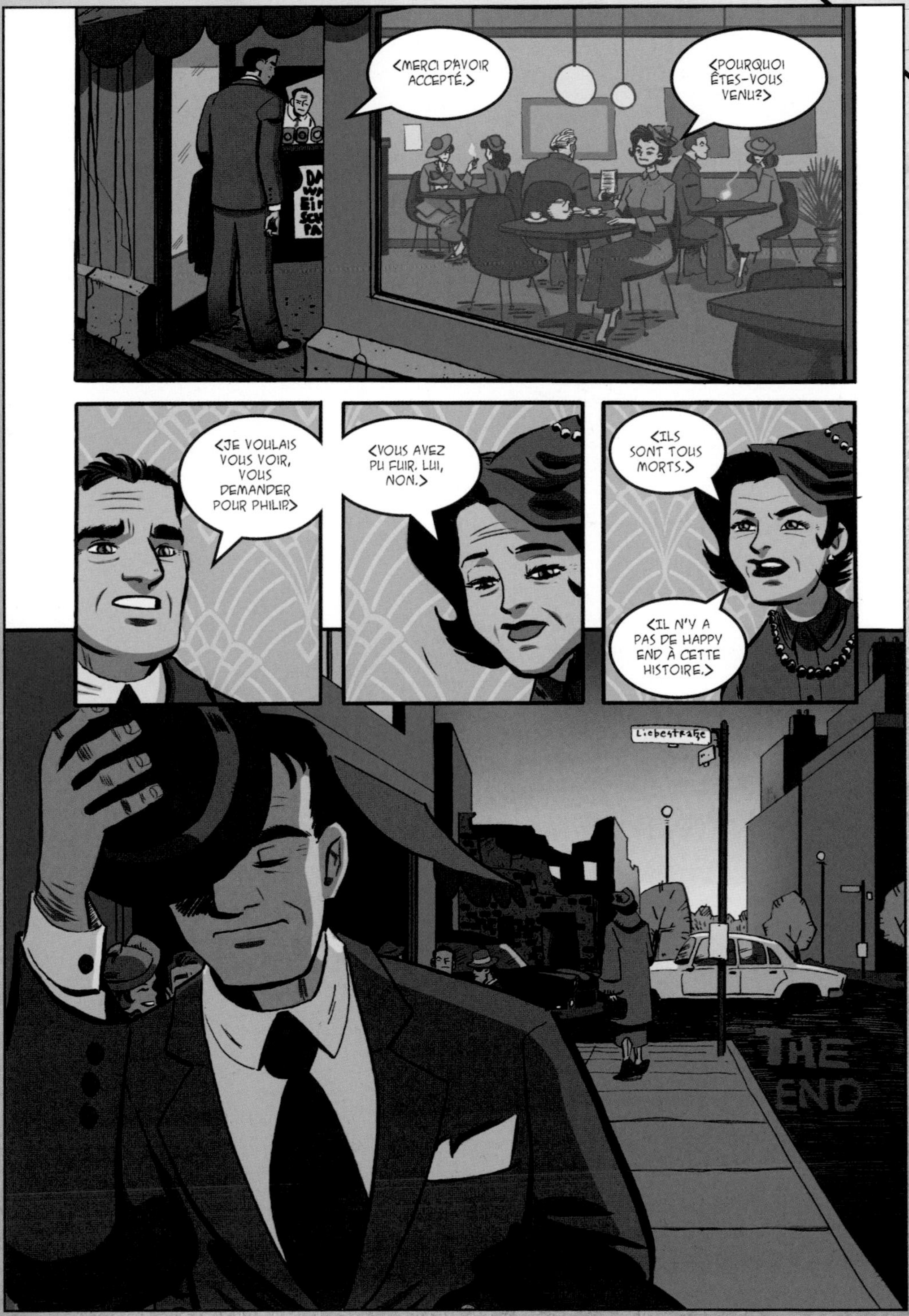
<MERCI D'AVOIR ACCEPTÉ.>
<POURQUOI ÊTES-VOUS VENU?>
<JE VOULAIS VOUS VOIR, VOUS DEMANDER POUR PHILIP.>
<VOUS AVEZ PU FUIR. LUI, NON.>
<ILS SONT TOUS MORTS.>
<IL N'Y A PAS DE HAPPY END À CETTE HISTOIRE.>
Liebestraße
THE END

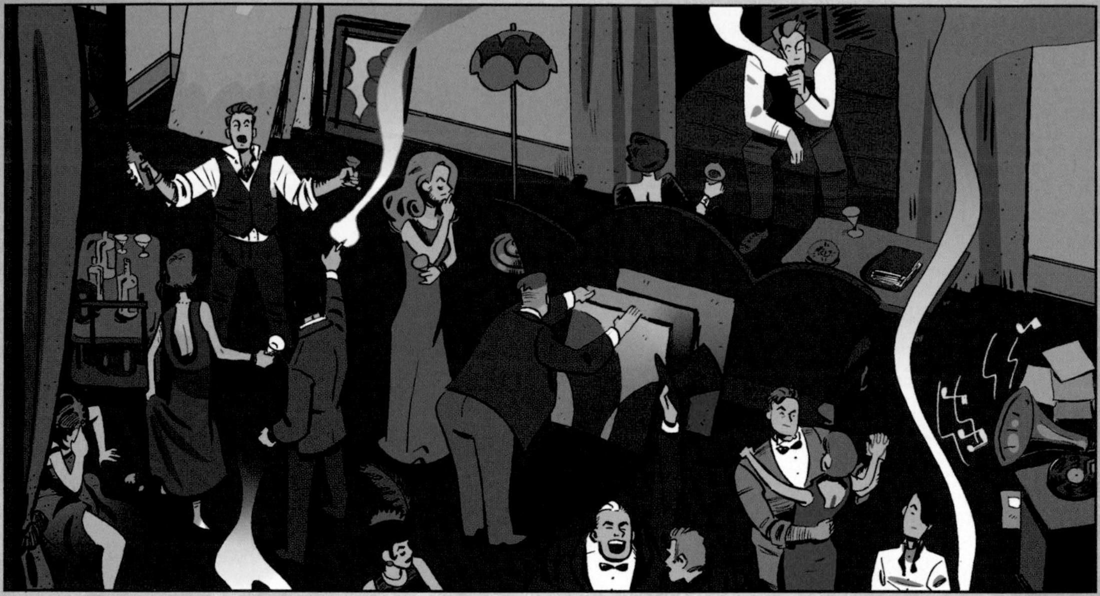

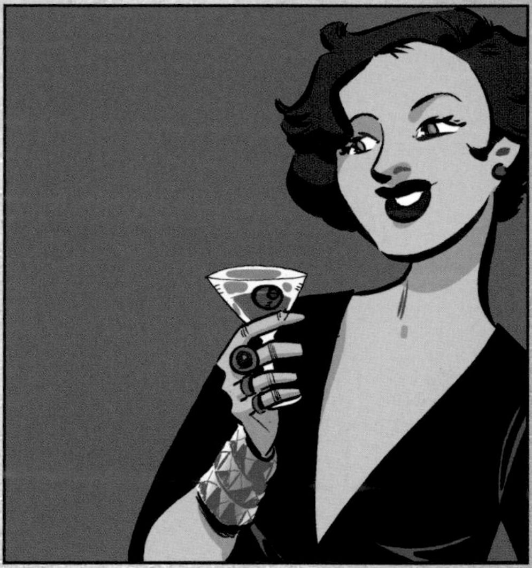

Greg:

The setting of Berlin in the 1930s came before the characters. We knew we wanted to tell a love story set in that unimaginably horrible time of Hitler's rise to power. Previous representations of gay/queer life in Berlin have been somewhat chaste in their presentations—we wanted a love story that showed two men truly in love.

Tim:

As a history student, the interwar period has always fascinated me. It was full of joy and hardship, progressive thinking and the conservative backlash. It was normal and then it was insane. I knew a lot about the Nazi rise to power and persecution, but walking through the Holocaust memorial in Boston was the first time I was aware that gays, too, were persecuted. It's a story that's not as often told.

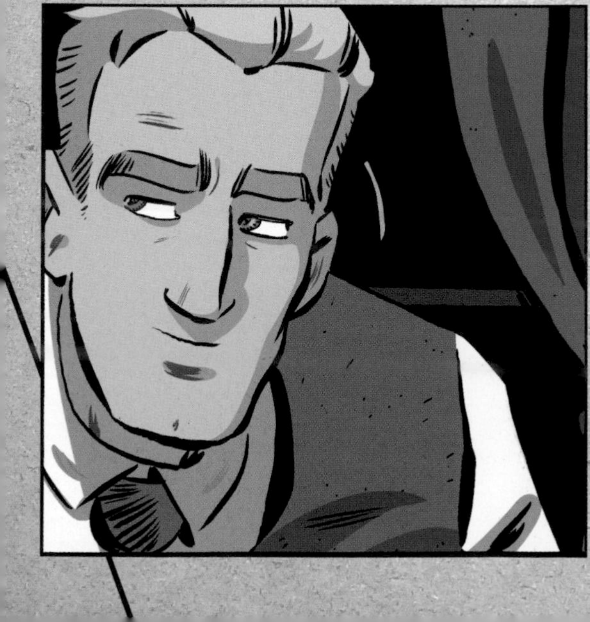

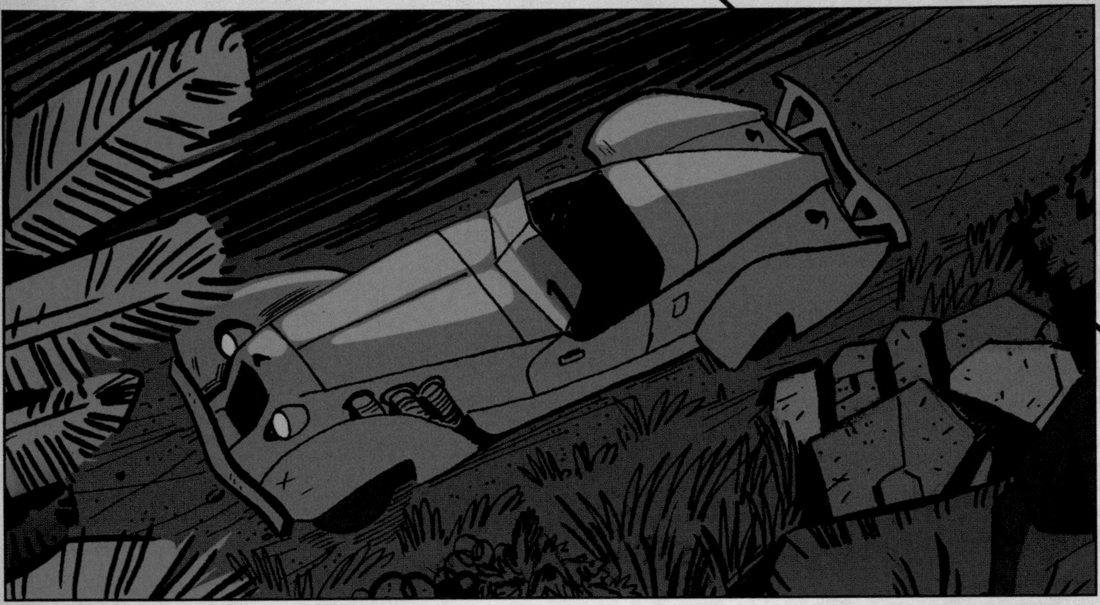

Tim:

When we first discussed the project, I offered Greg a few restrictions, but did request the opportunity to draw a few old cars I love. In drawing cars, I never use photographs unless necessary. Instead, I turn to my collection of model and Matchbox cars. How else would I justify the collection? But I get to position the cars any way I need to for the panel!

> Here, my penchant for the English-made Jaguar SS 100 and the American-made Auburn 831 Speedster consumes historical accuracy.

Given the quantities manufactured, plus the German motorcars of the era, it's highly unlikely that these two models would have made it to Berlin.

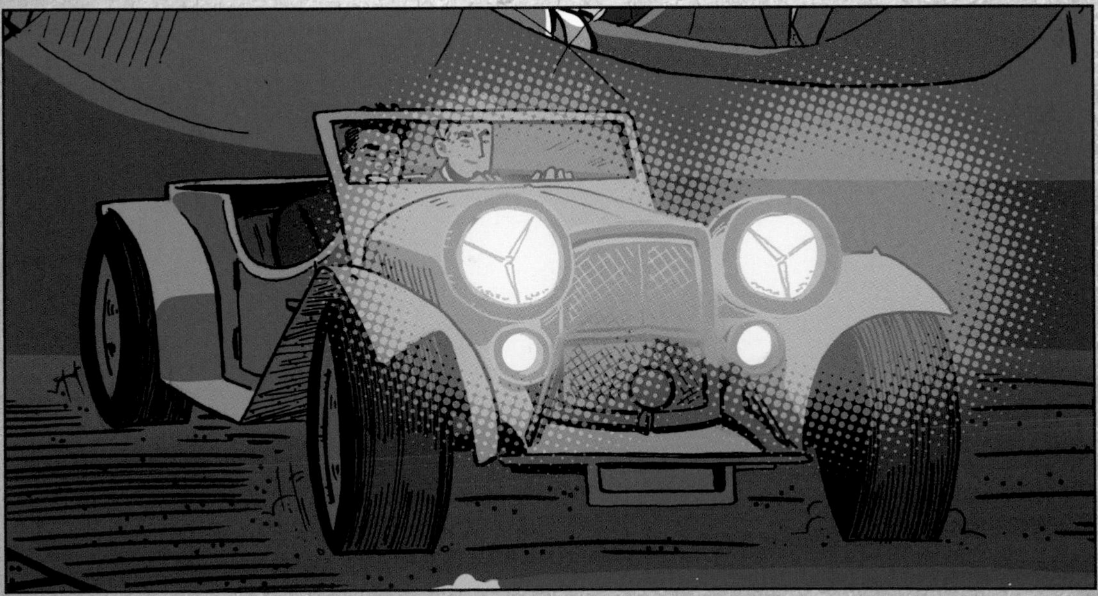

Ultimately, since we wanted to focus less on Nazis themselves than we did the other aspects, I made the uniforms more generic than accurate.

Tim:

For a past project, I'd researched Nazi uniforms enough to know I'd never get them 100 percent correct. The uniform system was highly complex, based on division, function, time, and region. So it would have been extraordinarily difficult to pinpoint the uniforms worn scene by scene.

We set out to draw the parallels between the 1930s and the political climate of 2016—today. It was a difficult balance to ground the story in actual events while avoiding deep discussions of Hitler and pervasive displays of Nazi imagery. But it was important for us to keep those elements minimized to help the reader stay connected to present-day events as well.

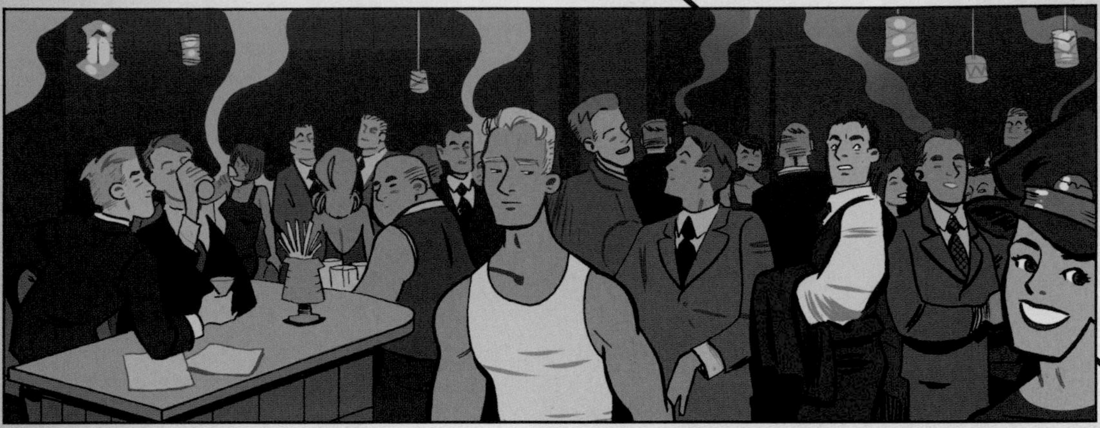

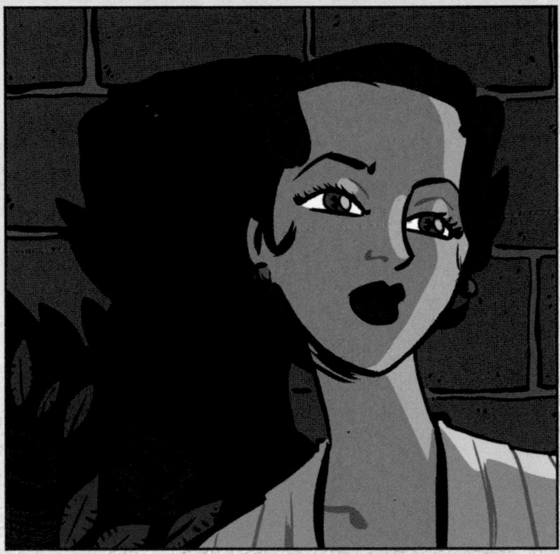

Tim:

I am terrible at drawing real people, which might be for the best . . . no mistaking my drawing for reality! My inspiration for Philip's sister, Hilde, was Myrna Loy. *The Thin Man* for early days and *The Bachelor and the Bobby-Soxer* for her later years. For Hilde's clothes, I opted for pattern books and magazine ads from the 1930s.

The patrons at the bar came directly from a vintage photo Greg shared. I understand why there was little photographic evidence from gay establishments of the era, but I love seeing the old photographs.

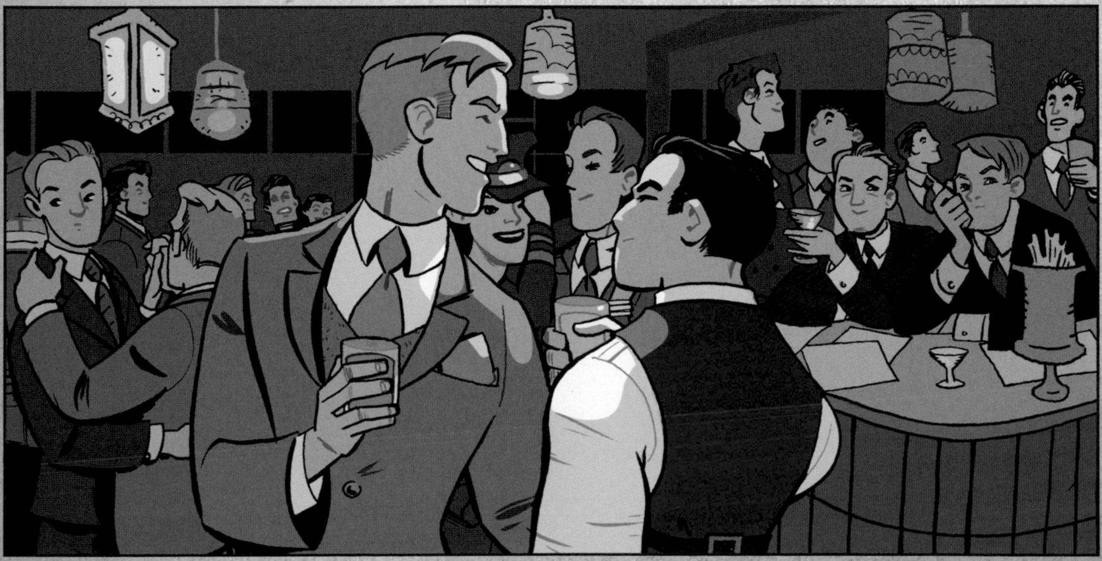

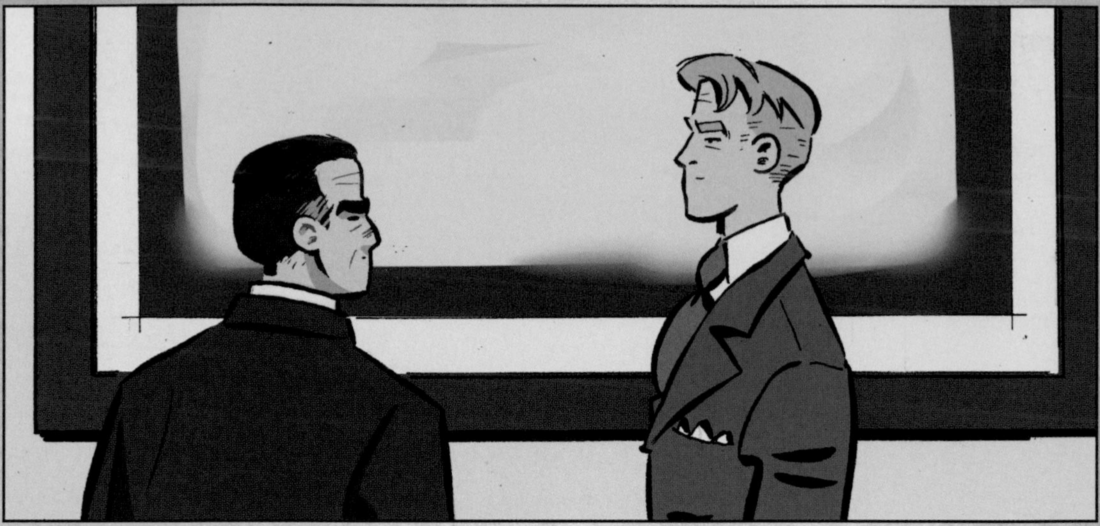

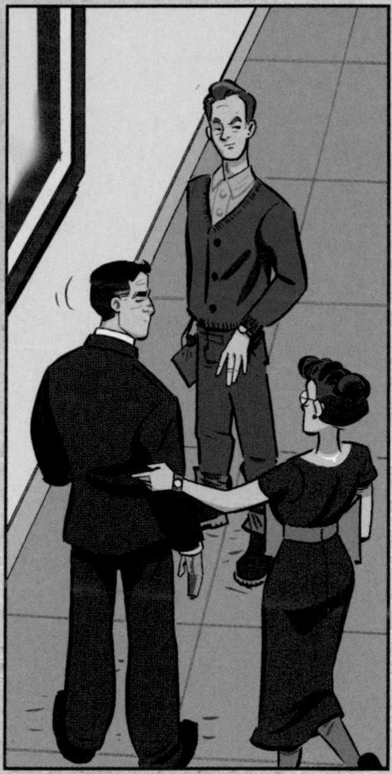

Greg:

After the war, Sam's involvement in the art world through a museum's board of trustees provides an excuse to get Sam back to Germany.

Not only was this a device to justify Sam having the right visas and clearances to return in 1955, but it also allowed us to show aspects of the prewar Berlin art scene that haunted Sam long after Philip's death.

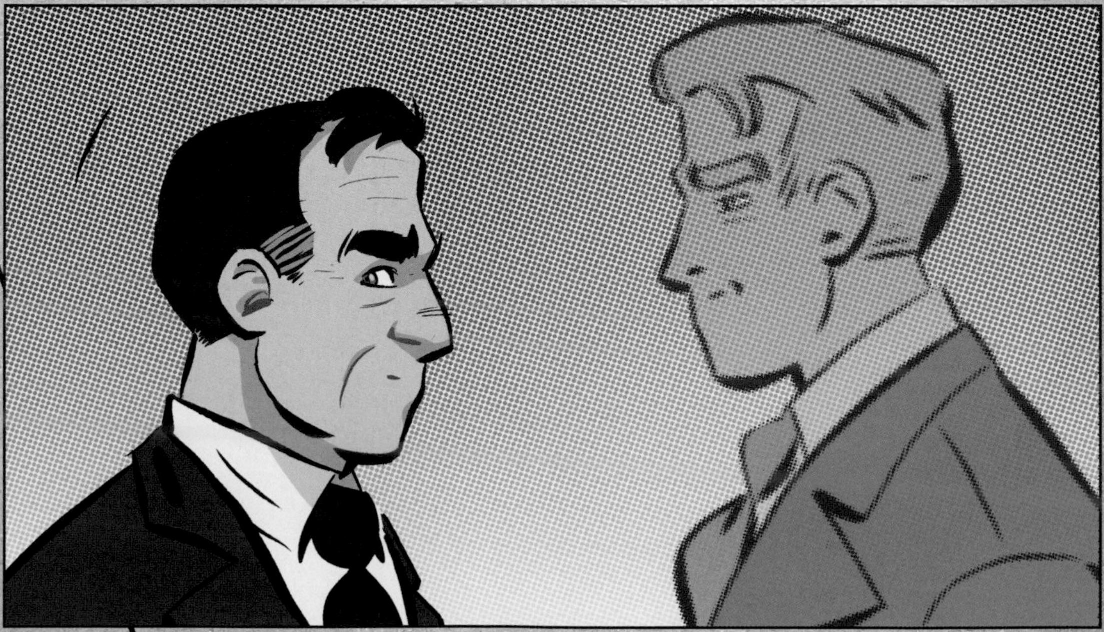

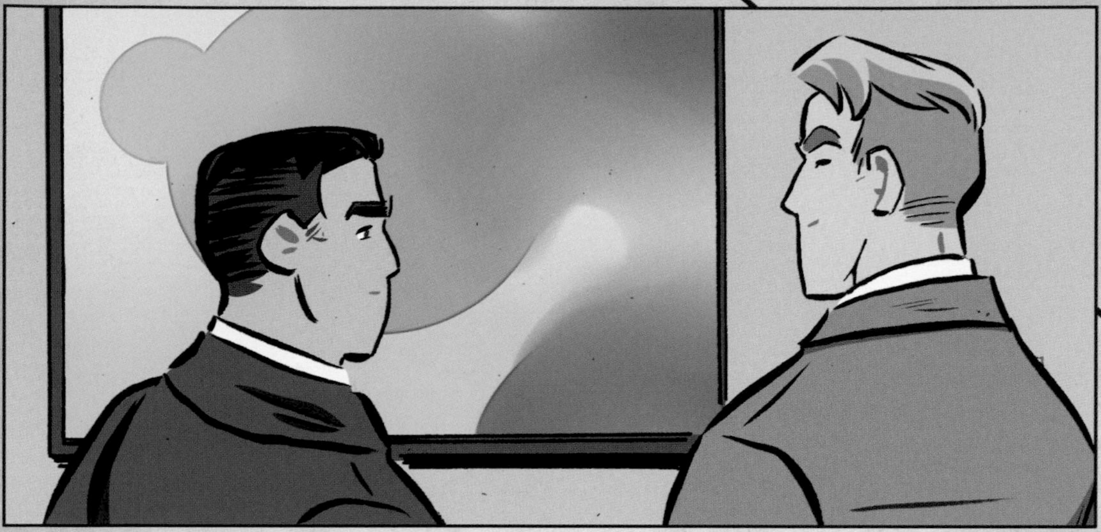

Greg:

Sam and Philip first see each other in a museum but they don't speak until they meet again later in a bar. I wanted this to parallel Sam's life in 1955 New York to give the readers a shorthand into who Sam is and a very simple way to show that he is haunted.

The art gallery interlude turned out to be a really nice way to provide common ground between Sam and Philip's sister, Hilde.

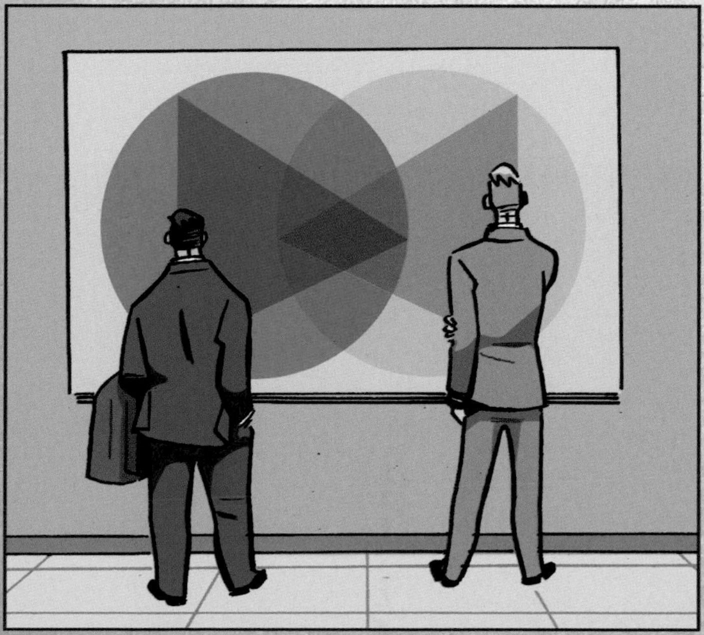

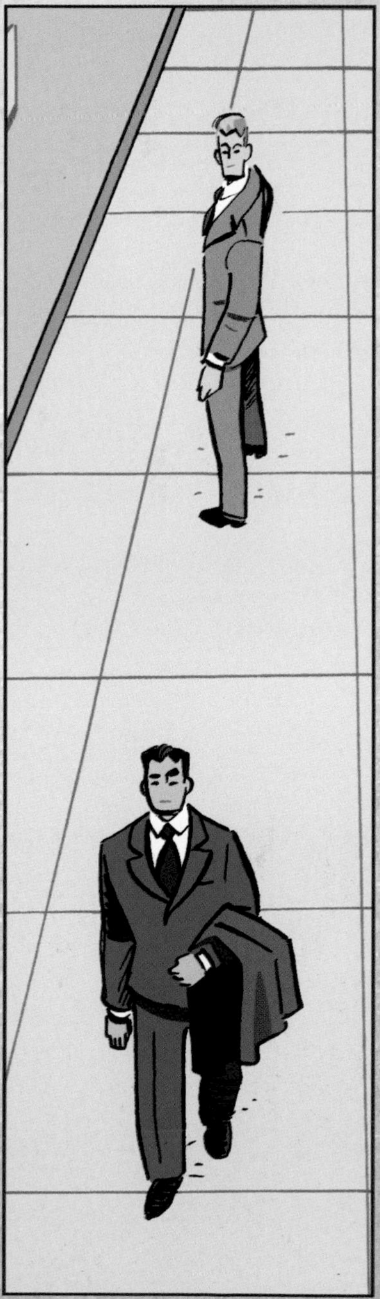

Research & Development

Greg:

I did a significant amount of reading research and film watching during the development of this story. Many creators (writers, artists, filmmakers, et al.) have returned to Weimar-era Germany as a point of inspiration, and plotting a graphic novel that starts in the Berlin of 1932 was intimidating. But the research was both amazing and heart wrenching, as it documents the great social changes that were made during that time toward a deeper understanding of sexuality and gender.

A partially complete list of my references includes:

Nonfiction and memoirs: *Gay Berlin* by Robert Beachy; *I, Pierre Seel, Deported Homosexual: A Memoir of Nazi Terror* by Pierre Seel; *The Pink Triangle: The Nazi War against Homosexuals* by Richard Plant; *An Underground Life: Memoirs of a Gay Jew in Nazi Berlin* by Gad Beck; *Christopher and His Kind: A Memoir* by Christopher Isherwood

Prose fiction: Christopher Isherwood's *The Berlin Stories*, Jason Lutes's *Berlin*, Philip Kerr's Berlin Noir trilogy, among others

Films and Television series: *Casablanca; Berlin Alexanderplatz; Babylon Berlin; Bent; Another Country; Christopher and His Kind; Cabaret*

Here are some notes in greater detail on these works:

Gay Berlin by Robert Beachy (non-fiction) —The most comprehensive portion of my non-fiction research was focused in this volume. A relatively recent scholarly text that gave me invaluable insight into our characters' world and the sociopolitical atmosphere in Germany. It also provided the historical context for much of those details included in our graphic novel. Impeccably researched and still very accessible for a motivated reader. Beachy's writing is clearly-voiced, unlike many academic texts, and I felt as if I learned a great deal while traveling through this period of history.

An Underground Life: Memoirs of a Gay Jew in Nazi Berlin by Gad Beck (nonfiction/memoir) —Beck has a flair for the literary while he recounts the harrowing events of his life in Nazi

Germany. A member of the Resistance and a true hero—we are very lucky to have his words in this memoir. The memoir begins at the birth of Gad and his twin sister in 1923 and continues until the emancipation of Berlin in spring of 1945.

Christopher and His Kind by Christopher Isherwood (memoir)

—Christopher Isherwood's fictionalization of his time in Berlin, *Goodbye to Berlin*, and its adaptations are frustrating to me as a reader (and viewer) due to their exclusion of Isherwood's homosexuality. I have empathy since they are the product of their times, but *Liebestrasse* is an attempt to provide a spotlight on the stories of queer and gay individuals forced into hiding or concealing their stories in the decades that followed.

—Isherwood himself uses this autobiography, *Christopher and His Kind*, to be more candid about his past and the community he was a part of in Berlin (and beyond). "His kind" were the "tribe" of connections he made as part of his sexual and intellectual liberation in Berlin. He also returns to the city in 1952 (with different motivations) but the nod was intentional in our story when Sam returns to Berlin in the same year. *The Berlin Stories* (which collected *The Last of Mr. Norris* and *Goodbye to Berlin* in a single volume) was a massive influence on the creation of this story and I hope represents a fictional response that is a little more truly queer in its representation of Berlin at that time.

Another Country, directed by Marek Kanievska, script by Julian Mitchell, adapted from his play of the same name

—There are plenty of films that influenced the creation of this graphic novel but I want to focus on a wildcard entry: *Another Country*. The movie was a very conscious influence in the structure of our flashbacks as well as the subject matter of queer longing.

—The 1984 film starred Rupert Everett as Guy Bennett (who had originated the role for the West End production) and Colin Firth (in his film debut) as his best friend, Tommy Judd. Cary Elwes also appears in the film (in his debut) as Guy Bennett's love interest. Loosely based on the life of a British spy, Guy Burgess, the film portrays two best friends at a boarding school in England during the 1930s. It's gorgeously filmed and tragically sad.

Berlin by Jason Lutes

—The collected edition of Lutes's *Berlin* was released as we were beginning to pitch our graphic novel. *Berlin* is a masterwork and should be read by everyone with an interest in the city and its history. This graphic novel transcends in its scope, as well as its tight focus on the two lead characters, Marthe Müller and Kurt Severing, as they navigate the years leading up to World War II in Berlin.

—Lutes is a fabulous sequential storyteller. The majority of the shots are mid to closeup, which ensures the reader is close to the characters while also bringing you directly into the heartbreaking and terrifying reality of the changes in Berlin.

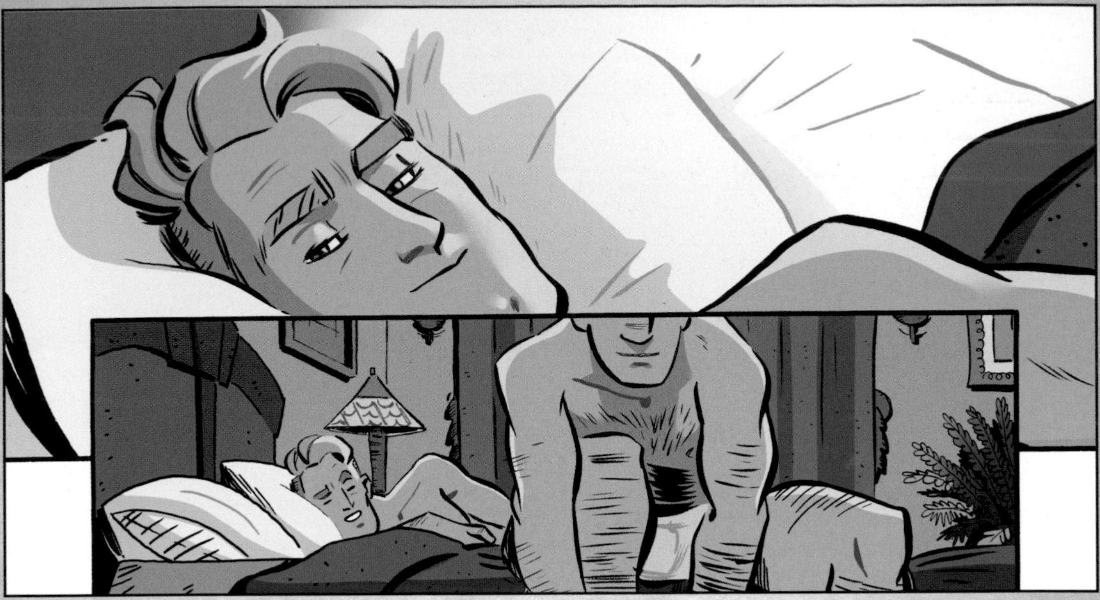

Greg:
I've never seen a single closeup this beautiful in all of comics. Tim's line art here is perfect: his "camera" placement, the look in Philip's eyes, the flop of his hair, the creases in the pillow . . . and Héctor's color and the subtle way the sunlight is hitting Philip's face and pillow is just so dreamy and wonderful it elevates the panel outside of the limits of my hyperbole.

> This is the exact sensuality I knew we would be blessed with in hiring Héctor when we started this project.

Color Process

Héctor Barros:
When I first colored the short story, I used warm greens, golden yellows, and purples for the scenes when Sam and Philip meet for the first time and when they are together, contrasting this in other parts of the story with more muted and neutral colors for the scenes set in the present or the world outside their bubble of happiness. I avoided red, except the bright red of the Nazi insignias and the scenes where their violence is shown or implied. The graphic novel allowed me to explore and expand those color-coded scenes in more depth.

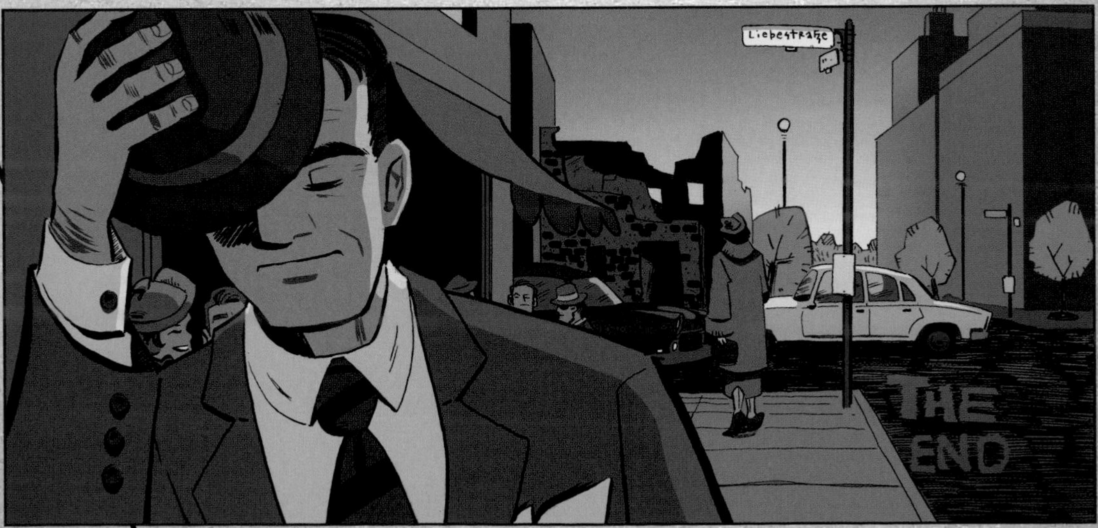
Liebestraße
THE END

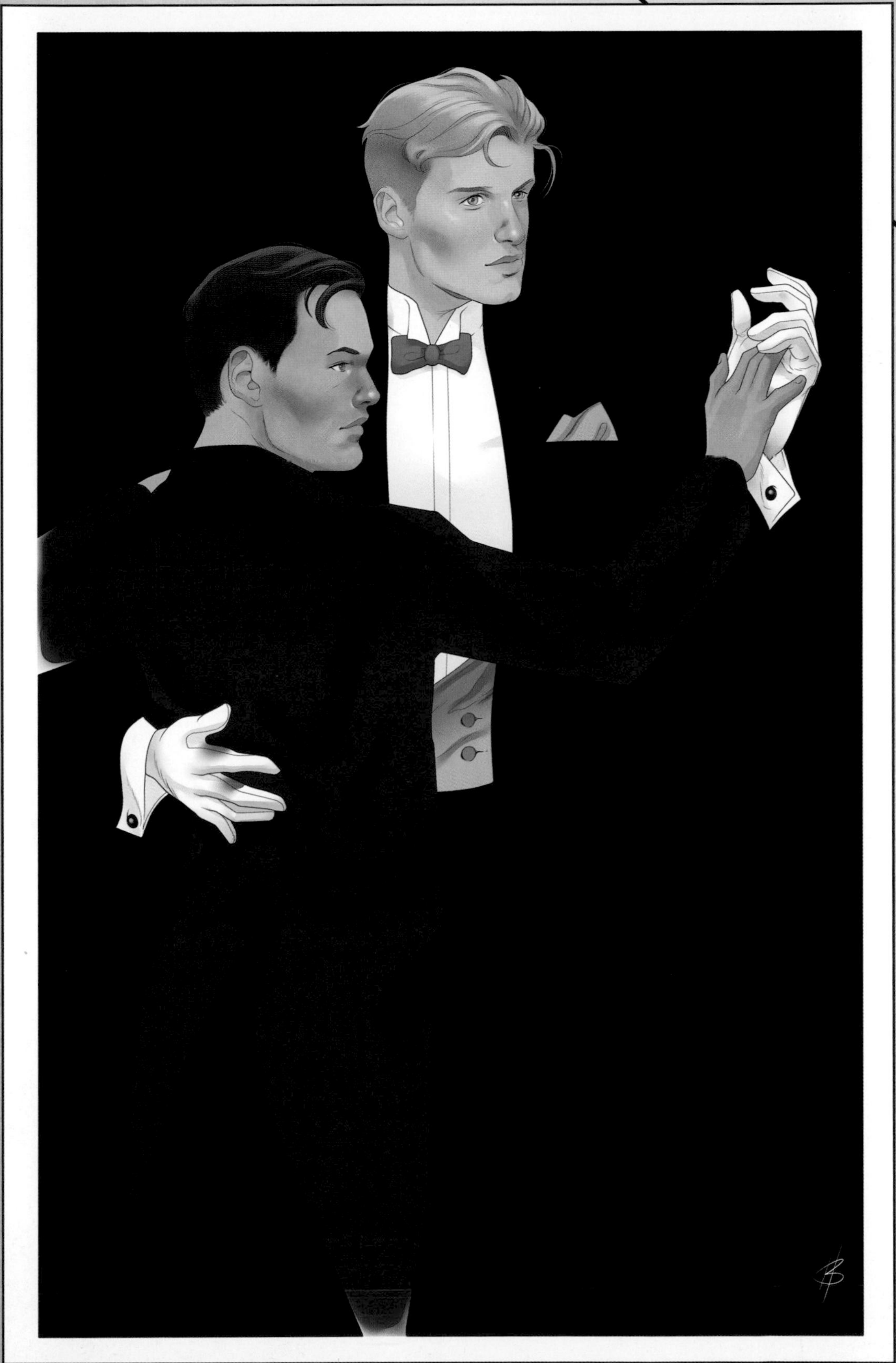

Illustration by Héctor Barros

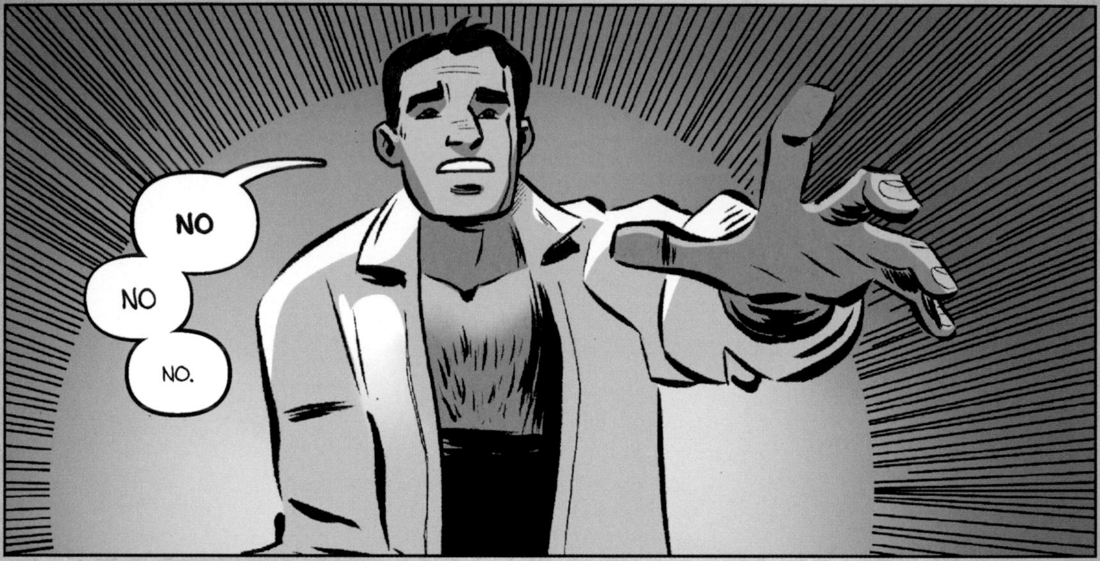
NO
NO
NO.

Lettering & Logo Design Process

Lucas Gattoni:
I remember the first thing I noticed from Tim's art was how much he was able to express just by modulating his ink outlines. So my instinct kicked in and I knew I wanted to use a typeface that could match this.

I had already discussed with Greg about trying to tie a European look to this book so I quickly thought of Fando's Fonteys Caps, based on Albert Monteys's handwriting. This wonderfully programmed font has four different contextual alternates for each character, so it was the perfect choice.

For a complete handmade feel, I created a custom brush for the balloons, and ***Liebestrasse's*** lettering style came to be.

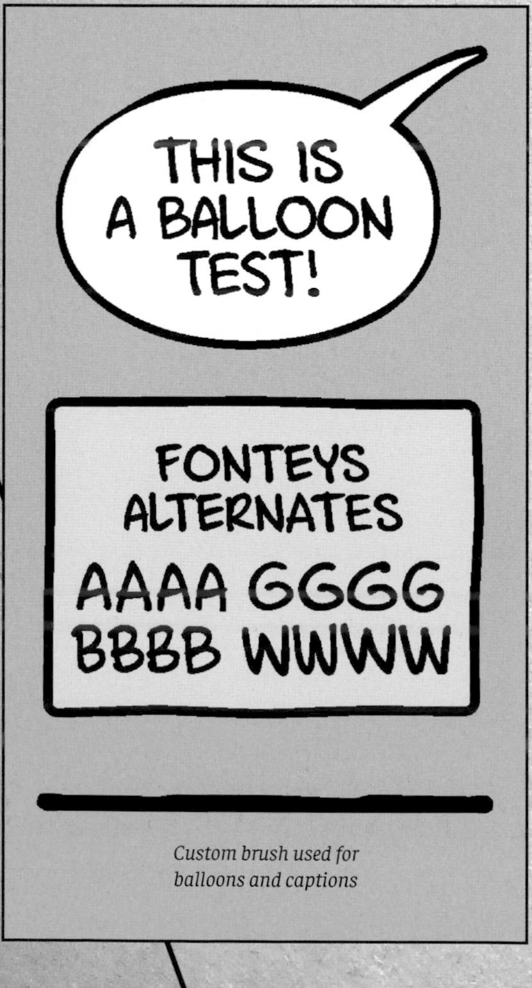
THIS IS A BALLOON TEST!
FONTEYS ALTERNATES
AAAA GGGG BBBB WWWW

Custom brush used for balloons and captions

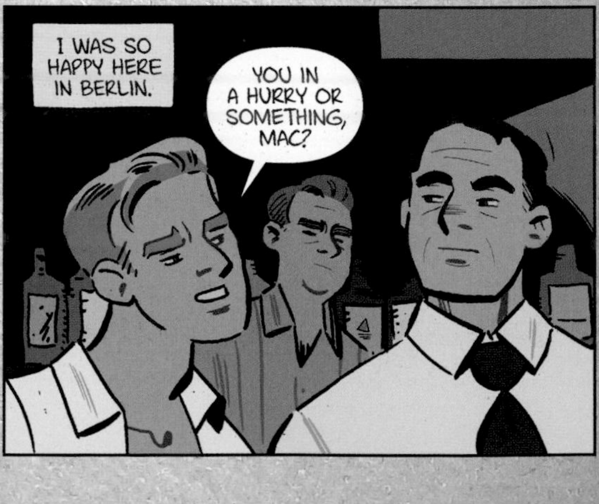
I WAS SO HAPPY HERE IN BERLIN.
YOU IN A HURRY OR SOMETHING, MAC?

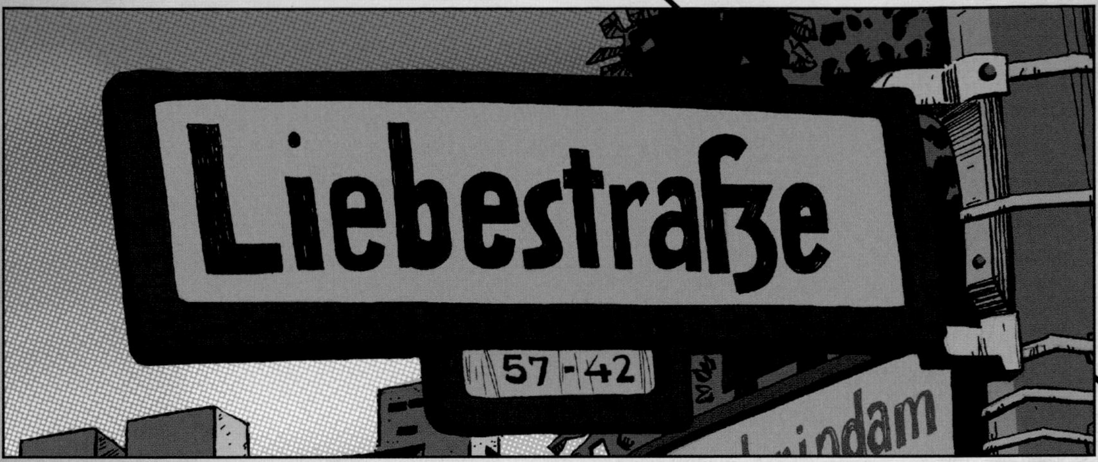
Liebestraße
57-42

When designing the logo we had a clear path; as ***Liebestrasse*** is the name of a fictional street, we knew we wanted to give it a street-sign look. Tim had done a beautiful drawing of it on a page, so that was my first inspiration.

After researching some signage from the era, I settled on two DIN-like typefaces I liked. To achieve a hand-painted look I loosely traced the characters on vellum to provide two different options, from one of which ***Liebestrasse's*** logo was eventually created.

We considered using the gorgeous German letter eszett (ß) but discarded the idea as it would've hindered readability for English readers.

Below are some unused sketches I prepared, inspired by old-time movie posters, in case we wanted to go a different way.

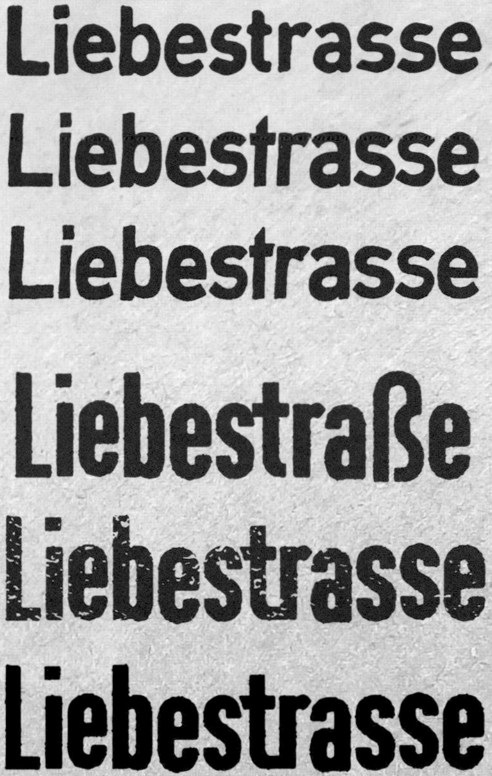
Liebestrasse
Liebestrasse
Liebestrasse
Liebestraße
Liebestrasse
Liebestrasse

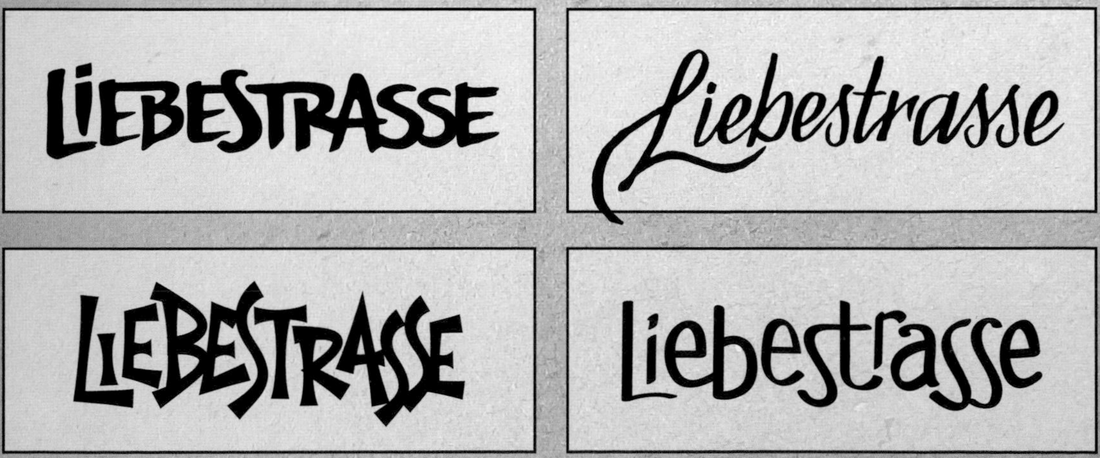
LIEBESTRASSE
Liebestrasse
LIEBESTRASSE
Liebestrasse

Location Research

Tim:

Berlin's history is a mixed blessing. There are lots of photos of neighborhoods and buildings prewar. But I think about 80 percent of the city was destroyed during the war. Researching the reconstruction was much more difficult. For the part set in the 1950s, I tried to capture the essence of the progression rather than have precise accuracy. Fashion was also fun to research, from old magazine ads and patterns.

As a tourist, I've visited Munich, and Berlin a few times, and throughout the east between Berlin and Prague. In Berlin, the reconstructed buildings, riddled with bullet holes and using the remains of the originals with new material to fill in, are haunting.

Bauhaus-Archiv
(photo by Greg Lockard)

> My visits to the camps created a long-lasting impression. I marveled at Berlin today and then was face-to-face with its brutal past.

Greg:

I have traveled to Berlin twice in my life and I was very lucky to have these experiences to pull from as we started the development of our story. It starts in 1932 Berlin, a time period in the city that is rich in details both terrible and wonderful. Having a living version of Berlin in my head to draw from helped ground the story in my own senses. These are some of the important locations I reflected on as I researched the project and completed the script writing.

The *Bauhaus-Archiv / Museum für Gestaltung* is currently undergoing a massive renovation but it is housed in a very striking building near the Kreuzberg neighborhood of Berlin. My visit to this museum in June of 2015 was immensely helpful to my research. The role of Philip's sister, Hilde, and her work as a painter connected her (and Philip) to the art world while allowing for their background to be complicated by their parents' role in traditional German society. The Bauhaus movement contained a multitude of female artists that have not been remembered as prominently, and placing Hilde within the movement (as a fictional figure) gave us another interesting perspective on the world of Berlin in the 1930s.

The **Memorial to the Murdered Jews of Europe** (also known as the **Holocaust Memorial**) is near the eastern end of the Tiergarten near the famous Brandenburg Gate. It is a massive memorial that is incredibly moving. It is meant to be walked through; you are eventually surrounded by massive concrete slabs that feel like an abstracted cemetery. I highly recommend the time spent in quiet reflection as you walk through the sculptures.

The **Memorial to Homosexuals Persecuted under Nazism** was inaugurated on May 27, 2008. Located close to the Holocaust Memorial on the edge of the Tiergarten, this sculpture is much smaller: a square cube made out of concrete, and within is a small video screen that plays a film of two men kissing. Near the memorial is a small plaque that explains the persecutions carried out by the Nazis and those who came after, using the Paragraph 175 law. The law wasn't completely repealed officially until 1994, which is a solemn reminder of how close we are to being illegal in love.

The **Soviet War Memorial** (in the northeastern corner of the Tiergarten) is another memorial that was very important to the construction of the graphic novel. The Soviet War Memorial is a massive structure erected by the Soviet Union to pay tribute to the eighty thousand Soviet Armed Forces soldiers who died during the Battle of Berlin in April and May 1945. My first visit was at dusk and it was extremely haunting, which helped paint a picture of the Tiergarten as a place for cruising in Berlin during the 1930s. This memorial didn't exist during the earlier part of our story but my visit to the site informed Sam and Philip's drive through the park, as well as other aspects of the story.

I think it is important that I met Germans on my trips to Berlin. I saw the city alive but also had ideas to help my imagination visualize the unfathomable amount of death. The city felt both haunted and vibrantly alive. During the trip in 2015, I stayed on Engeldamm Street near **St. Michael's Church** (Sankt-Michael-Kirche). The bombed-out remains of a Catholic Church steps away from the small apartment. It was strange to live near the ruins of a war sixty years prior. Even among all my friends in the city, there still was a darkness in the neighborhoods I couldn't ignore.

I think living among the wounds of the past is something we try to patch over in the US, but there are stories that we shouldn't stop telling ourselves, there are stories we must constantly learn from.

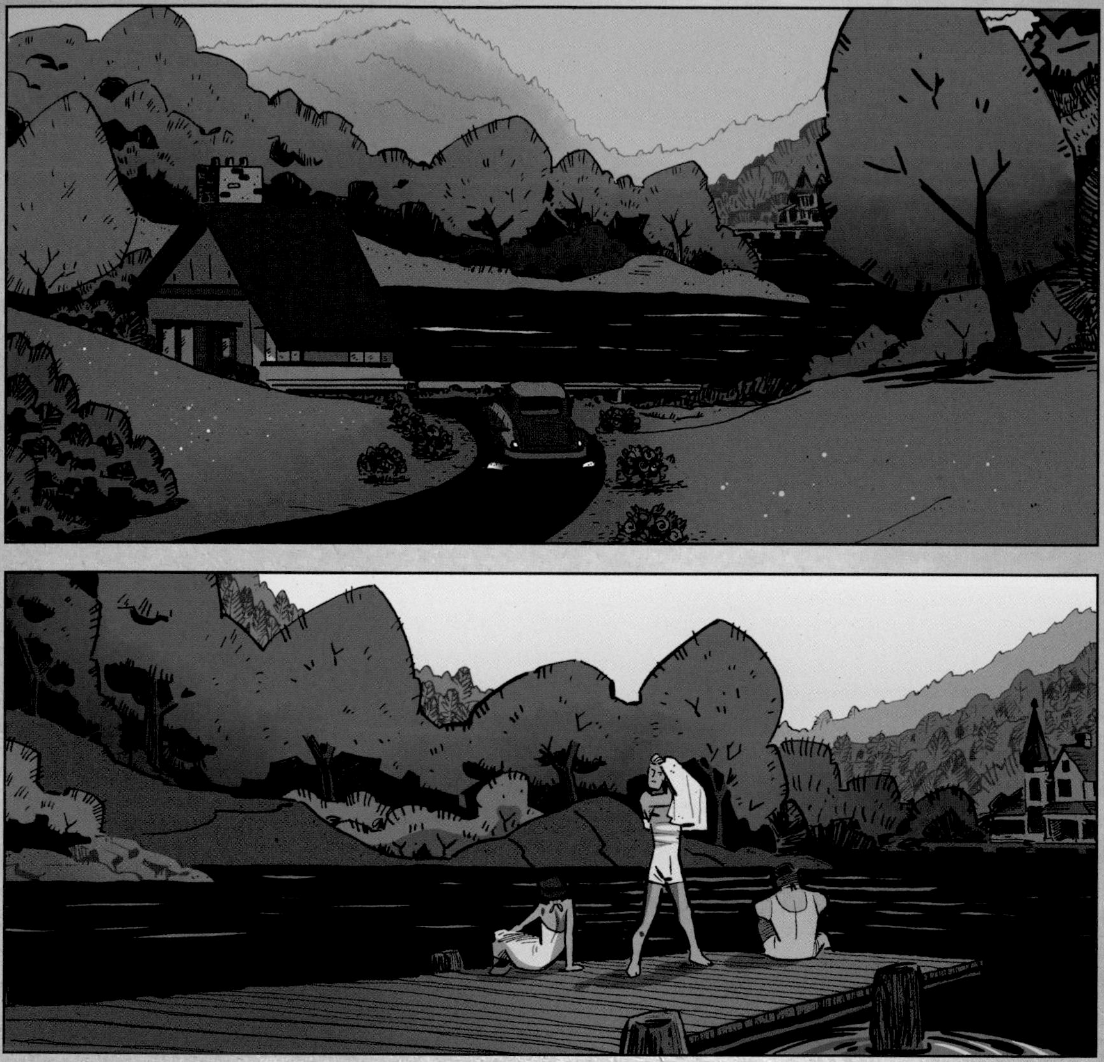

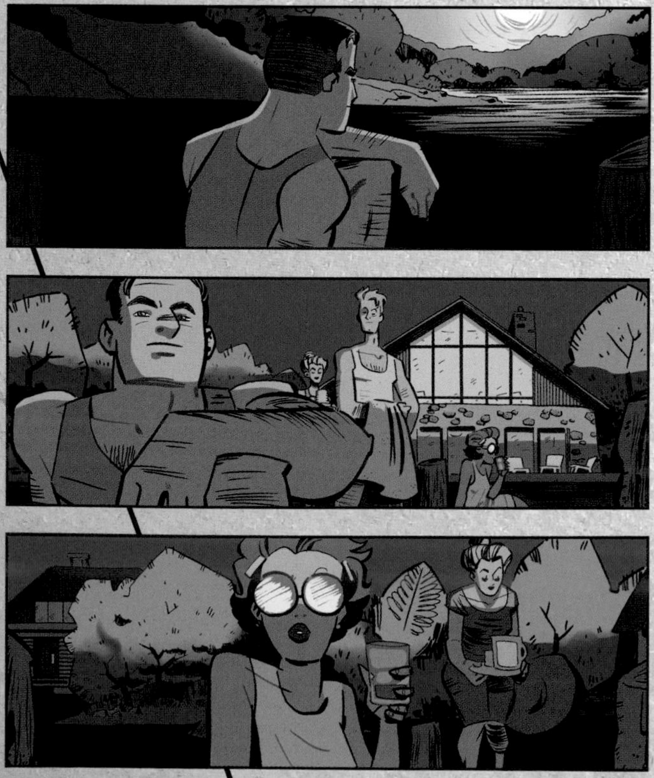

Idyllic Germany

Greg:
The ending to the original short story was much more harsh and quite damning for Sam. That was something I wanted more space for and was glad for the opportunity to expand in the graphic novel.

Moving Hilde outside of Berlin to the countryside helped in a few ways, thematically and otherwise. Showing idyllic Germany (and Switzerland) was helpful in drawing the parallels to contemporary American politics.

Terrible things are happening and it's a terrible element of human nature to ignore actions and problems that aren't immediately in front of us or affecting us.

Balancing the portrayal of the Germans and Germany was an effort to allow the modern reader a better chance at empathy in the comparison to the present day. Most fiction about this time and this country doesn't offer that same portrayal.

Still, Hilde and Philip saw what the First World War did to their father and they had the privilege of choosing to remove themselves from the conflicts in Berlin. Ultimately, Philip did not have a choice—but Hilde, and the American foreigner Sam, did.

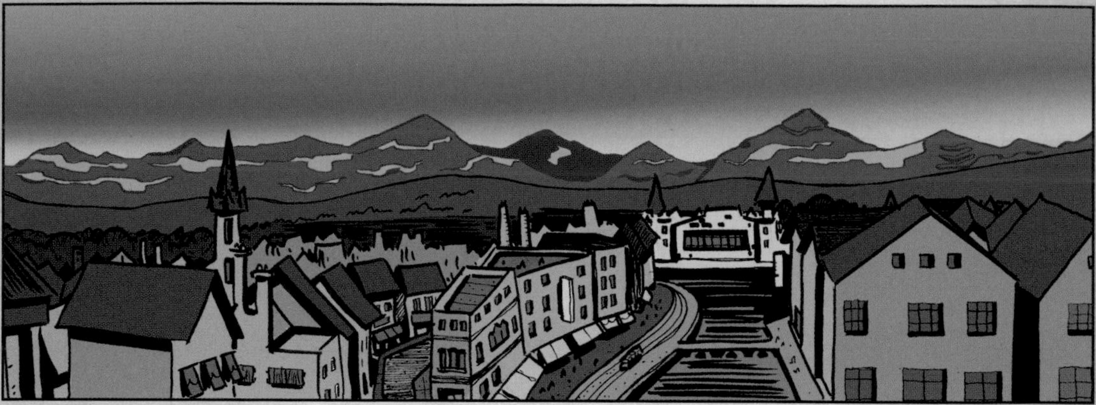

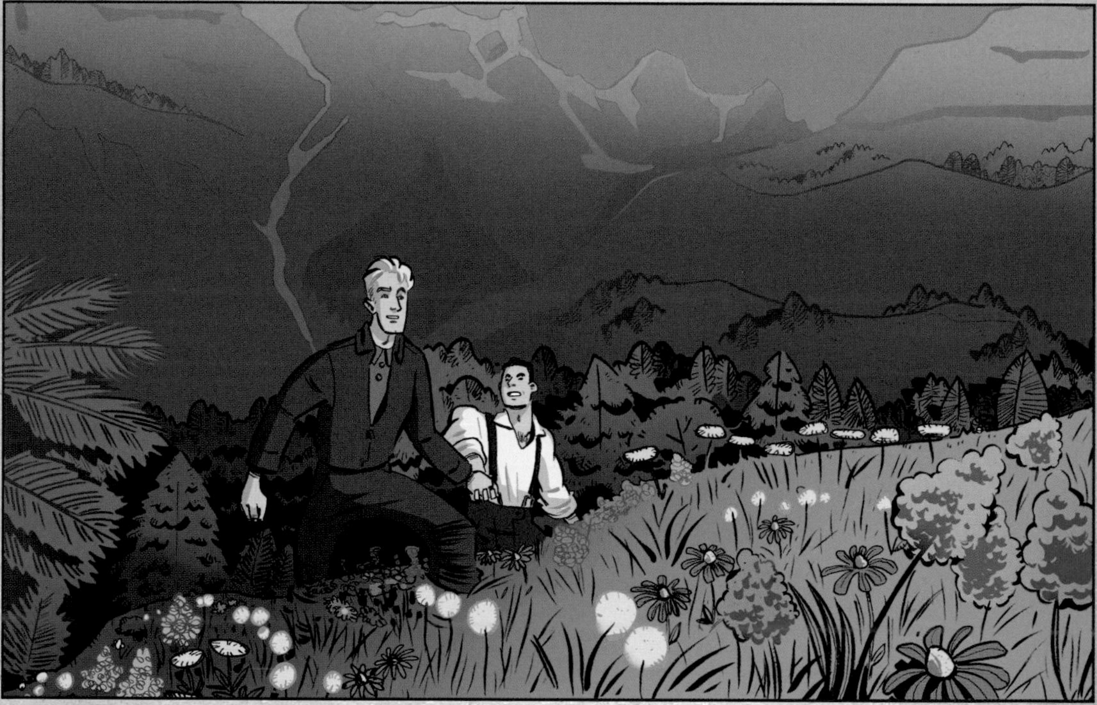

Idyllic Switzerland

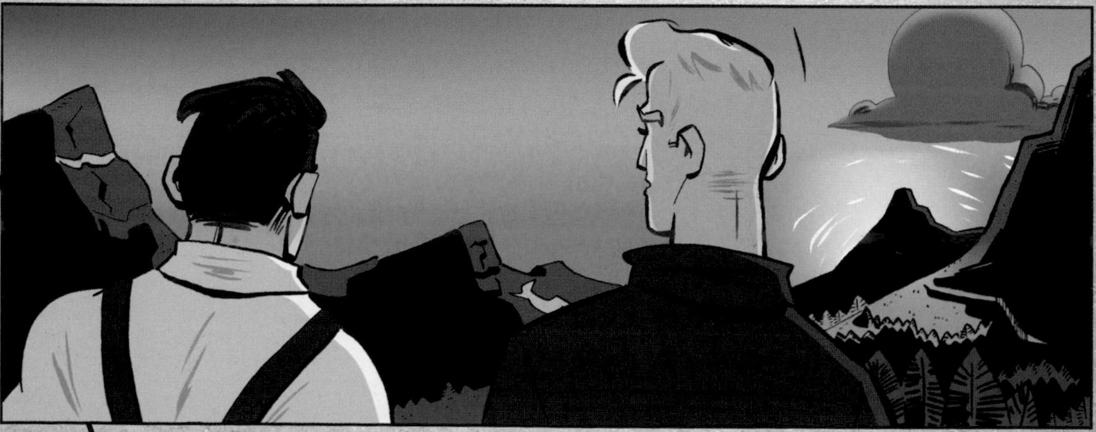

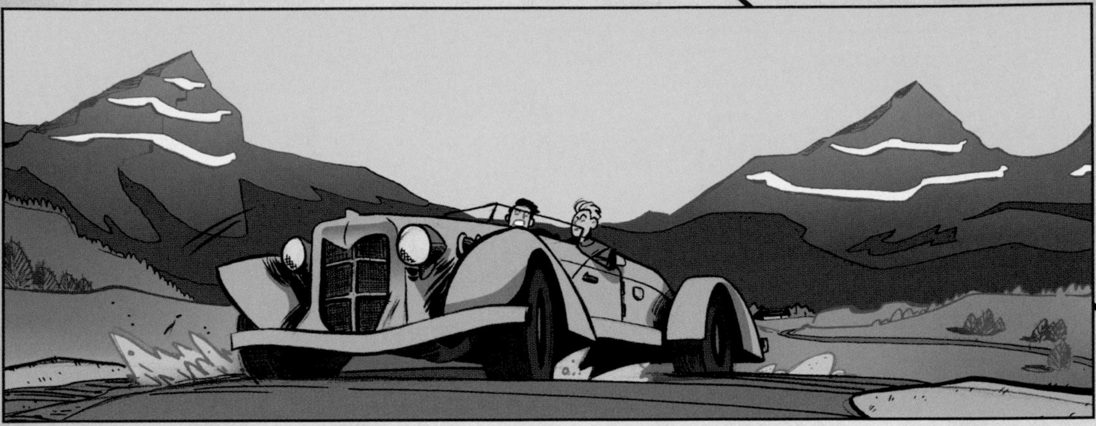

Tim:

Once I'd toured the Swiss Alps, I was frustrated by how inadequately photography and drawings capture the scale and majesty of the mountains. For this scene, I looked at a wide array of photos on the internet, as well as my own photos and sketches from Switzerland.

Very often, I like to let the memories blur, and then draw from my memory.

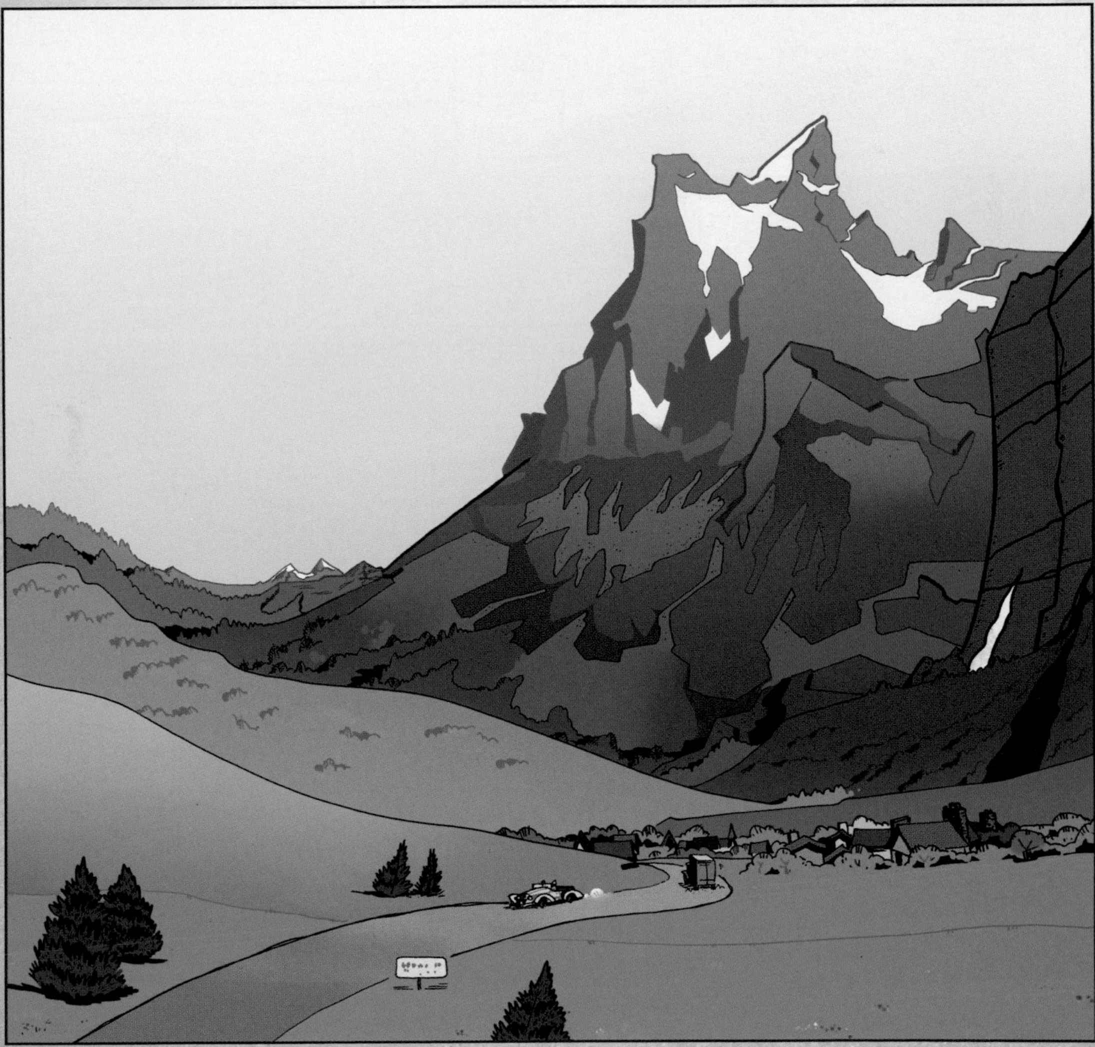

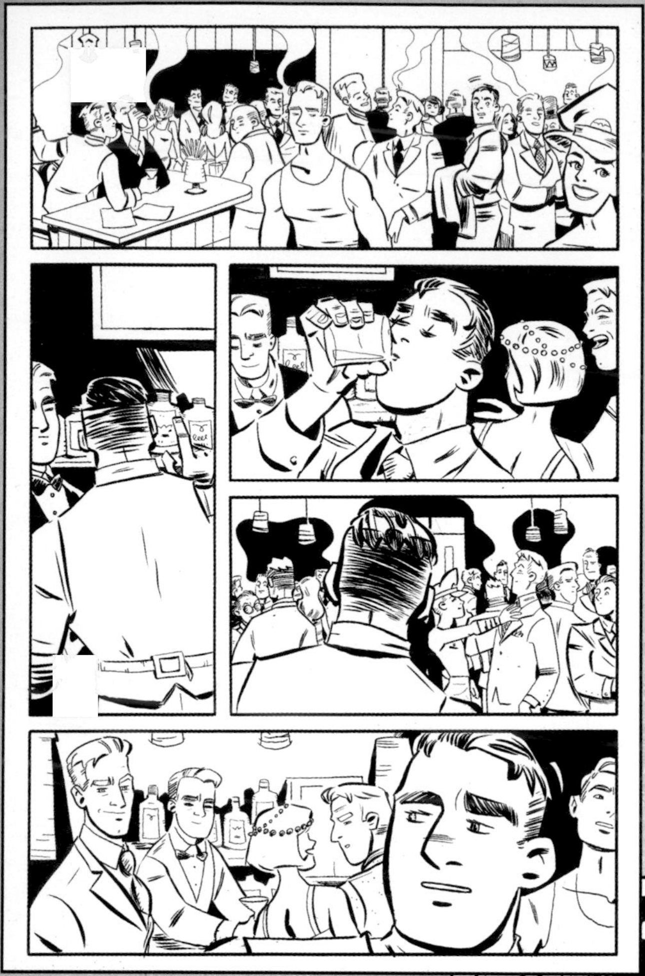

Berlin, 1932

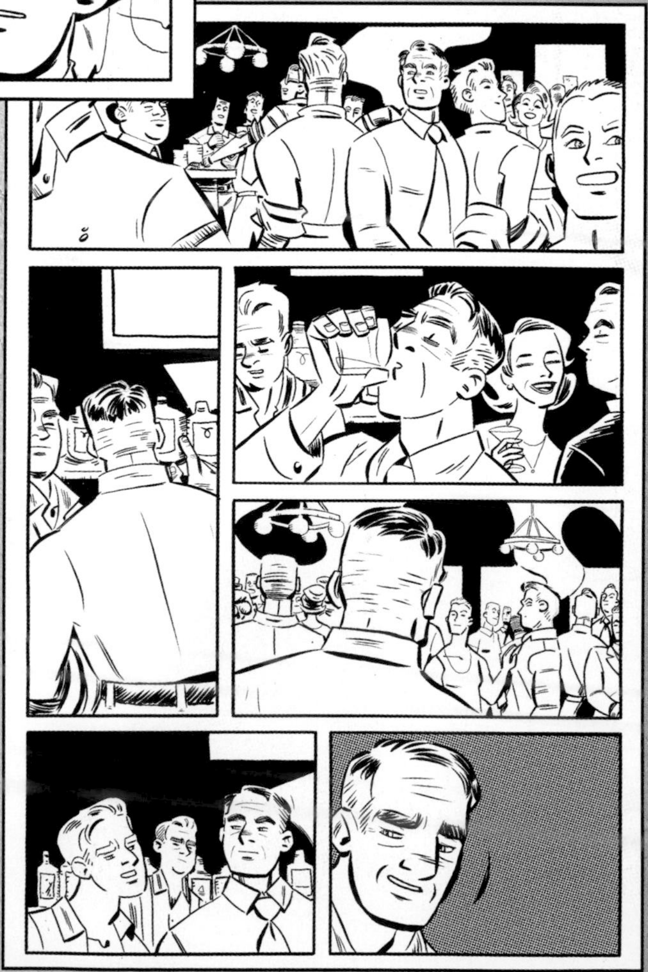

New York, 1952

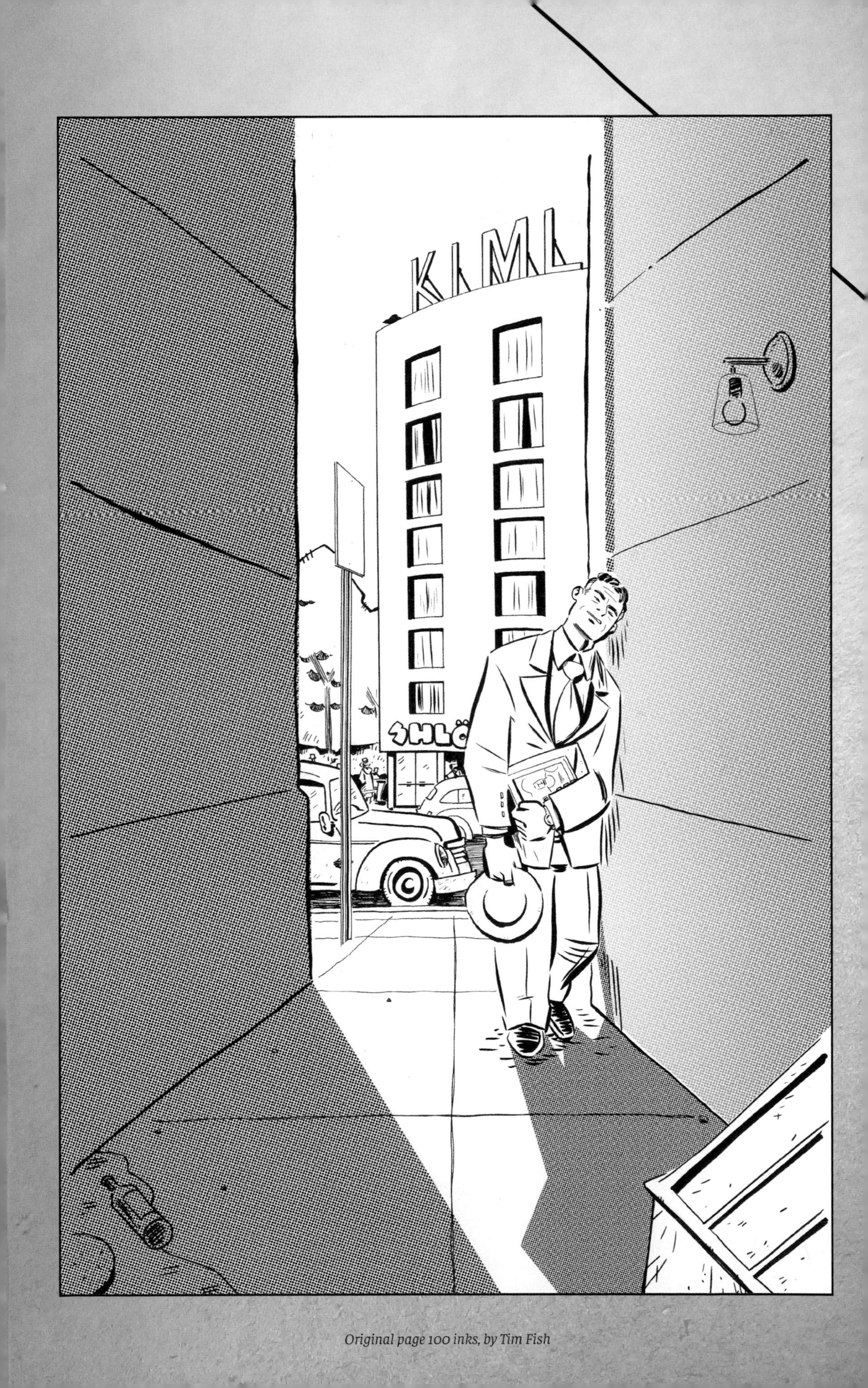
KIML
SHLÖ

Original page 100 inks, by Tim Fish

Greg Lockard is a comic book writer and editor. As a freelance editor, his clients include comiXology Originals, Image Comics, Einhorn's Epic Productions, and others. Previously, as a member of the Vertigo editorial staff, he worked on a number of critically acclaimed titles including *Dial H*, *The Unwritten*, *Sweet Tooth*, and many others. **Liebestrasse** is his debut graphic novel as a writer and cocreator.

Tim Fish is a comic book writer/artist, marketing professional, and part-time graduate student, best known for his gay romance series *Cavalcade of Boys* and its spinoff graphic novels. He was a principal artist for Roar's officially licensed comic series *Saved by the Bell*, based on the NBC TV show. His short stories have been published by Marvel, Vertigo, Fantagraphics, Oni Press, and more.

Héctor Barros is a Spanish illustrator and colorist based in Manchester, UK. Completely self-taught, he has worked as a colorist for Diábolo Ediciones (*La conjetura de Poincaré*) and *The Pride* Volume 1.

Lucas Gattoni is a pro comic book letterer with fifteen years of experience as a graphic designer and typesetter and a lifetime passion for storytelling. He's lettered mostly for indie creators around the world but has also seen his work published by IDW, Dark Horse, Scout Comics, and Action Lab. He lives in his home country of Argentina with his husband and their three unnamed goldfish (*oops*, make that two now).

Will Dennis was an editor at Vertigo/DC Entertainment for more than fifteen years, specializing in genre fiction comics and graphic novels. His award-winning titles include *100 Bullets*, *Y: The Last Man*, *Scalped*, *DMZ*, *Joker*, and many more. Since then, he has worked as a freelance editor for Image Comics, comiXology, and DC Entertainment, and also wrote *The Art of Jock* for Insight Editions. He lives in Brooklyn, NY.